I0641516

All This Thinking

RECENCIES

Recencies Series: Research and Recovery in Twentieth-Century American Poetics
Matthew Hofer, Series Editor

This series stands at the intersection of critical investigation, historical documentation, and the preservation of cultural heritage. The series exists to illuminate the innovative poetics achievements of the recent past that remain relevant to the present. In addition to publishing monographs and edited volumes, it is also a venue for previously unpublished manuscripts, expanded reprints, and collections of major essays, letters, and interviews.

Also available in the Recencies Series:

A Serpentine Gesture: John Ashbery's Poetry and Phenomenology by Elisabeth W. Joyce
Evaluations of US Poetry since 1950, Volume 2: Mind, Nation, and Power edited by Robert von Hallberg and Robert Faggen
Evaluations of US Poetry since 1950, Volume 1: Language, Form, and Music edited by Robert von Hallberg and Robert Faggen
Expanding Authorship: Transformations in American Poetry since 1950 by Peter Middleton
Modernist Poetry and the Limitations of Materialist Theory: The Importance of Constructivist Values by Charles Altieri
Momentous Inconclusions: The Life and Work of Larry Eigner edited by Jennifer Bartlett and George Hart
Yours Presently: The Selected Letters of John Wieners edited by Michael Seth Stewart
LEGEND: The Complete Facsimile in Context by Bruce Andrews, Charles Bernstein, Ray DiPalma, Steve McCaffery, and Ron Silliman
Bruce Andrews and Charles Bernstein's L=A=N=G=U=A=G=E: The Complete Facsimile edited by Matthew Hofer and Michael Golston
Circling the Canon, Volume II: The Selected Book Reviews of Marjorie Perloff, 1995–2017 by Marjorie Perloff
Circling the Canon, Volume I: The Selected Book Reviews of Marjorie Perloff, 1969–1994 by Marjorie Perloff

For additional titles in the Recencies Series, please visit unmpress.com.

Clark Coolidge holding the cover of Own Face *(published by United Artists, Bernadette Mayer and Lewis Warsh's press, 1978), Lenox, Massachusetts, 1979. Photograph by Bernadette Mayer. Image courtesy of Bernadette Mayer.*

Bernadette Mayer at a release reading for The Golden Book of Words *(Angel Hair Books, 1978), Lenox, Massachusetts, 1979. Photograph by Lewis Warsh. Image courtesy of Bernadette Mayer.*

All This Thinking

The Correspondence of Bernadette Mayer and Clark Coolidge

Edited by STEPHANIE ANDERSON *and* KRISTEN TAPSON

University of New Mexico Press
Albuquerque

Printed in the United States of America

First paperback printing 2024

ISBN 978-0-8263-6434-0 (cloth)
ISBN 978-0-8263-6627-6 (paper)
ISBN 978-0-8263-6435-7 (electronic)

Library of Congress Control Number: 2022950976

Founded in 1889, the University of New Mexico sits on the traditional homelands of the Pueblo of Sandia. The original peoples of New Mexico—Pueblo, Navajo, and Apache—since time immemorial have deep connections to the land and have made significant contributions to the broader community statewide. We honor the land itself and those who remain stewards of this land throughout the generations and also acknowledge our committed relationship to Indigenous peoples. We gratefully recognize our history.

Cover illustration courtesy of Nathan Dumlao on Unsplash
Designed by Felicia Cedillos
Composed in Minion Pro

Contents

Acknowledgments

First and foremost, we are incredibly grateful to Bernadette and Clark for entrusting us with this vital work, as well as to Philip Good and Susan Coolidge for providing information and support at every juncture. Marie Warsh shared ideas, located photos, and confirmed biographical details. The librarians in the Poetry Collection at the University at Buffalo and the Special Collections at the University of California at San Diego, especially Marie Elia and Heather Smedberg, were infinitely helpful. The Digital Scholarship and Publishing Services Department at Duke provided exceptional guidance at a crucial time, and Duke Kunshan University's support made the project possible. Marcella Durand shared resources and encouraged our work. Craig Dworkin enthusiastically agreed to host the remaining letters on Eclipse. Chalcedony Wilding worked tirelessly and invaluably on the manuscript, as did Shannon Lee. We are grateful to everyone at the University of New Mexico Press, especially Mathew Hofer and Elise McHugh, for their diligent work in bringing this book into the world. Finally, we are very indebted to our families, who patiently waited for us to finish our nighttime transcribing and listened to us talk about this project for years.

The letters are printed with the permission of Bernadette Mayer, Clark Coolidge, Special Collections & Archives at UC San Diego Library, and the Poetry Collection of the University Libraries, University at Buffalo, The State University of New York.

Introduction

"I Know I Mean We"

The Correspondence

"I think that there are always a few poets that don't interfere with you and feed you in a way so naturally on-going that you can't help feeling as if you'd written the work yourself. I've always felt that you and I work that way, and that's surely a blessing!" Writing to Bernadette Mayer on April 8, 1980, Clark Coolidge concisely articulates what is evident throughout their correspondence: their influence on each other is powerful yet so ubiquitous and sustaining that it registers as a kind of self-extension. This volume of their collected correspondence charts the duration and intensities of this unique relationship, a relationship that always remained both enmeshed in and slightly removed from the poetic scenes of their day.

Born in 1945 and 1939 respectively, Mayer and Coolidge were too young to be included in Donald Allen's watershed 1960 anthology *The New American Poetry*, which has long been credited with codifying the American avant-garde poetry scene into schools and movements such as the Beats, the San Francisco Renaissance, the New York School, and so forth. Both Mayer and Coolidge have strong connections to those movements; as poets and publishers of various little magazines, they promoted and circulated the work of their contemporaries in various streams of the New American Poetry scene. They also worked in other media and were connected to other art scenes—early in their careers, Mayer had a visual-arts practice and Coolidge was a jazz musician. Their correspondence emphasizes their proximity to New York School visual artists, the conceptual art scene of the 1960s, and especially the so-called Second Generation New York School, the group of poets that was slightly younger than Frank O'Hara and John Ashbery. Key members of the Second Generation included Ted Berrigan, Joe Brainard, Anne

Waldman, Ron Padgett, Alice Notley, and others, and the geographic base for the scene was the Poetry Project at St. Mark's Church in New York City, which Mayer directed from 1980 to 1984.

While this volume illustrates the strength of their relationships with these contemporaries, displaying a rich web of sociality, it also reveals other influences. Coolidge and Mayer both reference and admire poets such as Gertrude Stein, William Carlos Williams, Dante, and others, including their more immediate Beat predecessors, Jack Kerouac and Philip Whalen. More broadly, the letters capture their voracious consumption of other genres and media—a list of their repeated topics might include Nathaniel Hawthorne, Ludwig Wittgenstein, detective novels, and films by Jean-Luc Godard. Finally, as the correspondence details, both poets were taken up as influences for the Language poetry movement of the 1970s and '80s; Coolidge's work appears prominently in early issues of *L=A=N=G=U=A=G=E*, and Mayer's class at the Poetry Project in the early 1970s attracted many younger contemporary poets, including some who would go on to be associated with that movement.

Their connections to both the New York Schools and the Language school shifted between the 1970s and '80s and influenced their critical reception. In addition to her employment at the Poetry Project, Mayer was the only woman included in *An Anthology of New York Poets* (ed. Ron Padgett and David Shapiro, Random House, 1970), despite the presence of other women in the scene, while Coolidge's 1997 move from New England to Petaluma, California, put him in proximity to West Coast poets and critics. As a result of these and additional factors, Coolidge's connections to Language were recognized more quickly than Mayer's in the scholarship—and initially, Mayer was often more affiliated with the Second Generation New York School than Coolidge. The belated recognition of the complexity of each poet's aesthetic connections also means that scholarship has also been slower to spotlight one of the most compelling and tantamount influences on each one's work: their relationship with each other.[1] Happily, at the time of this writing, both poets have been the subjects of renewed critical attention. Mayer's *Memory* (1971–1972) has recently been published by Siglio Press with the original installation photos (after previously being available only as an out-of-print book), and new scholarship on her work proliferates; Coolidge is a subject of *Coolidge & Cherkovski: In Conversation* (ed. Kyle Harvey, Lithic Press, 2020).

Both poets continue to publish with innovative presses such as New Directions Publishing and Fence Books.

The correspondence, which exceeds 430 pages and is housed in the archives at the University at Buffalo and University of California San Diego, began in 1964 when Coolidge published Mayer in his little magazine *Joglars*; he also asked her for work in July 1966 at his reading at the Folklore Center in New York City (in a series curated by Ted Berrigan). Mayer subsequently published Coolidge in the third issue of her mimeograph magazine *0 TO 9*, which appeared in January 1968. Their first extended face-to-face interaction came in early 1969 when Mayer and then-boyfriend Ed Bowes road-tripped cross-country. The Coolidges were living in North Beach, California, and Susan Coolidge recalls that she and infant daughter Celia returned to their third-floor Vallejo Street apartment one day and found Coolidge and Mayer deep in conversation in the kitchen. It was the beginning of a conversation carried out in various forms for the next twenty-odd years.

The present volume contains the complete correspondence between September 1979 and October 1982. This period contains the most rapid and lengthy exchanges in the correspondence as well as sustained discussions of poetics and what it means to be a poet. These discussions occur alongside and entangled with descriptions of daily life, responses to the Language scene, and the poets' many acknowledgments of their aesthetic affiliation. For example, Mayer writes to Coolidge on September 21, 1980, "I wish I could say I think I'm a poet because you are, however nowadays that might be true but in the days when I was trying to figure out why I was a poet I didn't know you." In addition to documenting the significance of their friendship in relation to their writing practices, then, these letters reveal an intimate connection between poetry and correspondence throughout. Relatedly, this period of correspondence is intertwined with Mayer's epistolary projects *The Desires of Mothers to Please Others in Letters* (wr. 1979–1980, pub. 1994) and *What's Your Idea of a Good Time?* (wr. 1977–1985, pub. 2006). *Desires* is Mayer's "letters book" of "real & 'imaginary' (unsent) letters" written during her pregnancy with her youngest child that she references to Coolidge in her letter on August 14, 1980, telling him "there are many to you." The letters preceding and following those included in this volume can be accessed online in the Eclipse archive, which includes both facsimiles and searchable transcriptions.

In order to understand the significance of the present volume within the entire correspondence, we find it helpful to think about the letters as belonging to five periods, each one representing a different phase of the pair's epistolary relationship. In a preliminary period, 1965–1972, the poets move from mutual editorial solicitations to collaboration. On February 24, 1971, they read together at the Poetry Project, and in September 1972 they visit Eldon's Cave in Western Massachusetts, a visit that inspires their only published book-length collaboration, *The Cave* (wr. 1972–1978, pub. 2009). The second period begins in 1973 while Mayer is living in New York and teaching workshops at the Poetry Project; Coolidge is living in Hancock, Massachusetts, with his family, at a distance from the New York scene. During this period, which runs until Mayer and then-partner Lewis Warsh move to Worthington, Massachusetts, in July 1975, Mayer and Coolidge commiserate about the difficulties of the publishing world and exchange news about their friends. Both poets write long letters that revel in the details of reading, writing, and the everyday. "I really owe you this one," Mayer writes in a particularly sprawling and comprehensive November 25, 1974, letter detailing a trip to Chicago that we encourage readers to access on Eclipse. "I've been in transit. Since your last letter I've been carrying around your last letter in my pocket so, whenever I felt low, I'd take it out & read it, occasionally, in faav (in what?), in fact, I've had to read sentences of it to other people in order to cheer them." Amusingly, Coolidge's previous letter from November 3 neither praises Mayer nor brims with the optimism that might buoy most "low" addressees. Still, his inclusion of particular details unmistakably conveys his upbeat energy. He reports that his "longwork" is humming along,[2] shares that he has written a piece inflected by the work of Robert Smithson, rattles off a substantial list of recent reading, and encloses a book.

Mayer and Coolidge's geographies overlap and allow for more in-person communication in the sparse third period, from 1976 to 1979, when Mayer lives in Lenox, not far from Coolidge in Hancock, Massachusetts. This period is defined by a notable gap in the letters—the period's few extant letters are primarily written during travel—and we are left to imagine the development of the relationship that occurs between friends socializing in person. In this period, Mayer writes her lauded long poem, *Midwinter Day*. She consistently draws from the quotidian in her writing, and the move to a small-town setting, which dovetails with the experience of becoming a mother, marks a significant transition in her work toward domestic themes. During these years, Coolidge continues to work on the aforementioned "longwork," written between 1973 and 1981 and eventually released in 2012 as *A Book Beginning What and Ending Away* (Fence Books). Moreover, he publishes *Own Face* (1978), dedicated to Mayer, with Warsh's Angel Hair Press.[3]

Their correspondence resumes in the aforementioned fourth period, from 1979 to 1982, covered in this volume. Mayer and family move to Henniker, New Hampshire, for a year before returning to New York City so she can become director of the Poetry Project.[4] They spend the summer of 1982 in a house in Great Barrington, Massachusetts, near to Coolidge, resulting in a gap in the letters. The fourth period also involves transitions for Coolidge: his close friend, the artist Philip Guston, dies in 1980; he teaches in Naropa at the Jack Kerouac School of Disembodied Poetics; he travels to Peru. A fervent exchange between Mayer and Coolidge about the value of their work (discussed further in the following section) is an intense culmination of not only this volume but also the entire correspondence.

Finally, the fifth period runs from late 1982 to 1987, and the letters' contents shift toward personal transitions and especially Mayer's interaction with the New York scene. The death of Ted Berrigan, whose "absence is too much of a presence here" (Mayer tells Coolidge on September 21, 1983), significantly changes the dynamics in New York and contributes to Mayer's conflicted feelings about working and living in the city. For Coolidge, these years involve significant travels—to Italy, France, and Egypt—and both poets teach at Naropa. Major publications during this period include Mayer's *Utopia* and Coolidge's *Solution Passage* and *The Crystal Text*. The extant letters trail off in 1987 and end in 1995.

Cupbearing and Consanguinity

Despite, or perhaps because of, their broad networks of artistic associations, the letters underscore how both Mayer and Coolidge adamantly work independently of their "scene," even while developing group relationships. Given this mutual tendency, we might say that they work independently together. At several points, the letters return to a shared sense that their aesthetic rapport places them apart from their contemporaries. In an early 1973 letter, for example, Mayer writes, "Somebody asked me the other day if you + I were 'grouped' together in the same 'group' of writers. Who are the others in our group, please let me know." Coolidge responds on January 23, "I didn't realize that you & I were in a 'group.' . . . I don't think there are any 'others.' That makes us a 'duo'?" While they understandably resist the labels of the poetic schools with which they are often associated, their affiliation with each other is never so burdened; instead, it validates their similarly intense approaches to the writing process.

This introduction's titular phrase "I know I mean we," which underscores these poets' independent togetherness, comes from the third letter in a summer 1981 exchange that begins with an invitation to give a reading and quickly turns to ambivalences of writings' purpose alone or in a scene. As then-director of the Poetry Project, Mayer had written to Coolidge in that capacity on July 26, asking him to give the opening reading of the new season with John Cage. Coolidge, however, was suffering from a crisis of confidence in his work; on August 4, he refuses the invitation, replying that he is "going through a peculiar period" in which he doesn't like his recent work, a phenomenon he finds "very distressing," and his old work he "dislike[s] so much" that he "can't even look at it." This crisis is also linked to his broader feelings about the artistic scene. He explains that "the connections I once thought I saw, between individuals, between works of art and people's lives, are lost. . . . I get the feeling we should all be very quiet for a while or else go away (at least I should)." Writing is not the shared endeavor of an interconnected community, or even a career, but a compulsion created by habit, "just something I do that I can't stop doing." Describing the art scene as "an isolated island full of foolish people whizzing around," he points to egotistical careerism, a kind of art production completely severed from life. He finds it insidious, and the only adequate response he can muster is silence and removal. Though at no other point in the correspondence is either Coolidge or Mayer's discouragement regarding writing and the artistic scene this acute, over the years both complain about the superficiality of the poetry and publishing world.

Mayer responds to Coolidge's discouraged refusal on August 7, 1981, probably the same day she receives his letter. Her dating of the letter suggests her haste: the heading reads "August 4 no 7th 1981," as if she's gazing at Coolidge's date when she begins to compose her response and perceives herself to be writing to Coolidge at the moment of his writing—the present of reading the letter overlays the present of responding to it, as in a conversation. She begins her response with a pep talk of sorts, reminding Coolidge that, though "maybe it's even disturbing to think one's writing has already had an effect on the world, before one even knows what one is doing," "as some part of you knows your writing is enlightening to all (& dont even count me)." Her letter quickly becomes a reflection on her own practice: "For myself, I've begun to ruminate that it's self-indulgent to take what goes on in the world as an excuse not to go on with what one has a physical and mental impulse to do—thus of course your mention of not being able to stop writing." In Mayer's view, what's "self-indulgent" is not the disconnect between art and world that Coolidge fears, but rather allowing the world to distract you from the work of creation, "what one has a physical and mental impulse to do." There's an understandable tension in her reply between recognizing the severity of Coolidge's crisis and resisting the temptation to presume to identify with it. This tension partly results from the sense of aesthetic affiliation that threads throughout the letters. Later she continues:

> I am not saying that any of us are the same, I am saying what I am thinking as a result of thinking of you. Ultimately none of it matters the present moment excepted. Only thing is I feel so close to you that it's hard for me to write write sensibly & to try on a small page to respect your silence when I just want to hit you! I want to jolt you out of your thoughts! but that's exactly what you asked me not to do! . . . Please I hope you feel better, I often think it would be wonderful to have someone to talk to about what I think about writing at this moment, I dont. But we are the cupbearers, which I know is a misuse of the word but it's the word I've picked nonetheless, and we must still be doing this, your or my mishegoss notwithstanding, I know that much—dont you? And I dont mean just we, but I know I mean we. . . . Well you are my consanguinity too—I dont know exactly why—so I can make demands on you (should we have a self-criticism?) something otherwise I'll fucking mourn[.]

When Mayer states that "it would be wonderful to have someone to talk to about what I think about writing at this moment," she alludes to Coolidge's having been that person for her in the past. The word "cupbearers," meant to imperfectly convey the necessity of serving as a vehicle for the work, again puts the primacy on the work itself. When Mayer says, "And I don't mean just we, but I know I mean we," she admits that there are other cupbearers—artists whose work is vital—while simultaneously setting apart her and Coolidge's work. Semantically and contextually, the phrase "I know I mean we" elects the two poets to a circle of necessary artists; syntactically, the phrase clones the first-person pronoun. And it's hard not to hear it as "I know I means we" as well. This excerpt describes an extreme instance of encouragement, but Coolidge, too, supports Mayer when the difficulties of writing and publishing become discouraging. Ultimately, it is this support, plus their sense of mutual understanding—the "consanguinity" Mayer identifies above—that resonates throughout their exchanges.

This consanguinity does not mean, however, that the letters are without tensions and negotiations. Mayer describes the above exchange in a letter to Bill Berkson dated August 8, 1981, the day after she writes to Coolidge, collected in *What's Your Idea of a Good Time?* She acknowledges the extent to which Coolidge's letter and his silence have affected her, and she describes her emotions as well as the circumstances surrounding her response to him:

> I feel hurt and angry and only wrote back that he was of course right about what he said, I could say all those things too but that I thought there must be an end to one's self-involvement, I'm sure I said the wrong thing and to top it off I forgot to mail the letter when I wrote it but I stoically resisted rewriting it, oh fuck it, I still can say that I feel that many of my oldest friends make me feel very unsure of myself in my work at running the poetry project which is messy enough as it is without the benefit of generous enlightenment that I need. (I take all of this back.)[5]

Mayer's acknowledgment of this fracturing moment with Coolidge underscores the difficult negotiations involved in sustaining an intense poetic correspondence that is also a significant manifestation of the poets' friendship. Or to put it differently, to regard the content of the letters as exclusively—or often, even primarily—directed toward reflection on artistic practice underestimates the coconstitutive roles of friendship and poetics at work in their letters. The content is directed toward the correspondent. Each poet mentions particular topics and pieces of gossip that the other will enjoy.

Sometimes a poem is included with or within a letter. Thus, one important vantage that readers might want to further consider is how the correspondence positions each poet within the "plurality of social affinities" explored on the pages of *Among Friends* (ed. Anne Dewey and Libbie Rifkin, University of Iowa Press, 2013).[6]

Within this plurality, the correspondence is exceptional for its duration and intensity even as it remains in keeping with their correspondence more generally. Mayer and Coolidge have extensive letter-writing practices, including interlocutors some readers might find unexpected. Both corresponded about poetry and everyday life alike with Anne Waldman, Larry Eigner, Charles Bernstein, Bill Berkson, Lyn Hejinian, and Alice Notley. But Mayer also corresponded with Laura Riding Jackson and, briefly, John McPhee; Coolidge with John Cage and Peter Straub. In *The Letters of Bernadette and Rosemary Mayer, 1976–1980* (ed. Marie Warsh and Gillian Sneed, Aachen, Ludwig Forum; Bristol, Spike Island; Munich, Lenbachhaus; New York, Swiss Institute, 2022), a complementary collection to the present volume, readers can find a side of Mayer's correspondence even more oriented toward intense affective response, details of the everyday, and conversational intimacy.

The Letters as Writing

Ultimately, the duration and intensity of their correspondence also authorizes each poet's experimentation with epistolarity itself during these years. What are epistolarity's forms, and to whom are those forms directed? A personal letter is obviously intended for the addressee: we want to communicate with someone in particular, sometimes to *talk* to them; Coolidge and Mayer periodically lament the limitations of writing letters. For instance, on August 8, 1986, Mayer writes that she "wish[es] we were conversing in person instead of just these silly letters that have to end!" Or they reference times when they were together, writing as if having a late-night conversation over beers. Mayer and Coolidge's correspondence is deeply personal in this way, replete with gossip and details of their respective domestic lives that sometimes make readers feel as if we're snooping—and of course we are; the letters weren't written for *us*. The letters are often a rollickingly entertaining read and occasionally frustrating in their gaps. In those gaps, we are reminded that letters hold only one part of a relationship that often exceeds epistolarity.

Even as they conceptualize the writing as "talk," the letters reveal how epistolary "talk" is alternatively inadequate and liberating. On January 21, 1980, Coolidge writes, "I persist in thinking of these letters as 'talk,' though we both know they are also really writing. How many illusions one needs to keep on with correspondence! And how much I miss those all-night conversations we had here years ago, that seemed so perfectly germane (ha!) to the life of our thoughts and work then they seem to have been taken for granted." Epistolary intimacy is, alas, no substitute for in-person varieties of intimacy, such as "all-night conversations," but its very inadequacies—the dissatisfactions Mayer and Coolidge have with the form—also imbue it with potential:

> and now pretty much up to real time in this very sentence wondering what or if you can make out of all this thinking grammar. It looks like one can be even more giddly longwinded on the letterpage than on the phone, yes? Wouldn't it be great if we could keep moving talk in these letters constantly out into possibility what we didn't even realize we thought yet? Or would that be embarrassing and/or dangerous?

This excerpt, from a September 12, 1979, letter from Coolidge to Mayer, hints at the ways in which the writers keep grappling with epistolarity's communicative and formal possibilities beyond talk. A compelling quality of this correspondence is precisely this toggle between intimacy and a self-reflexivity about epistolarity, which has a potentially "embarrassing and/or dangerous" flipside, "public" writing—for the letters are "also really *writing*" (emphasis added), Coolidge says in that 1980 letter.

Though the tone and modes of thinking about the letters as *writing* vary considerably, that "public" self-reflexivity about craft runs underneath both poets' letter-writing practices and their reading of each other's letters. We suggest thinking of this writing as literary, appealing to a wide audience, with many potential addressees. Mayer, as mentioned, explores epistolarity as a poetic form, and both poets are thinking about the eventual wider audiences for the letters. On February 23, 1986, Mayer writes to Coolidge,

> Oh and I have been meaning to write to you for some time also to tell you

> I wound up reading over all your letters from the more distant past which is a way of putting it I've always secretly loved. Alas because I sold them to the University of California. And reading them was a great pleasure in a couple of ways—one because I realized I kind of had them memorized and so would never actually "forget" them, and another joy in them was the way we speak. & what a great sense of etiquette we've got!

Etiquette is not necessarily a "public" phenomenon, but it is a social and group-oriented way of thinking about what has been discussed in the letters, reminding us ("the way we speak") of "talk." Mayer's memorization makes the letters a cherished text that can be personal and/or literary. Finally, Mayer's rereading is done as if through yet another person's eyes in the archive, adding another layer—letter as archival document—to the writing.

The letters are thus complex documents that maneuver between various audiences and conceptualize talk, writing, and epistolarity in multiple ways. They are also a valuable resource for readers seeking greater access to the lives and interests of two poets whose writing can be difficult to approach. These moments of "meta" commentary are distinct partly because neither poet is particularly interested in putting forward a reflective, cohesive poetic philosophy elsewhere. In their interviews, classes (several of which are recorded), and other writing, both Mayer and Coolidge are gracious about sharing information about their writing procedures, but they are reluctant to reframe their poems in retrospect or discuss how readers might engage them. In their correspondence, though, they are far more willing to riff extemporaneously on the writing process and to take chances with what they say. On November 19, 1979, for example, Mayer writes:

> What I seem to have to do is to have someone to address in order to begin, then lose that, mix it up, get mixed up myself, let the language take over, work out some structures within that, see an ending, bypass it and then see how much longer I can last, having more or less abandoned the addressee, then collapse at some false ending, casting the work aside with the unspoken hope that I may have made some discovery. Then the next time I just start all over again, assuming I'm taking it all in.

Importantly, Mayer's discussion of an "addressee" here—as opposed to a potential reader or audience member—suggests the degree to which the epistolary genre inflects her writing in this time period. Moreover, these and similar comments indicate the extent to which she and Coolidge are using the correspondence as a space to work out issues of poetic practice as they encounter them, as well as the extent to which they each perhaps imagine the other as an ideal reader for not only letters but also their literary output.

If we imagine Mayer and Coolidge to be working both *with* and *for* each other as each other's ideal readers and the implicit addressees of entire books, then yet another way to read the correspondence emerges—as collaboration. In addition to being biographical and self-reflexive documents that supplement their poetic oeuvres, the letters become extensions of said oeuvres. Taken as a collection, they might suggest an emergent and expansive collaborative project—one in which both authors are deeply aware of the many possible forms that thinking with another person over time might take. "Thinking together," for Mayer and Coolidge, is a practice inextricably entwined with the materiality and mode of the letter-writing process. It requires the momentum of frequent correspondence as well as a willingness to engage, reframe, and enter into the ideas of the correspondent. As Coolidge suggests in the January 21, 1980, letter, this particular kind of epistolary relationship is rare:

> I must say that like you I'm pissed and depressed by almost all of the other letters I get. They don't seem to want or be able to talk about what I think to set in motion. So much of it seems keep-the-touch/take-the-temperature type correspondence, which it seems to me by nature can't be continued with any frequency.

Here, Coolidge's frustration with surface-level correspondence unfolds into an expression of desire for a partner who "[wants] to talk about what I think to set in motion." This phrase amplifies the tension between the acts of establishing a particular line of thought for the addressee to trace and of grappling with what is "set in motion" (including letters themselves, crossing geographical and temporal distances) on purpose, by accident, in unexpected confluences, and more. In again underscoring his consanguinity with Mayer in this lament, Coolidge draws attention to modes of thinking and writing that are contingent, improvisational, and ephemeral within their correspondence.

This volume is ultimately an enterprise of innovative collaboration that illuminates the many tributaries of reading, writing, and engagement that lead to artistic production. When Coolidge writes in that September 12, 1979, letter, "and now pretty much up to real time in this very sentence wondering what or if you can make out of all this thinking grammar," he's projecting himself into Mayer's addressee position, "wondering" about how his account will be received, while also characterizing the writing as "thinking grammar." The thoughts he "sets in motion" are in-process. Over and over, the correspondence provides a place for Mayer and Coolidge to try out ideas, to both reflect on process and adjust it. This feature of their correspondence is entangled throughout with the more ordinary operations guiding each letter, suggesting the extent to which they welcome quotidian practices such as letter-writing into the realm of artistic invention. As capacious "thinking" in which they can try out varying types of content and imagine varying types of readership, including self-projection of the writer into the position of the addressee, Mayer and Coolidge's correspondence foments their artistic friendship and celebrates the generic possibilities of epistolary collaboration, the many *we*'s behind each writerly and readerly *I*.

A Note on Transcription and Editing

This volume attempts to balance attentiveness to each poet's style with accessibility. We tried to preserve as much of the original formatting of the letters as possible: both Mayer and Coolidge were sensitive to the way they used the space of the page when writing to each other, and they frequently comment on the material text. We also want to acknowledge the importance of the typewriter to the writing—Mayer and Coolidge frequently discuss typewriters and comment upon aspects of the material writing process. You can't easily erase on a typewriter, so the page bears extra marks of thought, observation, and emotional state.

We also wanted the transcriptions to show the kinds of editing the poets do as they write and reread. Both poets make corrections with the typewriter and by hand, some presumably done midstream during the writing process and some afterward while proofreading. We silently changed letters or words that Mayer and Coolidge corrected with cross-outs ("x's"), words that were repeated by mistake or at the beginning of a new page, and spelling errors that were corrected by hand or type and were not later commented upon. Both poets do sometimes remark on their own misspellings, as when Coolidge asks on December 7, 1981, why he insists on spelling "obsession" with four *s*'s. These misspellings and creative punctuation are often improvisatory, playful, or generative; we preserved many of them, but have corrected obvious typos for accessibility. For both poets, we kept abbreviations and most capitalization, and we avoided additions of words.

We also endeavored to preserve the material traces of the movement between thoughts. Instead of indented paragraphs, Coolidge consistently uses dropped lines (on a typewriter, using the platen knob to drop down a line without changing the indentation, as opposed to using the carriage return lever to return to the left margin) to signify movement between thoughts in his letters; Mayer sometimes does the same and sometimes uses regular indentations. We have reproduced this important feature throughout. In cases where the formatting is unclear, such as when the previous paragraph ends at the right margin or the dropped line looks like a regular indentation, we have assumed dropped lines are the general style and have often used them. Generally, bold brackets mark editorial insertions and comment on formatting. In particular, bold brackets around unbolded years indicate that the letter was dated by the archive; bold brackets with bolded years indicate that it was dated by the editors. Page breaks that are commented upon explicitly or obliquely by one of the poets, or that make it unclear whether the paragraph on the previous page continues or not, are marked **[Page break]**. Additionally, the typography and spacing for dates and sign-offs has been stylized in the book.

Finally, the letters occasionally retain markings suggesting the conversational aspects of epistolarity. On two of Coolidge's letters, Mayer adds notes in the margin that she then incorporates into her next letter, and these are included, along with her initials, in bold brackets **[BM]**, approximating their location in the original letters. We've indicated notable in-text additions with brackets and marginal additions made by a poet who is writing with an arrow. In most but not all cases, in the original these marginal additions are written out by hand; Coolidge more frequently types his P.S.'s and asides but makes handwritten corrections or additions from time to time, whereas

Mayer's asides, P.S.'s, and marginal notes are mostly, but not exclusively, handwritten.

For much of this project—including letter transcription, editing, and the writing of this introduction—we found ourselves in an epistolary relationship similar to and drastically different from Mayer and Coolidge's. One of us was located in North America and one in Asia, and the time difference emphasized e-mail's epistolarity. E-mails and edits threatened to cross in the mail, as it were. Like Coolidge and Mayer, we often worked late at night, while children were sleeping. Our understandings of our roles as cupbearers gradually shifted: When we transcribed, our hands became mechanical, transferring the content of the letters from one medium to another. Transcription, we found, is often the work of light attention, or the attention of surface accuracy and not depth; when we began to edit, we had to go back and reread letters we'd already "read" multiple times while transcribing. And then finally we began to conceptualize how the letters work as their own text in the ways we articulate above.

In order to help readers of this volume better conceptualize the original form of the letters, we have selected a letter by each poet to be reproduced following this introduction. These images suggest some of the challenges of representation that the work of transcription produces, and they gesture toward the letters themselves, sitting in archives on opposite coasts. And yet the physical process of transcribing, dating, and arranging the letters into a coherent text is also a collaborative process. During it, we sought a balance between text as perfected product and text as useful resource. Some days, our ideal form for such material would be a giant stack of photocopies clipped together in boxes. Other days, we'd have preferred to highlight the brilliance of this work by extracting particular passages and collating them into a fine press edition. What you hold now is the result of a series of discussions and negotiations that, we hope, showcase the incredible work—provisional and cumulative, improvisatory and collaborative—done in these letters.

Notes

1. Marcella Durand's work on *The Cave* is a vital precursor to this volume, as is

her discussion of Mayer and Coolidge's correspondence, located at http://writing.upenn.edu/epc/authors/coolidge/durand.html (accessed February 22, 2022). Lytle Shaw's "Faulting Description" also foregrounds the significance of their relationship, noting that they "encouraged a kind of extreme experimentalism in each other that far outstripped the primary modes of quotidian and occasional writing that were coming to be associated with the later generations of the New York School." Shaw, "Faulting Description: Clark Coolidge, Bernadette Mayer and the Site of Scientific Authority," in *Don't Ever Get Famous: Essays on New York Writing after the New York School*, ed. Daniel Kane (Champaign, IL: Dalkey Archive Press, 2006), 152.

2. In a 2013 interview, Coolidge addresses both the idea of the "longwork" and his and Mayer's shared interest in pursuing it, which sets them apart from their peers: "I felt kind of embattled even within the poetic scene to a certain extent in terms of length of readings and the extent of the work. Both [Mayer and I] were writing what would be more formally called poems at the same time but it was the longer work that we were really pushing. We were trying to make ourselves go beyond our abilities." Clark Coolidge and John Melillo, "Operating within the Irreducible: An Interview with Clark Coolidge," *The Poetry Project Newsletter*, no. 234 (February–March 2013): 6; see also 6–11.
3. Anne Waldman and Lewis Warsh started Angel Hair with a magazine of the same title in 1966. The magazine ceased production in 1969, but Waldman and Warsh continued to publish books under the press name until 1978. Mayer worked on *Own Face* with Warsh, and the two started their own magazine and press, United Artists, in 1977.
4. We chose to divide the third and fourth periods of the letters based on Mayer's physical proximity to Coolidge rather than placing the division at the more intuitive rupture between her time in New England and her return to the city. That is, in the context of Mayer's biography, her year in Henniker would be considered coextensive with the Lenox years, but in the context of the letters, her move to Henniker reestablishes her epistolary relationship with Coolidge.
5. Bill Berkson and Bernadette Mayer, *What's Your Idea of a Good Time?* (Berkeley, CA: Tuumba Press, 2006), 142.
6. Anne Dewey and Libbie Rifkin, eds., *Among Friends: Engendering the Social Site of Poetry* (Iowa City: University of Iowa Press, 2013), 5.

Wednesday 12 September

Dear Bernadette,

Here I am, nine in the morning, brain slowly rising to the surface, fingers dumb from driving this insensible typewriter, legs aching from newly-instituted exercise program (more on that later), doing my best to reach back for some semblance of epistolary ability answering yours (feels like it's been ages and it has). We missed your moving day partly because I wrenched my back again and it felt best when lying down but mostly it was suddenly all too sad and we didn't want to say goodbye. Somehow it began to seem that you were already gone and we'd best get on with the new dispensation. So, it feels odd here in this here letter at the first but maybe the chance for new thoughts or whatever to arise that haven't in some time and be worth going on with. It's certainly the first time I've felt like writing a letter in many's the moon, dark ages of doused connections. Perhaps you do finally find out what's worth continuing and precious little of it is? Shit, I hope most of this letter doesn't get taken up with bitching, however necessary. That sounds silly. Imagine starting a letter with "I must tell you that I have taken up with bitching". We might accidentally revive several old styles in the process! Hopefully instead we revive several "old"(?)(you said it) human beings: us. Interesting maybe to see into particularly how this poetry pursuit has aged us. Right now I'm feeling it's aged me back to (possibly useful as refresher?) infantilism. Like, how ancient Beachboys stuff sounds great today (beyond any later/present use of "california" before anybody'd even been there to see how the "sun" there was a dustier form of neon at noon), as in "Help me Rhonda" (the single). Possibly useful as unadorned craziness? Or is craziness now (post-acid) helplessly baroque if not rococo? and any use of the art-historical terms is just such dignity as I mean?? This is starting to go everywhere at once, which I absolutely want and don't want. Let's sit down with cheap rye in our dormitory room and discuss this. My problem then was I never got to hear the birds in the morning, sleep or no sleep. My problem now is I can't surely tell if things I think/feel (no distinction?) are mechanisms resultant of my age or the world's, general confusion of self and world being mostly unforeseen part of this gig as poet anyhow? And I don't get to hear many birds anytime in this basement room anyhow, unless they actually peck against this here wall or die against my window (which they've been doing increasingly lately, even causing most of a poem called "... " wait a minute, gotta look it up... "Glare Spreads"). Olson's hysterical disregard for same has absolutely taught me to close all parentheses, which I spose just means that within the big thing that can never be closed we can enjoy fiddling with closing all the near and thus smaller things. This is known as self-contextualization, which is always self-starting and which Creeley has never learned (Connectual Energy Reduced from Ignorance Dept.). How's this for prime head-in-the-bucket-of-everything start to further investigation and illimitable silly sarcasm? Poets' letters are never fully publishable even if they get to be. I guess I never believed in a steady state of language (like my mother?) so I'll never get there ("there" meaning "understandable"). Dick Hunley's review of you was certainly understandable, no? At least the things he got wrong don't seem to matter much, and it certainly makes me feel hopeful for all such further outside reception of our writings to see a person with no background in the writers we praps think of as developmental in-our-lifetime background getting off on the writing as if no problem and showing fairly simple delight in the process. Maybe any prior consideration of such background is bullshit?!!? I tend to think so, hope so, chattering away in the room with Milton &

Typed first page of letter by Coolidge to Mayer, dated September 12, 1979. United Artist Records. MSS 12. Image courtesy of Special Collections & Archives, UC San Diego Library.

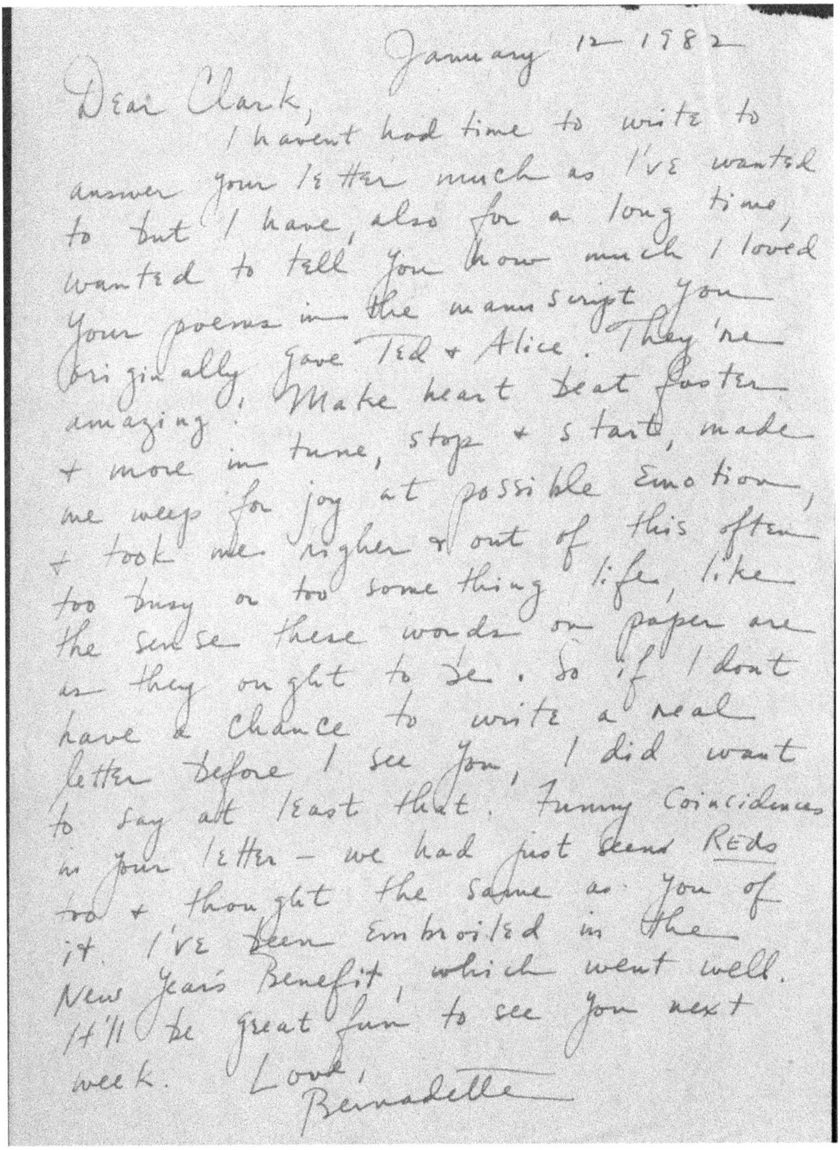

January 12 1982

Dear Clark,

I havent had time to write to answer your letter much as I've wanted to but I have, also for a long time, wanted to tell you how much I loved your poems in the manuscript you originally gave Ted + Alice. They're amazing. Make heart beat faster + more in tune, stop + start, made me weep for joy at possible emotion, + took me higher + out of this often too busy or too something life, like the sense these words on paper are as they ought to be. So if I dont have a chance to write a real letter before I see you, I did want to say at least that. Funny coincidences in your letter – we had just seen Reds too + thought the same as you of it. I've been embroiled in the New Year's Benefit, which went well. It'll be great fun to see you next week.

Love,

Bernadette

Handwritten letter by Mayer to Coolidge, dated January 12, 1982. Clark Coolidge Collection. PCMS-0101. Image courtesy of the Poetry Collection of the University Libraries, University at Buffalo, The State University of New York.

The Letters

THURSDAY SEPT. 5 1979

Dear Clark and Susan and Celia,

So where were you? Hope you guys are o.k. When you didnt show up for the moving I got worried about you but it was so chaotic, I didnt call. Did you think it was Sunday? Anyway our able-bodied men were surely that, and they moved us, more or less, into the truck, in two hours! Then we started feeling ineffably sad, then Sophia had a few tantrums Sunday morning while we were trying to have a fast breakfast at the Lenox greasy spoon, I cant even remember most of this, all I know is, like the rest of us, Marie keeps asking me when Celia is coming to visit us! And, Celia, Sophia's haircut is looking better every day! In fact her hair's getting curly, but I think that's from the hurricane we had today! ?What a welcome to this place. This place, it turns out, is unbelievably beautiful, I mean exactly where we are. I had forgotten to put that on my list of good things about it. We're surrounded by all these seas, veritable ones, of erudite mountains, on all sides, and we can see all the different parts and kinds of sky from here, if we just keep running out all the different doors, and the doors are myriad! So myriad, in fact, that it's impossible to keep track of the children who are driving us crazy, and with two sets of stairs too! But we seem to have done it, or be doing it, it's kind of lonely, did I say that before? We met Russell Banks and he seems kind of nice, sort of chubby, a little dull, I cant agree with a thing he says, he loved the Scarlet Letter version on t.v., and so on, but what can one expect. I mean after all, as far as we know, we maybe getting paid tomorrow, just for looking at these mountains and hurricanes so far. And then we can go have some lobster! There's no good bread in this neighborhood but I do have a cast iron stove with six burners and, in the kitchen at large, there are three ovens, so, I keep thinking, in the words of Mississippi John Hurt and others, it's nobody's business but my own, in a way. I am entranced, I almost hate to admit it, by this landscape, it's so fucking dramatic you wouldnt believe it, it's frightening, it will be frightening in winter. And you know what else, it's not foreshortened after all, as I described it to you, but only my original vision of it was. The idea of the college And the teaching is a bit foreshortened though, and Lewis got some communication from them as a part of his "department" which was so horrifying in its tone, sarcasm, you can imagine, the usual, but we had forgotten about that aspect of things, where the academic teachers feel somehow superior to their students, and exempt from life itself, but I promise I will never mention that again to you in a letter. Strangely there are no birds to be seen or heard up here on our mountain, we are so overwhelmed with crickets and grasshoppers, it's like a plague, and their noise is deafening, I mean the male crickets I guess. A chipmunk got caught on the window, which was down, of our car, and stayed there a long time and then Marie had a dream about chipmunks who wore hats, and danced. Sophia's been having tantrums, she must feel very displaced, and we've not been feeling our own senses of humor that much, since all our helpers went home, but tonight we are somehow more solidified, because both of us are finally at our desks, have been able to get to them through the maze of hideous boxes. I dont know what this life is going to be like but naturally, I mean as nature will have it, it sure will be pretty, or even spectacular. There's millions of amazing lakes around here, and the pond at our house is totally freezing, we jump in and right out again, it's pristine I guess. The water from the tap is freezing, the windows of the house are long and narrow and have a certain charm I didnt credit them with before, having been so entranced by my Lenox windows. Grace drove the 22-foot truck all the way here, slowly but surely, we even ate in a Howard Johnson's where we were laughed at, but almost enjoyed. What I mean to say is so far nothing awful has happened, and, amazingly, we didnt lose or even break anything, though with our salaries now I guess we could afford to! Oh we did seem to somehow lose about half the bricks for my personal bookcase so that all the Hawthorne books are piled up practically to the ceiling, and one of our couches, the pink-like one, sort of collapsed and had to be left in a local dump and Russell told us our car would never pass inspection here because they were "very hard on rust here." Ha, what a joke it all is! Here begins the new life! And yet another and another! Arent we too old for all this, I keep saying to myself! But, in some funny way, I feel it's a joke specifically because, since the days when I lived in Great Barrington, I always wanted a place like this, with all the expansiveness of these mountains and this land, and money to support it to boot! But now I think I'm a cynical old person, or am I. Sharing a house with a cynical old psychiatrist. Well at least I can say we got here, sensibly, and it is sensibly beautiful and my desk is congenial, but alas I miss you!

Love, Bernadette

WEDNESDAY 12 SEPTEMBER [1979]

Dear Bernadette,

Here I am, nine in the morning, brain slowly rising to the surface, fingers dumb from driving this insensible typewriter, legs aching from newly-instituted exercise program (more on that later), **[BM: *No time*]** doing my best to reach back for some semblance of epistolary ability answering yours (feels like it's been ages and it has). We missed your moving day partly because I wrenched my back again and it felt best when lying down but mostly it was suddenly all too sad and we didn't want to say goodbye. Somehow it began to seem that you were already gone and we'd best get on with the new dispensation. So, it feels odd here in this here letter at the first but maybe the chance for new thoughts or whatever to arise that haven't in some time and be worth going on with. It's certainly the first time I've felt like writing a letter in many's the moon, dark ages of doused connections. Perhaps you do finally find out what's worth continuing and precious little of it is? Shit, I hope most of this letter doesn't get taken up with bitching, however necessary. That sounds silly. Imagine starting a letter with "I must tell you that I have taken up with bitching." We might accidentally revive several old styles in the process! Hopefully instead we revive several "old"(?)(you said it) human beings: us. Interesting maybe to see into particularly how this poetry pursuit has aged us. **[BM: *Cant stop rushing*]** Right now I'm feeling it's aged me back to (possibly useful as refresher?) infantilism. Like, how ancient Beachboys stuff sounds great today (beyond any later/present use of "california" before anybody'd even been there to see how the "sun" there was a dustier form of neon at noon), as in "Help me Rhonda" (the single). Possibly useful as unadorned craziness? Or is craziness now (post-acid) helplessly baroque if not rococo? And any use of the art-historical terms is just such aodrnity **[BM: *adornity?*]** as I mean?? This is starting to go everywhere at once, which I absolutely want and don't want/. Let's sit down with cheep rye in our dormitory room and discuss this. My problem then was I never got to hear the birds in the morning, sleep or no sleep. My problem now is I can't surely tell if things I think/feel (no distinction?) are mechanisms resultant of my age or the world's, general confusion of self and world **[BM: *babies*]** being mostly unforeseen part of this gig as poet anyhow? And I don't get to hear many birds anytime **[BM: *(birds back)*]** in this basement room anyhow, unless they actually peck against this here wall or die against my window (which they've been doing increasingly lately, even causing most of a poem called " . . ." wait a minute, gotta look it up . . . "Glaze Spreads"). **[BM: *Gargling w. Marbles*]** Olson's hysterical disregard for same has absolutely taught me to close all parentheses, which I spose just means that within the big thing that can never be closed we can enjoy fiddling with closing all the near and thus smaller things. This is known as self-contextualization, which is always self-starting and which Creeley has never learned (Connectual Energy Deduced from Ignorance Dept.). How's this for prime head-in-the-bucket-of-everything start to further investigation and illimitable silly sarcasm? Poets' letters are never fully publishable even if they get to be. I guess I never) believed in a steady state of language (like my mother?) so I'll never get there ("there" meaning "understandable"). **[BM: *sound like Kerouac + I do cept not*]** Dick Nunley's review of you was certainly understandable, no? **[BM: *like he?*]** At least the things he got wrong don't seem to matter much, and it certainly makes me feel hopeful for all such further outside reception of our writings to see a person with no background **[BM: *Corbett's fan of Nunley*]** in the writers we praps think of as developmental in-our-lifetime background getting off on the writing as if no problem and showing fairly simple delight in the process. Maybe any prior consideration of such background <u>is</u> bullshit?!!? I tend to think so, **[BM: *hope so, then dont have to be dutiful*]** hope so, chattering away in the room with Milton & Melville. And incidentally I'm not sending you any copies of said Eagle since Mathew told me he already shipped you a great pile of same. He told me that yesterday in his lonely bookstore. Only person came in while I was sitting there drinking M's horrible toothpaste coffee was an elderly guy who immediately asked for a copy of the book "I understand written **[BM: *"fuck"—Vaughn*]** by a young lady from Lenox"(!?) and there it was right on the desk before him, Mathew handing it to him with cocaine aim and the guy says "Good, I'm sending this to my son in Berkeley." Then he opened the book and I heard him chuckle. Random Poetry Commerce in America. Such anecdote is typical of the edgy nothing that's been going on around here of late. The Mall **[BM: *The Fair*]** will evidentally(evidently?) not happen, who cares? And I can't find a decent new typewriter though have entered every store around here I can think of might provide but don't. Walked into that bizz/machinery place we used to xerox in and asked for Olivettis (they used to have the franchise before they converted totally to gizmos with TV-screens on top) and this guy in a 3-piece gave me a look that said What kinda creep would want such a thing anymore anyway? I have the feeling of having missed the boat by a feeble few weeks. Seems there's nothing between the price ranges of IBM ($800 to $1000) and the useless-looking plastic forms of Olympia, Smith-Corona etc($100 to $200). Whatta I do?? Joe told me he can "get me a deal" **[BM: *stolen*]** on Smith-Coronas in city ($150) but who wants that? I get the feeling almost nobody thinks of typewriter as personal precious tool anymore. It either comes in a gross with the corporation or you buy the cheepest possible **[BM: *no types here*]** to send off with your college-age kid. As you can no doubt see, this machine is on last legs. I took a close look at the platen and there's the problem: totally punched in/worn through. No wonder the ribbons (sleeze as they are) wear out in a week! I may have to redevelop a readable handwriting. (and learn how to spell) I seem to have strayed far off the beam, the one holding up any possible roof to this letter. Light another cigarette in disdain. Another form my new infantility has taken is focus on physical refresh. I gotta stop all this wrenched-back nonsense, so have layed out a daily "course" whereby I have to huff up this misery motherfucking trail out back on the mountain everyday without fail. Bought some good climbing boots at Arcadian Shoppe, which weigh ten pounds easy, clomp up in those. Actually **[BM: *still?*]** I can't believe I'll really go through with this (only 3 days so far) but am set to try. Reminding myself in feeling of John Cleese last night on Fawlty Towers calling his stalled car a "vicious bastard!," somehow perfect. Kick shit out of a mountain grade and tell yourself nothing in the process. Turns out there's nothing can be philosophically appended to this sort of activity, just nails and oil. 'Course to really get anything shipshape out of this madness I'd have to stop smoking too (mind and body giving eachother that well known and worn hard time again), realizing I'm working against any possibly cardio-vascular perfection. But, legs starting to feel better already anyway. Shit, how do you like this "self-help missile" this has somehow degenerated into already? **[BM: *thee generation*]** Dangers of synthesizing chat in typed form. And I can already hear you complaining, He doesn't tell us anything about Susan or Celia. Self-centered old thump! Right. But how do we order this, Susan writes you about her herself or what? OK, dig this. Susan had to go into Berkshire Med Center to have IUD removed/replaced/revived (has to happen every 3 years they say) since Rahagi(sp?) couldn't get it out in office without mucho pain, and in preparation for this so-called "operation" they gave her: (1) a valium (2) a shot of morphine and (3) sodium pentothal. Can you believe that shit?!? Enough to knock down a mountain of horses. They're insanely free with the dope these days, no? Needless to say Susan slept through the next couple days. Man, hospitals! The deeper I walked into that place the more I felt like the whole fucking building **[BM: *IUD*]** was a descending elevator. Nix to that whole set. Reminds me of those old westerns where the guy keeps a gun on the sawbones throughout whatever operation no anesthetic or nothing (well, maybe a few slugs of redeye). Well, she's ok now but piss-off residue remains. She'd tried to get a local only but they always arrange least hassle for themselves. **[Page break]**

In the switch of these sheets I've, eaten a small bowl of gratenuts (should be that spelling?), discovered we have almost no more seed for **[BM: *feed birds*]** the birds (why do we still want the birds in such proximity?), heard mysterious earth moving-sounding equipment somewhere down but definitely on our hillside, **[BM: *house bldg near*]** wondered how best to continue this letter to any sort of rude pertinence(sharp continuance feasibility), noticed that it's still cold upstairs but not so down here (temp down to 40 lastnite and fall-angle of sun **[BM: *fall*]** clearly visible in mornings), wondered how I could possibly be "interested" in the Beachboys(which includes such awkward but stunning in its seeming irrelevancy knowledge as an entire precise history of Brian Wilson's gradual turning himself into one of his own vegetables), realized that at the moment I have absolutely no desire to read anything (may have something to do with having read The Empty Copper Sea and Cage's Empty Words **[BM: *Obit.*]** on the same day last week), wondered but not too lengthily what sort of writing-sharpness I might be losing in taking all these weeks up totally (almost!) with retyping the longwork (which seems from this short focus to be alternately a great cosmic array of brilliant play of knowledge and thought-gap realization and I can't stand it it's so great I love it etcetcetc. AND sheerest unraveling insanity in no uncertain terms (good title)), and now pretty much up to real time in this very sentence wondering what or if you can make out of all this thinking grammar. It looks like one can be even more giddly longwinded on the letterpage than on the phone, yes? Wouldn't it be great if we could keep moving talk in these letters constantly out into possibility what we didn't **[BM: *cld there be anything?*]** even realize we thought yet? Or would that be embarrassing and/or dangerous? There were things in that new letter-work of yours that would be a good starting off point to this notion of letter-writing if I could only remember them(!), so you'd better send that on soon. I mean, I could go on and build this all further on the basis of lapses (your famous "lapses"?) but then the danger would be that I might accidentally reveal **[BM: *secrets*]** some of my real secrets (you always kidded me to come on go ahead reveal anyway why not?). But the problem with <u>that</u> could be that what were actually my secrets might turn out to be just things you have no notions of or interest in. Into the depths/heights of that Private Language problem again, are we ever far from that one? Like, a stalagmite from a quarried-away cave in Pennsylvania may be about to slip from its tentative lean against the window frame and crash right through the glass. Believe it or not, an example I can grab easily here of the actual portal to a secret. But how could you or anyone make the same plunge through all the residues **[BM: *by . . .*]** (and residue-futures) of that one that I can. Thus this might all become poised on a diamond of the vastly-dense or the incredibly-stupid. Another point entropically (but enjoyably-hysterically) being that one arrives this way very rapidly at not any longer knowing what one is talking about internally or externally to any initiating proposal. Sheerest windfalls gleaming in total intellectual absence? This is starting to feel like that dorm room again. Or else, one would have to take endless time going back to the beginning of everything story-of-my-life-and-mind-in-detail fashion a la Neal Cassady on a limitless nightride? It's real appropriate that all these sentences that I no longer understand where I am when I get to the end of them end up as questions. A question mark might there equal three little dots spreading off into a booming waste. And a further problem (fun, no?) is while I have a delight in going back **[BM: *yes*]** over everything in infinite parse and shuffle I also have a strong (maybe stronger at the moment) desire to shuck all that and start all over again fresh. Yes/But, indeed. And still I think the real craziness is any settling for the one rather than the two(does the three always follow or does it just lay around out there waiting in ambush?). Well, shit, I'd rather push through this sort of muck always than find ourselves in the well-known letter-welter of so&so's book is better than so&so's, or I just saw Days of Heaven and it's really just a pretty slide show.

Can we have our [**BM: *cant "remember"***] sparkling rude or otherwise original heads and keep them too? Luckily I probably won't be able to include much poet-biz gossip detail in these letters since I seem to have junked all those correspondences that would have provided input for same. Come to think of it you're my only source [**BM: *8th st., Harris***] for such anymore (in mail), so watch it! This letter's no doubt different than one would be in midst of writing something (not just typing and looking). Though I must say that in retyping the longwork I get an amazing amount of precise memory-flashes/dream-flashes (some from long ago) as well as particulate recalls of how passages were written, what was in mind at the time. More than I thought possible, especially since the first parts of this work go back easily five years. What would such a packed-field do to a reader? Maybe this is why reactions to the writing are very seldom exact and the work gets quickly relegated to the avant-garde drum? If only the speed of readers in retreat could cool one's head on a hot day. [**BM: *readers like cigarettes "Enjoy the mud in yr mouth"***] This particular cigarette tastes horrible, put it out. Sometimes the words are only passing familiar and I grab one on the way to momentum. Shit, how much of writing (I mean the actual use of words) is memory anyway? That's still a damn good question! How come you womenfolks are the only ones to keep bringing that up? Another at least interesting question (to me anyway). And how come you get to write such long beautiful sentences without the feeling of the need to stop them on the way? [**BM: *no punk***] I often feel lines with no punctuation as bodyless floating nowhere. How come? And yet, sametime, a period seems only a point to move from. Only in art I guess could indecision be touted as structure. I feel like I'm on the edge here of going into a whole lot of personal stuff I don't quite want to do in this letter. Later maybe, if you want. But [**BM: *40?***] being forty surely is a great strainish business. A good time to crack up. A hell of a time to find oneself negatively incapable. Feeling forced to reconsider everything in not enough light is kinda miserable. Need [**BM: *short time or long, all same, babies***] larger-scale chalanges and not sure if I got the gyz to push 'em. I don't mean it to sound that way, just concerning. Hard to believe in another month [**BM: *bef. Frisc. Liquor #23***] I'll be hurled to Frisco in another tin tube. Hope they stock in some JD in those little bottles. Gottago now and run up my daily mountain. Write soon.
Love to you all,

Clark

P.S.—Still nothing from B.B. Send his address & phone if you have it. I probably should get in toch or touch or something?
PPS: Tell Lewis there's a live Talking Heads album put out as DJ-promo by Warner Bros that's great! Maybe their best disc. They sound a great LIVE band, with interesting ad-lib moves especially on Byrne's vocals.

[BM:
Go on forev.
dont wanna
plan

———

religious
+ poetosity
Brodey   Yom Kippur
Oldenburg
Dylan, etc.   Pope
Fanny + fall
***Russell*]**

OCTOBER 2 1979

Dear Clark,

Here I am, nine at night! Well let me begin this letter with a few more excalmations (is that what they are? I dont feel calm at all!): What an astonishing lack of time I have! It's the combination of the new life being new plus all this debilitating teaching for which one prepares two nights a week and then recovers two plus all the people we see are what you might call new people, not that we see so many of them but always their being new consumes energy which is my old-woman (to old man!) way of thinking, now conserve all that for later, for writing and so on. Now Lewis and I have begun to believe we'll have to eliminate all people, except the ones in our classes, and thus our classes must replace the socalled social life, because otherwise there is not the proper kind of time. I never thought a "Job!" could have this effect (THE JOB), I mean six hours a week, it is not so much time consuming as just consuming, plain consuming, and I have such a distinct image of what the kind of time I need must be like and since I absolutely have to have it, I just keep eliminating what is not necessary right down to the elements of what might turn into being crazy, as you say, too. However, I will not spend the whole letter, whatever a letter might be, complaining either; I think a letter turns out to be writing, as I am learning in doing my book, yet it is not quite writing but something else I can come close to doing and then turn away, like a seduction or something, which I enjoy doing, coming close to when I'm writing for the book (for the books?) but then when I'm writing a real letter I can see what the differences are and they are just as distinct and clear as my demands for time. Now tonight Russell stopped over, in great need of a drink after his long class and he was much freer in talking, for the first time really, about his inability to do writing writing, as Gertrude Stein might have had it and kept calling himself an artificer or fabulator, all these great words, some culled from Hawthorne, and remarking on how us guys could write so much about ourselves. Now something is happening to my self-machine and it refuses to space properly—maybe it doesn't have time! **[Page break]**

Perhaps another kind of paper might or would more please the machine, oh I forgot what was supposed to be one of the beginning exclamations—wow what a great letter you wrote! It's like an intellectual exercise to answer it! I could make notes! You see I can let myself use exclamations in letters, and nowhere else! Meanwhile the rest of the world's claims on my time most temporally involve vivid visits from Harris Schiff who cannot decide when he gets here whether he is escaping the city and all his other plights in life or visiting with us, lonely as we are, and he feels just as back and forth about the children, and he is such a baby himself that we are all nowhere, and he is embarrassing, I must admit he (and other poets I can think of) make me feel like my old eighteen year old self where I couldnt speak and feel ashamed somehow of my normal feelings like saying, "what a beautiful tree!," "what a great rain," and so on. They make you feel like a fool, perhaps (and I'm hoping) because it may be those very simple things they cannot express easily, but, however, it's a real strained way to feel and the whole thing made Lewis and me think maybe we werent so lonely after all. And now of course there's more (and I havent even gotten to be having a real conversation with you in this letter yet, that is still to come), Lewis's father has had some embolism, small and just in his eye, which seems to have wound him up in the hospital for tests and the rest of the family in a turmoil where they are thinking maybe Lewis's presence is necessary in

New York, which at this point would only freak both his father and me (the calmer members of the family) out, however all this is new like a cutting edge and I sure do realize that parents, especially at a distance, become old and maybe even sick and perhaps even die and I am only kind of sad that my own experience with all this is by itself so old and of no use to anyone but myself, with all its consequent weaknesses and strengths (and secrets, we'll get to that later). So except for describing what the teaching has become like, this is my present situation, this is mostly just tonight. And tonight is too a beautiful warm false pre-Indian summer night, with warm air coming in all the doors our landlord has told us to lock for fear his ex-wife will try to come in (is she a wild Indian?) perhaps to steal away the ski poles they are fighting about, or something. The life of transients does include these absurdities, I know. But it is inspiring, the mountains are very like those Persian shawls Monument Mountain was supposed to have worn, by Hawthorne, and the local trees, the parochial ones about our house are all in a different state of changing, and though I am determined to remain the same and thus still cannot identify with my old love of autumn, perhaps out of a stern reluctance to adore what I have not been able to have for a while, in such profusion, I still can almost deify the return of the birds to the environs of this house, they have come back, I think because the crickets, and their noise, have calmed down, just winter birds, bluejays and chickadees and such, and the old aging crickets like me are wandering about inside the house in such a funny way, I mean they really do have possibilities that other bugs have not because you can scare them and they'll jump, and one by one they are pleasant and lucky to listen to, but I sure am relieved of their incessant noisy drone outdoors and also the chance of being stung by one of those myriad hovering wasps who had begun to become so lethargic as to hang on my clothing, as if waiting for a handout or something. You see I have a problem with all these commas, I've been using alot of them but sometimes I dont exactly know where to put them. I had a student today doing an imitation of an excerpt from WINNING HIS WAY and she kept putting commas in and no one could understand why I told her to keep them out! Though I did try to explain all about it. However these students are rather like how the nuns had hoped I and my cohorts would be, and never turned out to be—unrelenting logicians of the most unintelligent sort (I have some good ones though!) who have taken life literally so far and dont want anything to fuck it up, including words like fucking, I've had to defend that one already. No more exclamations!

Now there are so many things in your letter that require answering I dont know where to begin (I have forborne to call you up!)! I know I havent been reading my art magazines lately, though the college library (which I've never been to yet, can you believe it!) has a big stack of everything, but is adornity one of those words, I like it, as I like being old, I wish to be older, after all it's the only chance we have, however the problem I see with it is I cant stop rushing, being pregnant is like being older for a while and I see while I am it that I have to slow down a bit and that's one of the things that makes me detest pregnancy, yet I still adornity the babies, and many women I meet say the opposite thing, they say everything's o.k. till after the baby is born. Well I just like the people, in whatever stage they exist and persist in not being able to see why they have to interfere with my own functioning, that is if I adornity them with their needs and lots of love and then I should be free to do my work, not still encumbered as I am, pregnant, with a preventative measure so as to be supposed to be "resting, etc.," I do hate that and I've never been good at indulging myself though I know always it is this same old difficulty with rushing through things, even this book that I thought I was more or less quietly working on, the kind of book I thought I could adapt to things like moving and having another baby, and now I find myself suddenly just as involved in it as I was in Midwinter Day and when I cant work for a while, like when Harris was here, I begin to see images, it's like when the alcoholic person sees his dream in the d.t.'s because he cant have them because he cant sleep, so I see as I've always known that I am this subject, and there's nothing I can do about it, and this gets more extreme (one of my students, a Dutch woman, used the word "extremized") as I get older, if you'll forgive me I see it as a race against embolisms, or something, but however the one thing I do learn, getting better at this, or just more experienced, is that the pregnancy is temporal, and not lasting forever, and really is becoming such a short time and so I am beginning to see that if I can adapt to that I can find it analogous to adapting to the baby afterwards, which I've begun to find easy, long as not many other things impinge on time, like people! Ah, I've written myself into a corner again! It's crazy, isnt it, this life in present America, where you absolutely cannot function best, one way or the other! Is that so or not? Ah now I've had a million thoughts, when Harris was here he made some remarks about how it wasnt **[just]** him but all of us were sexists and it was just ingrained in us and I felt very elated to tell him that I felt if I didnt feel writing poetry, or whatever it is that we do, changes all that and somehow frees us from the parts of being human that are necessarily small, why then I would throw it all up because it had then necessarily become less than a beginning, less than a way to take you higher, sometimes it seems like everybody forgets all that, where they are, under the stars, on the ground or pavement, next to the trees or buildings, a human—I spend half my time, the kind of time I was talking about needing, reminding myself of where I am and what I am. However if you want to talk about confusion of self and world, then I see that, very individually at this time, as babies and the New York Times (and what I've been learning in my classes relates to this but I dont know if I can even explain that). **[Page break]**

Sorry for the variations in the papers here, but in a new place, I havent been able to conquer certain things yet! I think the most unforeseen part of being a poet is having to deal so much with everything which for me, seeing myself somehow determined in time to be timing everything, and still for the things I start as experiments to, in my older age, to be turning out to be so necessary or even right, if I can say that, it all throws me for a loop and when the birds come back or Harris pretends to fix the battery and then the next morning the car doesnt start, well I just feel I know something that perhaps others do not. However I know I dont know enough to be what others might call confident, isnt it like gargling with marbles I was thinking? Once I experimented with gargling with salt water (this is what a person who doesnt take drugs does, I guess) and when I swallowed a bit of it, it was true, my esophagus rejected it and closed up; I have always been astonished that I could trust my body to react in the predicted ways to things so that I feel quite free nowadays to tell the doctor (or midwife) that I'm certain I will be just like a statistic, but for my unexpressed (now) knowledge of the tinier workings of my soul, and on my body they work. But they dont matter and they are what metabolically almost translate into the poetry, not to write about them maybe but to present them to the meditation between me and the rest of the world, the world that exists and the meditation that exists, but in that case I do not exist anymore. As far as I can see. Sometimes I feel like in my new work I am trying to sound like Kerouac, and I have been so obsessed with him again lately, remembering how I was so tempted to go to his funeral, I was living in Great Barrington, practically with my car, and I do wind up sounding like him except that I do not and I cant string the words along as well and surely I think in some ways I am becoming even more understandable, but then I cant tell. Reading that biography of him took up all my thinking, all surrounding this moving I was reading it and beyond and it was the usual Kerouac scene—horror and amazement and love. When we were in Boston Bill Corbett made fun of the Nunley review I showed him and I was aghast at his reaction, but I didnt say anything. I think Bill thought I wouldnt like him to like it! Meanwhile it turns out that not only is it Bill who practically got us these jobs but it is him who's telling us (much to his own dismay at revealing it in a somewhat drunken moment) (and you must not say anything to anybody about it now!) that there is some chance that both me and Lewis will get NE grants this year which means that we neednt have ever moved here, which mainly means to me time lost and leaving Lenox which I loved unconscionably, please definitely dont let on about this, or else I'm afraid Bill will shoot himself as he regretted mentioning it about a minute after he did. But anyway, here we would be, if that turns out to be so, and what would we do then? With alot of money? I understand the exigencies of the life I've chosen (have I chosen it?) and I'm not complaining that way, at least I'm not a waitress or something, but really couldnt it be more civilized? Oh you'll have to forgive me for saying it that way. Anyway about Dick Nunley's review, I was tempted to write him about it, in fact I had the whole letter of praise phrased in my mind, and it would be to say I hope you can write this way about me and then that begins to be meaning that the duties of the poet may be much reduced, as regards reading. But he was very good and I was pleased with that.

Hey, speaking of riches
it's been brought up to me that the thing to do is to get oneself a STOLEN
ibm typewriter, for less than 300 bills, as they say, whaddayou think? I might
indulge in that, if I can and it would work out, you definitely have to get rid
of that boat you're driving, however if stealing avails none of its charms to
you, why dont you get yourself a second-hand Royal, an old manual, I think
it might be the best thing you could find, dadaptable and sesweet. And I'd use
one if I could find it, but we still need to replace this thing of mine, to type

stencils electric, but otherwise you could do with a manual, if it was the right kind. But it's got to be a Royal, And so, like the aging typewriter, you and I are now climbing up and down the mountains for exercise, isnt it boring? isnt there some way to just stay high, i mean minimally high, high enough to just feel right enough to write, without all this shit? I think it's great, actually, and could never understand why you abhorred that mountain all this time, ignored it, when it's such a great one or nice one, to walk up, I mean it's not as if you're subject to hideous fears about it, and so on, or are you? I mean if Lewis has to go to New York I might think as is my wont that I suddenly cannot drive the car which so far I've never driven the awful automatic non-romantic car I hate so much! However, since fears are always so sexual like fears of a mountain (I'm not saying you have them, but I do, without doubt, so I'm putting myself in what they call your place,) I would have some forsworn pleasure in all that too. **[Page break]**

Now it occurs to me, as if I almost didnt exist, in this chaos of papers, that in the course of telling Russell Banks about what Paul Metcalf thought of my and Lewis's works, if that can be so, I had a sudden inspiration that if I were a member of the me-generation, then Paul was one we could scalp off as the "thee generation," how about it? However that is not the same as changing one's iud and you must tell Susan that the midwife showed me yesterday what they call a "cervical cap," a new kind of more efficient diaphragm, all the while encouraging me to convince Lewis to have a vasectomy, which she could not understand my explaining that his being Jewish was preventing him from having! However (also) if you tell Susan that I can barely reach my cervix, because of the way things are, then we all decided perhaps the cervical cap, like other methods, was not going to work for me. So perhaps it's being monks, like I always hoped, will be the thing for us! No sex at all! Nothing! Absence! Forbearance! Brother and sister and so on,—finally I'm the Virgin Mary! Well, we'll see. Maybe I would have to change my poetry name. Bernadette Joseph et al. And all. I hate this New Hampshire korec-type.

But I will feed the birds now that they're here and see what we can set up and there's someone, even in this woods, building a house right near us, we can hear their radios as they play them, building, across the field and Obituaries by William Saroyan is a great book but it's not as good as Kerouac, or even reading about him because Saroyan's walking, almost in his sleep, is not as good as all that fast driving, though not in real life and now we get to the problem of secrets and letter writing. I do think the letters are better for that, even just for the typographical erros, you see what I mean? There's nothing dangerous I feel if we just swear to get rid of everything, the evidence, tear up the letters, burn them, I could even say in them I am disappointed in life, I am bereft, and I am sometimes, I am lost because what I want to do, feel determined to do, cannot be done, and I am always finding some man in me to tell me that I am not the moment I exist in and sweet life acts unfairly and then they tell you that's because of what you know, and that it's true. Well it is not and there is a purer state or estate, and that's the existence of secrets there, and what's it worth beyond death and the ranting about that that we can do, however we are also all so fraught with this penurious wisdom we've got, which we've learned from somewhere which makes us want to be babies. **[Page break]**

Now I hadda start a new page again, isnt that silly. I know everything I know is stupid, that's why I'm afraid to read more books, I have that immigrant instinct. It's got to be something new I discovered for myself, I know that sounds insane—could there be anything we think that we havent even thought yet?—well yes, there could be a few things, hidden in the syntax of the awful memory of this language, I hope so. I mean that memory replaces what we know of life, say as children, so language is what's left to us, and color too and the rest. So that that memory (and I resent that biography creep, McNally saying that Kerouac shouldnt have thought he was a genius, like Stein did too, after all he was one) turns into genius and the genius becomes what's left to us, does that make sense? Genius of language, the ultimate pause, almost as far as I can see the one way to discover something that neither new or old, but now I'm getting waxing eloquent without the justification of the limitless nightride of sentences we'll either have or not, it's kind of handed out to us; lately all these poets are becoming religious, namely, Jim Brodey, Patty Oldenburg, Russell Banks, Fanny Howe, "bob dylan," the Pope and so on; it makes me nervous. I know that religion if it is something is like poetosity and I know I can go on forever and dont wanna plan anything, however I "cant remember" being a poet, any better than I can see afterwards that tree of yellow or red, whatever it will eventually be, nor can I remember what came in the mail, I never could, today, I remember the eighth street bookstore closed down for good, it said that in The Times today, but readers retreat like the pleasures of cigarettes and Saroyan said to one of the men he was obituarizing, "Enjoy the mud in your mouth." It's amazing and now I feel desperate to say, like Pontormo, I am thirty-four and having another baby now and you are forty and either the time spent is short or long, I am rotting no I dont mean rotting I mean rooting for us to go on long, because it seems that's the best way of knowing if only I could stop rushing (I wont have any more babies now!), sweet is the typographic sleep that's allowed to us either way. Well it may be horrible to get so telegraphic as is allowed to us in letters, I cant write poetry lately, hope this reaches you before you go to Frisco for the environmental reading, these letters may be long lost to us like taints on our characters but they will get there.

Love,
Bernadette

OCTOBER 19 1979

Dear Clark + Susan—

Thought you might enjoy reading about the long-winded local UFO's as annotated in this radical newspaper "we" have "here." This photo was taken on the hill we live on + I swear a few weeks previous I myself saw one of those same red + green phenomena I had seen once at your house, while looking at the stars. Well if being here only turns me into that sort of lunatic I'll feel I've gotten off easy. Wouldn't it be nice to have an identity—finally? We are so lonely, we think of you often + I for one even have a nostalgia for "Lenox," whatever it was. I sure cant write about this place that way. Do you think, as you go north, the people get less friendly? Or is it just our peculiar straits—teachers with a family among teachers without one, poets who are teachers among teachers who are not that, townspeople who are with the college among townspeople who hate the college, and, finally, among the few people we do know here, the only ones who don't flee the place as if it were Hades on the weekends which means between Thursdays + Tuesdays! So we are so without even acquaintances that Lewis [→ with "pregnant" leg] had to walk four miles today to have the car fixed + the UPS man said it took him a week to deliver a package because "nobody on the road or at the school had ever heard of you"—! Meanwhile the college secretaries have accused me of "acting inappropriately" because I tried to put an ad for a playgroup in the "faculty bulletin"—am I allowed to say now "sic transit gloria" or something? Tell Sylvia this college's motto is "Dura Duranda Alta Petenda"—I couldnt agree more! I need somebody to strive to talk to! And to be loved + praised!! Oh well, just the usual demands—Be in touch, as they say,

Love, kisses + everything—
Bernadette

THURSDAY ONE NOVEMBER [1979]

Dear Bernadette,

I'm finally back, it has seemed a long time away to me too, and you've had to wait for this answer I'm sorry about that, but time . . . Your letter so rich I want to take off from every point of words in touch but that's beyond me at this point I fear. Try my best and anyway get on to the next point of meeting (almost wrote "meaning," why not?). This business of going somewhere as a poet is like landing on another planet for a while (whistle stop), even if you are wonderfully taken care of by good friends in a home, as I was by the Palmers. In fact I wonder if I would have been able to do this (as well as I did anyway without sickness creeping in) without such replacement-home. I imagined living in some drear hotel room to go back to after the tingling exhaustion of pouring the poem out each night, no cooking in the room and nothing but street noises for company. No doubt though then I would have had thoughts and especially dreams that were not allowed by the replacement hominess. I only recalled one dream I had while there: an elaborate thing of hexes being arranged for me and everybody I know by someone invisible, placing of complicated strata of stones with special papers leaved in between, but nothing came of all of it, 'least that I remember. And certainly nothing in real life as the whole length of the readings went so much better than even I had hoped. The pointed result of the whole attempt I spose: to hear the poem coming back to me, from inside my head around out in the air of a room and back in, justified! Even forgetting the audience, who were at least respectful and even sometimes seeming inspired. I did get to quite a few real highs in the reading, transported back close to the source of the writing, maybe, is it that? Anyway, I really held the floor, as they say, inviolable as the feeling I remember in playing high music, you are the whole space in time for a fraction. Funny thing was though, surprising me beyond plan, I only got exactly HALF way through the 500pp! I had had the purely intuitive feeling beforehand to read in two 45-minute sets and that seemed to work out best keeping me and everybody fairly bright throughout, though of course it kept me from finishing the whole length but maybe saved my voice, which was no problem, I brought I thermos of honey & tea & lemon & rum for the last night but really didn't need it. So, half way, which led to jokes about "you'll have to go for another week," which I could almost at that point see doing except they had someone else scheduled, but mainly I figured then it would really seem like some sort of conceptual-athletic event which I dearly wanted to prevent, that kind of reception seeming to want to creep in enough at every point anyway. I think most of the poets thought I was crazy to attempt such a "marathon" anyway (marathon is a California term nowadays), but after all I wonder what they did think. The Language Guys very much in attendance, sometimes in shifts it seemed, but they kept a fairly respectful distance, guess I'm lucky that way. I mean, they didn't lay any of their misthought "Marxism" on me. Excepting Barry, of course, who mainly just goes on revealing how his mind never stops to pick up anything but just keeps talking to no point. And he really is very uncomfortable around people and told me how he has these months-long stomach aches the doctors can't cure (ha!) And Grenier kept on with such praise for my work which he always seemed to connect with his own so I finally just couldn't believe any of it. But, I liked Bob Perelman & Kit Robinson (especially, an instantly identifiable personal resonance sort) & Lyn Hejinian is so nice I wish her work was better. But, shit, you know, now that I think of it (and use all these commas!), nobody really reacted in any way (excepting Michael, but then we go back a long way in sympathy) that led me to realize anybody even got near what I think I'm doing. Is it our fate to be taken away? What am I looking for out in that room anyway? And wouldn't it be great if praise were actually that next step (even an inch) forward into someone else's realm? Otherwise even the best audience seems a great vacuum cleaner. So much so that I feel least-poet the exact moment after I step down from up on the work. That step is really the long fall. Which leads to all that stuff (interesting actually if one could use the write vocabulary) (that "write" a slip for "right") about where does the poetry come from, feelings of inside/outside & all that, right, stuff. I sat in on a class Michael was teaching about Spicer at the New College and of course got into his "dictation," which reminded me of that thing you once expressed to me about always having(?) to feel you are somehow addressing a specific person (or place?) when writing a poem. Say more about that if you can, it's always intrigued me. Now what can I say about that. I always seem to have to have all these things and places and people (specific) somehow there in the mind of the writing and sometimes I feel I am addressing them and sometimes not, depending. And "depending" does seem a big term, no, more a big action in the chemic/physic of the writing a poem. What that WCW poem always seems to me to be about, that verb like a big arm bending at the elbow and brought "upon" the everything else. It's the image of the working of the poem but of course also endlessly mysterious (generative). I have a big elbow drawing by Guston here, the hand working the brush, that rings with that poem. And yeah, it's getting to the sex angle here, sure. Sex, flex. I always get sexually obsessed when I go away that long anyway, road blues road dues. Which leads to a completely nervous compression, language image whatever. But, thank god, as I get older all that is more totally focused on Susan, so I'm spared that random craziness many are prey to. I just tend to contract around a very specific lack. And scribble pornography in notebooks. It's like being on a planet where everybody is the wrong sex! So you get strung in memories of possible futures. How did I get off on this. So I do all this reading and then one day it's over. And then I go off to the mountains and try to push myself up there after years of not, and the fascinating thing there is that day when we got stopped, by weather and feet, just exactly at the shoulder of Half Dome, it was so absolute and amazingly so that we couldn't even imagine going even one more step! So clear drawn, it's hard to believe now. You go up against that really alien universe and it just draws the line, at some perfect point that's the stop, you just don't get any further. Something that seldom happens in my writing (I always want to urge it a bit further, just to see . . .), but when it does it's great (at least in retrospect!), you're finally allowed to have a squint at an absolute edge. And edges are so active. As opposed to, say, notions or issues. All issues are false, because they don't issue forth.

Break here to try to get your letter better, but that ain't gonna happen exactly I can see. Richness is motion, and I'm over here already. Good, we go on. And maybe it all applies (to what you said too) anyway? Mirrors. Did it ever cross your mind that in that famous "holding a mirror up to nature" speech Shakespeare might have actually simply meant showing nature to itself, as if nature were some kind of "being" able to receive and respond? Now that I disposed of "notions" I say that! Then you can never see your life from outside. Like Michael telling me that in years to come lots who weren't there will claim they heard my reading of the longwork. I mean, I love him for telling me that but I just can't believe it. That's all happening to one of those guys in the past we all read and read about. Which is me too!?!? Or like Guston saying about Dore Ashton's book: Hey, that's a kind of interesting guy she's talking about. Seems things get past quicker as you get older. Always a speedier trip past succession of various yourselfs, but it don't really help the view? Feeling like I've left myself all over the lot. And this great mass of what I have left "in here" so transformed I often can't even tell where it came from. Like your saying "I never can remember being a poet." It occured to me long ago that all this "making it new" might be just function of memory loss, or your once-upon-a-time "lapses."

The sun finally came out, filtered through a lot of misty layers, 2 P.M. After the Albany radio said "sunny today" at 7 this morning. Sure. Been going to bed early, getting up with everybody, watching little TV, hope it keeps on this way and I get back into a lot of work done. All the trees are bleak, just as I thought I'd return to. Novemblear. I can spell. . . . Ha! SMELL the snow. And I have a big miserable story about typewriters to tell in a minute. But first I was going to say that with all this performing I haven't read any books, or even seen any movies. Listening to music mostly at Michael's during the days, he has a great various record collection. It's great not to read sometimes, just listen and look. The words always going on inside anyway, helpless. We went over to Duncan's house one afternoon, and of course he never shuts up so I just looked all around at all the crazy nicknack Victorian and whatever pictures and hangings he covers everything with. It's funny, his house right in the middle of one of the worst Spanish Mission neighborhoods, lowriders lounging on every corner. And some rooms in his house are libraries, completely different from the room you just came through, with professional-type stacks and even a card catalog! And Jess's collages, one in color he had just finished, about six feet wide, seemed to include everything like a Bosch landscape or something, he said he had tried hard to "for once" keep death out of. He's very nice, taller than I thought, kind of heavy and funny, he and I laughed a lot about coffee making difficulties (he made some great strong brew) and the insanity of Hi-Fi while Duncan carried on. I always get that impulse to put everything in, I guess I'm an amasser! Like, even of the Catholic Mass I always thought it was at least supposed to suggest everything, no? But then they took the Latin out and diminished the returns. The brain is a full place. Love of Kerouac I spose is somewhat a love of that. And by the way, you don't sound like him at all, though I know what you mean and I often feared I would end up helplessly sounding a bad imitation. Funny how that turns around. I used to fear Stein in the same way, would avoid reading her, the very real pleasure of reading her for long periods. Actually, when you think on it, nobody has ever been able to imitate her. Same with all the great irreducible inspirations. The ones that set you a realm.

Oh, the typewriter, sob. Seems like this is all about typewriters and mountains, how they are similar in fear. Susan and I were in Bennington one saturday for lunch at the Brasserie and stopped for the hell of it at that Business World store on the main street where they happened to have one Olivetti Lexicon 82 machine in stock, so I figured why not? I'd been having so much trouble finding anything in this parched neighborhood and it was only $275. Took it home and used it for 2 or 3 days, specificly to help with my longwork retyping project of course, and I'm just getting the touch, even learning to enjoy it, when suddenly I hit the return key and the carriage jams. Immoveable, can't even turn the platen. Shit. So I take it all the way back up to Bennington, where it's been sitting ever since. They can't get parts! Serves me right maybe, buying on such an utter whim. And you're probably right, I shoulda got an old Royal portable, which would be so much like going back to the beginning for me, my first machine was one of those. What to do. Pissed off and back to this old horse, I ended up having to finish the longwork typing on. Bought a new ribbon and what the fuck. Trouble is, now with so many things we haven't paid any attention to in decades, there's really nothing in between the cheepy plastic Joe College models and the high price IBMs. I used Michael's out there and it felt really solid and sure, one of the first models with a ball he got cheap from Duncan. Sure, if I could find a hot one I'd go for it in a minute. But you probly got to be in the City to catch those deals?

Nuff about that sob. Naropa. Anne called and described this Shakespeare project; one week, four lectures, two on S., two on whatever, plus a reading. Pick one play. Natch, Allen already reserved The Tempest (the bastard!), so I think I'll do

Timon and also not avoid bringing in the Sonnets somehow along the line. It intrigued me, so I accepted. What would you have picked? At least it gives me something else to think of and I'll probly have fun this winter reading through and thinking about him. Or maybe I'm nutz.

I left the longwork with Michael to be copied. He has a friend with his own copying service. So you'll be getting a copy hopefully soon, he'll mail it from there. How's the copying scene there? Hope you can send your letter-work soon as I'm dying to read it. Or are you going on with so much it's really incomplete so far? Send some of it (like what you showed me in Lenox that night) anyway?

Feels like I really haven't answered or continued anyway most of the things in your letter I wanted to get to. But let's keep on as it goes, and anyway I did want you to have something before much more time passed. This much single-spaced is probly hard enough to read? Should I 1½ it? Fear of running out of paper maybe. Certainly enough to say. Hope you're not too lonely up there. Sounds like you're busy enough, and busy will keep you from totally woebegone. I'm beginning to feel really at home for the first time today, writing this letter and the writing rebeginning. Actually, in midst of the typing project a new work popped up and I got a good start on it somehow even though I'd thought I was totally distracted. It's this: two sets of twelve poems each. Wrote the first six of the first set, each poem about 1½ page length (so far anyway). What a funny "form"! This may end up being the winter's work. Plus continuation of the long one, reading Shakespeare, etcetc.

Larry sent me a postcard from Arezzo saying "The true cross sprang from a seed in Adam's mouth. Why aren't you here to see it?" And the Piero detail on the other side looks like Christ's head is springing from the grain of the tree of the cross.

The sun's in my eyes. More soon.

All Love,

Clark

NOVEMBER 19, 1979

Dear Clark,

These letters weigh too much, I'm trying to trim them down, our house is too big for us, that's small talk. You sure do need a new machine, your letter looked like it was typed on a sandwich, can't wait to see the results of the Olivetti, now my machine is in the shop for complete overhaul & major repairs, $55 by a nice man, one of the few, in Concord. Everybody in Concord looks retarded, not a nice thing to say. Let's see I was thinking of writing you an essay on the nature of the New Hampshire people but that might turn out to be as dull as writers corresponding about their machines! Suffice it to say that Lewis and I cannot figure out how these people have fun & yesterday we went to the two Concord libraries for the first time and not only were they dismal and depressing, one like an airport, one where you were forbidden to "see" the books but could only call for them through the card catalogue, but I also asked the librarian if this was the place where (Russell had told me) the Franklin Pierce–Nathaniel Hawthorne correspondence was housed and she paused for a long time, looked at me like I was crazy and said, I dont know whatever you are talking about but we do have an interlibrary loan service. You see she didnt know the meaning of the word correspondence and had never heard of either of those two famous New Englanders! <u>La lutte continue</u>, or something like that.

Should we have paragraphs? Your dream of the strata of stones sounds like it was your work itself, for sure, and you are the invisible one, but—arranging a hex for yourself! & everyone you know! Not bad, actually, maybe the word hex has some other meaning too, all I can think of is rex. Arranging "hecks," as in aw heck. It's a nice dream to invent while away from home. Hecklers! Ah I give up, you're the only one who'll know. Your trip sounded good, a good way to open up the serious winter season. Here it has been so milk, I meant mild, all this November so far, no snow and 60-degree days with actual sun, I'm beginning to like November but this place continues to be weird, I'm writing you in the midst of our Thanksgiving vacation and on the eve of our leaving for NY, believe it or not, we're driving there, to be staying in a vacant apartment in Brooklyn of an aunt of Peggy's, ah what would we do without Peggy! It seemed timely to go and we need a vacation, a true one, from our own restraints here. Mostly I need to remember what person it is that I am because as a result of our pretty superficial relations with people here, and some of the ridiculous things that have happened which I wont go into, I'm beginning to think I'm this person who thought of myself in the past as liking people and being generous and somewhat fair but that it turns out I'm some sort of inadvertent misanthrope, and probably cruel, so I've gotta go be with friends who know me. Also I think that's sort of a need of pregnancy. Being pregnant makes you kind of doubt the world to begin with so it'll be nice to be able to slough that feeling off for a while, like temporary relief from a phobia or something, this teaching at this particular college making everything seem kind of drafty and fraught with a sort of unavoidable and admitted failure. Does this make sense?

Well if that doesnt, this may make less. First you've gotta tell me which play that mirror to nature speech comes up in, it's come up in various readings of mine recently three or four times and in your letter and I must say I think of it often on my own too, but the play's skipped my mind. Now I cant figure out my thinking on this but thinking on that makes me want to say that when I read something I've written in the past—doesnt matter how distant, as long as it's "over," done with—I'm always finding I'm being (in the writing) more interesting than I thought I was and then I always think, well that is because one's "values" or even just sense of things gets slacker and surely less precise when you are not in the moment of creating the thing; at a remove from it then I guess, thus maybe the mirror. Also that the thing, the work, isnt supposed to exist in relation to me anymore, anyone but me is o.k., so my reading of it is sort of surreptitious and almost evil, I'm not "supposed to be" doing it, it's like peeking, something forbidden. But, if I can pursue this even more, the "person" (apart from work) that I admire in myself is always the person of the past and not the one of the moment and this sure is memory loss, because perhaps here like the writing, I forget in my view of the past what was "bad" or hard about being that person and only tend to wish I could regain some figurative lost momentum, just as I forget about the exigencies, the circumstances of writing and thus distort everything. But the writing does do this one thing—sometimes, occasionally, not too often, the whole thing written in the past can seem to me clear as a bell and in some stage of perfection and as a result of knowing that that can be, or seem so, maybe I try to inform my life so. Boy do I begin to sound mixed up, tell me if you see what

I say! Maybe I can bring in the famous lapses again here to say that they are the spaces in between that dont exist in words enough in the writing to somehow render these distortions of memory impossible! So that when you say "everything" is in there, you can mean it. Which is why Kerouac . . . , etc., being prolific, etc., being voluminous even, being unending. Oh I guess we just want to be immortal in some over-intellectualized ways! This that I've just written to you seems to me now like one big circle, though poorly expressed. See what you can make of it. I guess I want to say why should it take longer to read something than to write it (I'm not counting typing). And I will persist till I am feeble in knowing (having been rendered feeble by this belief) that my state of being is the same as my work. So, nature/nature, just to try to bring it back to that. Maybe I'm actually saying something quite simple-minded, I now see! I think I'd better be quiet!

Lately I cannot end anything, it's funny you would mention that, in relation to edges, I come in my (prose) writing to some perfectly good and sometimes acceptably great ending and I just stubbornly keep going past it, I dont want it, it's all a part of trying to write myself out of my poetry's style (which I think I've succeeded in doing, from some little scraps of poems I've done recently) and out of rhyme and all that I was doing, but now of course this thing of writing myself just past every real ending is becoming a sort of trick too I guess. What I seem to have to do is to have someone to address in order to begin, then lose that, mix it up, get mixed up myself, let the language take over, work out some structures within that, see an ending, bypass it and then see how much longer I can last, having more or less abandoned the addressee, then collapse at some false ending, casting the work aside with the unspoken hope that I may have made some discovery. Then the next time I just start all over again, assuming I'm taking it all in.

To get back to what I was saying before, which I cant seem to forget about, I was doing this thing in my classes where I was trying to "force" the students to liven up their language, looking for mechanical tricks which is all there's time for with them to trick them into writing something good so they could then perhaps see how they did it later. So I decided to make a list of what I considered to be great phrases and images from Shakespeare's Sonnets, phrases that had some color the students' language doesnt, and when I sat down to do it I was amazed to discover that the Sonnets dont have the kind of language I thought they had in them, that they are rather sparse and every simile is really a metaphor extended throughout each poem anyway, so there is not any way to cheaply make my list of tricks. Then I began to consult other great poems to find somewhere examples of the kind of language I was looking for and I look everywhere and cannot find it, I begin to think it's all in my imagination which of course is where it belongs, in relation to any poem, and that all the great poems are like these absent metaphors for an abstract beauty with no dereliction to sudden isolatable phrases in them, and phrase by phrase they are not like my own sensible, sensate, synesthesic image of them at all. Again my memory is playing tricks on me when I'm trying to be in charge of all the tricking! So I compromised and made an alternating list of stuff from the Sonnets and Desolation Angels which actually I'll include here so you can see it, it's not what I expected it to be, but I did read it to the students and made this explanation of what I had done and told them it was simply my vacation gift to them. I wonder if any human being is ever "right" about anything!

However the Shakespeare play I am most partial to is King Lear, I know you'll laugh but that is what I'd do, & second choice, Twelfth Night I think. Hey how come those guys didnt ask me! It's an enticing prospect though these days I must admit I can never think of anything to say about some work of writing but, look at this. I would love to see an anthology of that sort of class about Shakespeare, or an anthology of all essays by you on the subject, not a bad idea. I've been thinking of putting together a sort of "anthology" of my own, not a real one but a work made up of a mixture of all the great American writers' words, an idea I got from Ed actually who asked me if I had any thoughts about sound-tracks for a series of t.v. shows he might be doing. Just part of my endless love of structuring things.

Well I will have my work copied for you first chance I get, though I dont know when that'll be, maybe in New York if I dare to bring it with me, it's now getting beyond 200 pages, I've just numbered them in case I drop the thing (I mean on the floor). I've been enjoying reading alot of "evil" books lately, Notes from the Underground & Junky & even Maldoror again, it must be this stage of pregnancy. I even tried Ned Rorem's diaries but couldnt take his prissy, rich-boy attitude at all. Read Philip Lopate's novel too and it was awful but I'm trying to summon up some good trash for the rest of serious winter so if you know of any recent excellent bad novels, let me know of them. Tell Susan I'm saving her letter to answer till we get back from New York in the hopes that by then I'll have graduated from this recurrent state of complaining I've been in, I know that we can make something of all this being here, oh and I forgot to even mention! we both got our grants so by next year or sooner we'll be richer than ever before or since! Did you know about them before we left Lenox?! Boy I must admit I think I would've campaigned to stay there if I'd known for sure, I think of Lenox now as this peaceful time—you see what my memory does already! But it was so clearly manageable at least for me there and I think my theory of (my) life is beginning to be that the only excitement I want, beyond the need for people to talk to even, is my writing and I want everything else to be dull. Is this old age or just devotion? And am I still human? It's just it seems to me there is so much to do, luckily the page prevents me & I must end. *LOVE,*

Bernadette

THURSDAY 6 DECEMBER [1979]

Dear Bernadette,

Sorry to have to continue with this "sandwich"(right!) machine (and also to have somehow to start out this letter with more reference and complaints about typewriters!). Those bastards have still got my Olivetti hostage ("news" coming in here) and when I call each week dutifully hopelessly and ask they just repeat that they're still waiting for parts. How can that be?! A new machine for Christ's sake. I can't help feeling I made a bad mistake on a whim again. Well, cake and eat it, to mean you inevitably get the bad as well. See if you can sight this through anyway, put up with conditions. Bad enough my thinking seems to me often as confused as you think yours to be, though I always find what you refer to clear as a bell.

That stone-hex dream does seem a good traveling dream: you go to a new place and immediately set things up for yourself by inter-bedding sheets of your writing with stones of the region. I remember that a big feature of that dream was textural (not far from textual?): the friction alignment and slipping of the papers inbetween the flat rocks, almost as if the syllables on the paper could have an actual physical exchange with the grains in the stone producing an actual magic chemistry of largely my own devising. How egotistical! But of course! I mean, most deeply, I never was kidding about all that "arrangement of objects" business. "Proper" layout could be the key to the locks. One of my strongest daydreams as a kid, and also probably a big kid ego fantasy about bypassing all that knowledge they told you you had to master in order to effect anything that I always despaired I could ever get to. Magic settings. The spacing of the stars as visible from here (I never bought all that connect-the-lines zodiac animal and hero stuff). Hex. Means "six." And also, as a noun, means "witch." Greek. And wasn't witch also a verb, as "to witch" somebody? Hecklers, too, yes, one could certainly be hexed by an audience. Though this didn't happen to me, though Barry for one tried his best at times, though I don't think he thinks he's doing that, he's just trying awkwardly to appear bright or something hazardous.

That "mirror nature" speech (I had to look it up too) is from Hamlet's lecture to the Players, the one that starts "trippingly on the tongue" (Act III, Scene II). So famous it's everywhere, so you can't find it anywhere. Re mirroring your own old work, right, I agree that it's no longer "for you," you're getting a fatal peek and for the reasons you state. What's maybe even weirder though is the way the writing seems to change from day to day to week as you're in the process of writing something (one longish something), and I have no explanation for this. To put it grossly, the thing may look horrible when you're done one day so you put it away and then a few days later it looks more than possible to be going on with (if it does, not always of course). Maybe when you come directly out the end of working on something your mind is already "to one side" enough, or full of what comes next enough, that you're in the wrong position to see what stands back there(?) It can get very fine-grained so you lose the placement of even one word for awhile, then the next day, say, seem to regain it. Another sort of "lapses"? This being more temporary and finicky of course than the long-term thing you were speaking of where you seem to lose that former self so it might be somebody else who's a genius. And then sometimes when I stop I get the sensation that everything (else) falls in displacing what I've just written. Whew, I can see maybe why nobody talks about all this: too many factors occurring too instantly and at every point. But, everything is the challenge (chalange?), right? I sometimes want to title my longwork EVERYTHING, but that's probably too dumb?

Then there's that thing about if you couldn't forget there would be no remembering. And Guston's always thanking his lucky stars for the aid of the Angel of Forgettal. Somebody should write a work called FORGETTAL? Is there even such a word?? And then there's the distortions and the reversals of the mirror. Now Shakespeare uses the word "pressure" in there, so I'm sure he's not forgetting those mechanisms. There's another equation, as in memory-forgettal: if the mirror reflected exactly then there would be no mirror, or given an absolute twin the whole universe itself might get displaced? Ah, dire and silly speculation!

Yes, deeply finally I too feel "my state of being is the same as my work." Trouble being that only in the work does it appear that way (to oneself anyway) (to others, who knows? or we too seldom get to know even a peep). Kit Robinson wrote and sent me mss of a very nice 14p report on my Langton St week, including excerpt quotes from the question period discussions (Langton will soon publish and you'll get a copy to read). I dug it especially since he really paid attention (attended) and got so much of the work (lots more than I thought anyway) from this necessarily audial side (not having read the pages). So that's hopeful. I always feel it goes by too fast, I feel I have to keep to the momentum or I'm dead (maybe a performance neurosis?). Anyway, some better feedback for a change.

Your sentence re how you proceed in the writing (bypassing false endings etc.) is wonderfully clear. The kind of thing I envy, and that should be saved if you ever feel the need for printed "explanation" or other. The sentence (a long one, natch) even has the rhythm of all those stops & starts, changes of tempo and attack. Great. Maybe we can know what we're doing and still not give away any helpless secrets! In my "case" (right!) I have millions of rapid blank spots, each, when it's going right, to be filled by a word or phrase I can almost feel dropping down into the slot. Life is full of Holes. And of course we don't want to stop (some death secret lies in the breaking of habits). During the Langton St Q&A session somebody (a woman) said "It's not the end when you end something" and I thanked her. I sometimes have thought if I stopped writing (as Cage said about stopping smoking) I'd forget to breathe.

Your page of Kerouac/Shakespeare parallels is great. All the linkages are glowing. It's a work, and you musn't mind if I borrow it for Naropa. I've always felt so much Shakespeare in Kerouac's language anyway(and as he himself points out). I think he got his word "pity" from Shakespeare(as your page also points out). And I've had the same experience of assuming some poet's language is colored in a precise way I can no longer find when I go back and look. That's somehow connected in what we were talking about before, no? It's pretty amazing genius I spose that (re The Sonnets for ex.) it turns out it's the whole poem that carries that bright weight in your mind afterward. This seems to approach some dumb "wholeness" idea that teachers once put in my head, 'course it's no doubt true finally but they hadn't a clue just why and we're even now just coming to realize the intricacy. Then there's the factor of one's divergency from the work that has inspired, how it gets worked on in one's head so that at some point you have your "own" Shakespeare etc. (what I hope to get to for Naropa classes). What Kerouac too did, "mindful of how poetry is done by mouthings and brainwaves and wizardries of inwit." And then comes in here something Ted once said to me years ago that I think continuously wise. I was raving about some artist or other and he said, Yeah, but the guy's work has to survive your fascination with it(as he said O'Hara's had for him). And this has to do with Bill Berkson being presently unwilling to cast a hard eye to his heroes (we've been hassling over late-de Kooning in letters). Or at least to see how one's own work has changed them. I was thinking the other day how unchallenging lots of Sixties painting looks now (Rosenquist, Stella, etc.), like colors on the supermarket shelf. Warhol's portraits as if they'd been invented by the board of U.S. Steel. Well, no doubt I'm being willfully hardass again. **[Page break]**

Another page. Well, I'll try not to go on too much longer this time. Only when need be. I feel a tendency here to drop into a mire of useless gossipy doodads. But, I was told by Michael Palmer that your grants were "practically a sure thing" but that something "could still go wrong" so don't tell, etc. It put me in a horrible bind, believe me. I recall desperately trying to find any other way of telling you, that you had "a real good chance" etc. But I would hate to have told you it was definite and then have some screw some loose so you stayed in Lenox on the basis of my comment only to have no money come finally. Shit, how stupid it all is, the blather we finally have to base hard decisions on. But, anyway, now you have all these bucks and can splurge on great food and books and all. Bill wrote how you all had a big preposterous lunch at PJ Moriarty's, great. That place by the by (if it's the one near the East 60's)is inextricably linked to an old love affair of mine (early sixties). But, for now, I'll go on to the next thing without telling that long dark tale. I was in the Lenox Bookstore yesterday only to have Jo thrust into my hands a letter you had written to "Math." An embarrassing gesture, so casual(she didn't even ask Mathew if it was okay), so I tried not to read it (while secretly doing so, but not all) and saw that you were ordering Van de Wetering's latest, etc. I haven't seen that one yet, would like to. Tell me how it is. I haven't found any great terrible books lately so can't advise you of such. Just got and read Creeley's latest (LATER) and it's certainly more substantial than HELLO (thank god), though it struck me as odd that in so many poems not so much the actual words but the thought has a kind of dying fall at the end of the poem. Mysteries of a Middle-aged Hipster? And I keep hearing the title as hipster inflection, like "Later, man . . ." or "Later for all that!" And, nothing to do with Bob really but, I hate that shiny grey look of N.D. books, like old filing cabinets or something. The cover photo and lettering seems inappropriate to the works inside too. The stairway to Denise Levertov's attic?

Well things are proceeding okay enough here into the inevitable Xmas Gulch. No snow yet. It got cold (teens) after that warm spell but seems to be warming up again today, rain predicted. Pale sun on birchsides this noon. Celia has a cold, which doesn't hinder her sax practice. Our road got fixed but collapsed again in the mire of rains. Had a nice thanksgiving in Providence with my folks, turkey dressing and walks around the Lovecraft streets. Saw no movies except LIFE OF BRIAN, we all three went and dissolved into constant tears of laughter, it's hilarious! You'd love it. What else? I've been reading Kafka's diaries and Rilke's letters. Do you know of a good biography of Rilke? I found two in the Lenox library (one by Butler and one by somebody else), but they both seemed too awkwardly teacherly judgemental and I finally left them there. All I want is the facts! Lenox looked kind of dreary actually, and they've put awful white chintz curtains in your front windows. Mathew looked stoned. So what else is new? No word or sight of Meltcalfs(!!) in long. Susan's stepfather Tom brought a chainsaw the other day and cut down a big dead birch which promptly fell right on our phoneline snapping it off at the pole. But unfortunately they fixed it almost immediately. But, passing the phone the other afternoon I thought sadly how much I miss having those long talks with you! But we'd best not get into that from this distance.

All Love,
Clark

Think I'll append, as they say, here some notebook jottings you might find of interest, no big deal or anything, just in process feeling a bit disgusted with the daily grind.

Before I shall even decide whether to greet them or not they are gone. Some forms of indecision amount to a fine enough riddance. Even now I hear the relays in the wind clicking shut.

I only want my work to pierce my forehead from without. Sure knowledge only at the bloodflow.

There is little to gain but much to be shattered. The sign on the hill fence post rumbles, so quiet is my nervousness. The top of the hill grows blue and more blue. All that is active in "more" is to darken. When there will be no more windows where I sit.

Clashing birds are the spirits of these words.

I am afraid to watch there an imperfection.

A fearsome state in which water may come loose. Then haul up sticks. Then drop all ropes.

A house constructed of standing.

I run into the cat in the dark as if a moving stake. How could the small animal feel so solid?

I don't understand a thing, then I am penetrated. Each thing a volleying liar.

My typewriter wounds me.

In grasping or releasing the pen random strokes begin to cover my fingers giving my hands the expression of a redman.

The convulsive inner tension of my mind clawing/grasping at the words, as if vast jaws with massed force again and again closed on nothing.

The world keeps letting me go, leaving at least some gaps I then fill.

To finally not know whether I am reading or writing.

Ah, yet a new morning of incapacity!

Plans for writing are like sinks filled with dirty dishes.

Poems to the dogs.

At a loud report the lines of all the tree trunks and smallest branches on the far hillside volley across the cold space to become cracks in the window glass. The effect is utterly precise. Then the fragments begin to loosen and to fall into the room, the whole pattern bulging to give, revealing a blackness of space behind, howling with something that wants to get in.

The day dims and will molden.

The world clatters with willness.

How can one stand to be so full of people?

Before all the doors stand stones, as Kafka so properly said. But will anyone notice and then greet them?

There are places I am from that I have never seen.
There are faces in the dream that stop me.

The desk is a door that I am forever going up to to knock and then turn from.

Philip's picture is the Door of the Law.

Kafka died exactly one month to the day before his forty-first birthday.

We keep leaving hollows in the world to be warmed by others.

What do I stop from occurring each time I refuse the writing?

This pen is too long. I feel as if I am unsheathing a sword.

The weight of the writing at the tip of the hand just as it enters the page.

I no longer want any knowledge that will not immediately produce an even greater ignorance.

If I could write a novel suddenly so ancient that I would pause in wonder at never having read it before.

All the work in the world is as a pie before the gathering birds.

—30XI79

And since I have the room
a poem I don't think you saw. →

GLAZE SPREADS

If I wanted to jam these things in myself
why wouldn't I blossom when I heard about death.
The bird hit. Isn't there anything else to see
besides, blind as I am, seeds in the wind.
You come into your own, they say as how
I enter my room slipping in repeat.
The world is a shag of mass forgettal

and living in a forest loops the mind.
The effort is perhaps to die. Waft away
in standard bars or should I even keep a log of this.
As piano I stalking mind even the room then,
what is listening? You push around then
you turn into stalls. The point of a pencil is
razor of the moon burn. Watch through glass
birdeyes die and I hiss. Even through spring
things cool. Go up. What could the clouds
point out about lengths. One inside the music
still has legs. Partitions to provide you eat.
What you said I don't listen now I pardon to.
All the glad enoughs must exchange. Surely
as dated up to now the girl on tip's a woman
of tulip lip. Could be raised what as skin
the coming back from going where and touching
shows in its deepening rose. The stores
close now, and then the caves. The finger
press the palace and its lights all swim.
The point is pockets sealing darts spell dooms.
And I jounce out from under the stiff bird
holding the whole glass home in prim. Skies
shard in poise, rocks when they hum.

—16V79

1/15/79 [**1980**]

Dear Clark—

Life is chaos, we all know that, no I dont mean that, what I mean is a tolerance for chaos is an excellent thing—can you believe I've owed you this letter for over a month and still it hasnt snowed! Well and now I've had the most chaotic day and yours is the last letter I have a desire to answer before I have this baby, though of course I'm sure I'll have time for plenty more. It's not the absence of snow that signals the choas I'm talking about, choas like boas, but the cabin feverish children acting like two-year-olds all day and then the babysitter comes back from a short trip to NY during which she was "tripping" too and she's in a state even a hot toddy wont shake and Sophia wont settle down and Lewis's toes are tickling him unbearably, now what could that be, Sophia keeps shouting she wants something none of us can understand, now all this sounds trivial but you should feel the feeling in the house, I'm beginning to think the absence of snow makes us feel crazier than a blizzard, ah if only I could get away from this screaming, my tolerance for it is low tonight, my theory is I have what they call postpartum depressions in advance and that no matter how ambivalent I might ever have felt about being pregnant I spend some time in the last weeks sad to separate myself, to prepare to do that, from the baby inside who, just to say something entirely obvious, two years from now, will be demanding a paper towel in bed as Sophia seems to be doing now, what a day. It was in fact supposed to snow today but it was sunny and bright and warm and even the phony snow on the skiers' slopes is beginning to show some potholes after the other night, 55 degrees at midnight, reminded me of when Marie was born, I went out for a secret walk and thought, gee tonight I could be working outside!

I think EVERYTHING is a great title for your work which portion of I got in the mail the other day from Michael Palmer, noteless, this giant manuscript which though I'm afraid to take to the bathtub with me, where I spend a good part of my nights lately, doesnt balance too well on this big belly either, so soon I'll be writing you about it and I think the best thing to do about that is do a gloss on it for you, as you did for me, for what was it the Studying Hunger Journals, I love that sort of thing, and doing it. Your ms., in two bound volumes, is gianter than Kerouac's unpublished writings! Did you see the awful article about him in the Times magazine around Xmas time? Said he couldnt write, said he was a big influence on poets, but fiction writers had nothing to learn from him, said a few other crazy things too, then to top it all off, showed a picture of three people identified as Kerouac, Ginsberg and Burroughs only Burroughs wasnt Burroughs and <u>then</u>, further, said K. died on October 20th, another misinformation which kind of spooked me since that's the day, 11 years previous, my father died and I was always cognizant of the closeness but lack of congruence in their death dates, you see from my crossings out how I cant even get this into words! Though, to get back to where I started from in this paragraph, if it's one, EVERYTHING is a bit too much as a title but then I think <u>you</u> can bring it off, or, maybe it's just a clue to the real title, the way I thought for months that REMEMBERING was to be the title for MEMORY. Now I've just stopped myself and done a random opening of your book to see what "title" I would get and I got You and I, or rather, "You, and, I," not bad. But more appropriate for Maintains maybe than this book, I dont know, the only thing worse than getting into the title dilemma over the phone is to do it in letters I guess, no, I didnt mean Maintains I meant Polaroid, well so much for conversation! The fascinating thing about the book I'm working on is that I force myself before writing each "chapter" to come up with a title, no matter what, I just put one down, I rather love doing it, sometimes I stockpile them and thereby cheat, my stockpile at the moment is full of these two: Can Piercer and Rajaroots, the latter being a word Marie & Sophia made up which Marie says means the roots are growing but what it really is is that they do get obsessed in their gibberish talking between each other with certain sounds for a while and lately all the nonsense words they've done begin with Ra. Marie just makes up words at the drop of a hat, whenever you ask her what something is and it stymies her, up comes a brand new word and this penchant of hers is only aggrandized by the fact that much of Sophia's incessant talking now is not understandable but comes close so Marie, as interpreter, has another opportunity to create new words, just like we used to do, I often think! Forgettal and Chalance, still do! Ah well, come forgettal, I'll really be able to see myself as I am. I have so many plans to write and one is to write off that mirror speech and another is to write a short biography of myself in poem-form for my students and another an essay on mobile homes. There are hardly any mirrors in this house, I mean there are many small ones but you cannot see your whole self in this house anywhere but outside, if you look, like Frank O'Hara never did, at your reflection in a window. I am doing a series of photographs of this one view here, over a field full of pear trees, and everytime I do it I say to myself, this is only a study of the seasons it's turning out to be, so what am I doing, but for some reason this is the view and I am doing it, I do and I dont know why, perhaps just because I dont want to lose it as this is the most ethereal view on this place that seems so little mine still, I mean I cant possess this place but I can posses this view and when I photograph it it seems gentle and it changes in a way that permits me to see it.

Now Lewis's parents have called and I'm

doomed to be distracted, let me tell you a funny story, about state of being being the same as one's work, ah my work seems so mundane to me lately! Well first I have to add to tell you that the winter is acting pregnant, to my mind. Then I also feel you have to go on your nerve, even when you're nine months pregnant or 38 weeks as they say, or 39! Ten lunar months, did you ever see it that way? But when I read my sentences over, which I rarely do for fear, but when I do glance at them, I feel I've run out of things to do and as usual I am somehow in advance of my own plans and ready already to start doing some poetry but still chained to this book which I am only trusting myself is even a book, but like you in reading I keep to the momentum but I am dying for the moment in that where I am lying around after baby's born writing the last part, post-partum, sorry. What I've done is I've gotten myself headlong into fear, no, I mean prose, and I cant even envision what a poem is anymore, which is what I wanted and knew would happen, but now I'm scared. So I guess I'm forgetting to breathe, except I've cultivated now the long breath, the breath of being in labor but the short breath, the breath I've maybe denied in poetry but would like to know and to find, is still denied me, and I think—maybe forever! Ah, denied so many things—maybe I'm in for something! I cant think straight till it becomes my turn to talk to Lewis's mother, meanwhile I'm sort of half listening to what Lewis is saying to her so I'll know what it was. Just daily, I think so many things I can barely remember anything and I know as I've known for years, in writing, I always leave the most important part out; proved to me recently by digging up some old manuscripts and seeing how my book POETRY was really all wrong, well it's just the usual recriminations or what, but I had done that book, put it together so many times in the past without its ever being published and I liked the old versions with fantastic tables of contents designed in some old "open field" manner, well it's just the death instinct to even think like this! I think what you say about having your own Shakespeare, or whoever, is ultimately the point of it all—I cant really "answer" your letter, but I keep reading parts of it in between writing this and responding more as if we were in conversation which I fear we may never again be!—and it is the point of forgetting, the forgettal—you forget, or I should say I forget whatever it was that Shakespeare or Pound or Stein or Isidore Ducasse! ever actually wrote, but then you can find yourself saying something, either in writing or in conversation about that and you feel suddenly topheavy like you might be giving the lie to it all, just being smart, and then somehow it turns out to be true but you have to get somebody else to explain to you why, this has happened to me so many times in talking I've begun to realize I can trust what I say, I mean in writing I trust it instinctively and just go on.

For example—just finished my part of the conversation with Lewis's mother—I keep thinking there must be a way to tell the absolute truth about what goes on during pregnancy, maybe there is and then I think to myself, well why do these questions about writing, or even anything, always seem to have to resolve themselves into questions of just the truth all the time, not to denigrate truth at all as if truth were a woman named Ruth or something—I think I'm just as black & white, which is why I'm just as much as a Yankee as you!—as I was when I wanted to be a painter and I thought and worked a little and made this canvas of alizarin crimson which is a kind of maroon, off-red, and then I happened to be able to see the show of Ellsworth Kelly's primary canvasses at the Met and I thought, I've made a dreadful mistake in that art, I'd better be a writer where I can work more slowly toward the thing and not have to have all these objects to do away with in the meantime. And still I think often when I'm writing of the uneven and unprimary grain of that crimson painting where I know I sought the crimson for its greater sensuousness than any primary red, Godard-red as I think of it now. Old-fashioned thoughts, eh?

And if you'll forgive me for going on about myself, which I'm afraid is the condition of a pregnant person, "advanced pregnancy" and so on, I'll have to say that the problem with the work now I'm doing is that though it was to be a book of letters the letters have ceased to be letters and have become just works, again the problem of literalness and the form is not its form and the birthday cake doesnt look like one! But it is a cake, can be eaten and so on. And now I've got to sit and figure which of these "things" I want to print in the next U.A. which Lewis and I are conceiving of as our, what's the word, working-class issue—that wasnt the word but it was something like that, almost all typed now. Hey, you know what my latest theory is on what would've happened if we'd stayed in Lenox and then got the money—we'd have moved back to NY! I know Lewis wouldnt have wanted to endure another winter in Lenox though with another baby coming maybe we would've stayed on for a year, and gotten a car or something to stave off total craziness, I do know that time in Lenox, and I'm the only one who feels this way, was somehow perfect (for me) and Marie too because of the nursery school which we've only begun to see as such a great boon for lack of anything here and I do like order, I'm ashamed to say, and Lenox was so much that, but anyway, who knows? The thing that's happened instead being here is that I'm learning about circa 18-year-olds in advance of my own children being that age and what a survey of our culture it is! Albeit these ones are of a specific kind—privileged ones who are dying as a result of it to suffer and to be bad and often I dont think of them as much different from me and then I have to be reminded and they remind me, born in 1961 after all! So now I'll give birth to one born in 1980 and I must admit still between and among me and the students and my own children I still see very little difference which must mean I am learning something and I know I've learned it's torture to teach and if Lewis gets another job teaching as he's willing to do, I'm willing to abdicate it, I'm sure of that and I know it has nothing to do with my writing and I must admit I prefer spending time with my children though I dont mind either being forced to learn about everything else, if you get my meaning. Whenever I say to Marie "if you get my meaning" she says, I hate that phrase!

Well for trash I am reading MAWSON'S WILL, a book remaindered in NY about the Antarctic, badly written but pretty good, and KATHY IN HAITI by Acker and I just finished a Margaret Drabble book, THE WATERFALL, recommended by Fanny Howe, but though it's about women and children in some interesting way it takes such pains to be melodramatic and neurotic I cant say I'd recommend it to you and with my newfound wealth I just got a copy, my own copy of HAWTHORNE AND HIS WIFE by Julian Hawthorne, that's the biography of them written mostly in their own words from letters and journals they kept when apart from each other, a treasure to have, just like having one's own slight part of the Lenox Library all to oneself, and ARISTOTLE'S RHETORIC which I think will be good for a person about to turn 35 and not yet ensconced in any but the Western tradition and Lady Wortley-Montagu's Letters, a strange book in which I find a letter I once stole from to write this work called "The Sea" I wrote 15 years ago—I had found it in a book of 19th century etiquette for "ladies" but Wortley-Montagu is an

18th century person, a strange friend of Pope's, and so on. And I'm totally entranced by an old copy I found of CONFUCIOUS TO CUMMINGS, a book I havent had in my house nor thought much about for years, and I've also read some of Later which I like and when in NY I read the first chapter of Ted's Selected Poems and it was great, though Ted himself lately seems so off-base to me, he told Lewis that Alice was the Bernadette Mayer of New York now and things like that, if you'll forgive me he seems to be operating on only half his usual brain and so does Bill B. though maybe it's just me in my usual intolerant late-pregnancy state but Bill kept saying I had written him a letter that was "formidable" but then when I finally got his answer back, well it was simply just boring, he and I are supposed to be engrossed in this correspondence about some kind of ethics, we talk about different poets who are either "good" or "bad," but then I feel critical of nearly everybody lately and when in Boston for New Year's we spent time with Bill C. and Russell I felt unconnected to them too as I told you and Susan, I'm tired of being thought of as the child or naif, I'm to be 35, with three children, I know as much as they do about the world! Though I choose to live with Lewis who pretends to know nothing about chopping wood and insulation and cars! And I must admit I've gotten to the point, though in a different way, that you were at when you were suspending all or most of your correspondences, where, when I get a letter in the mail, I feel the answer to my own is somehow all wrong, insufficient, I know I have no right to say this but this is how I feel, and I dont want to answer. Just daily disgruntledness in this heartless forest I live in I guess.

Here's a work off your notebook jottings, kind of in kind:

I only want clashing birds are
the spirits of the fearsome state, a house
my typewriter at a loud report plans
the day dims and more is to darken.

This pen is too long, I refuse
I run into, I dont understand, in grasping
the world keeps letting me to finally
not know, reading or writing,

Poems into the room, wants to get in
before I shall if I could write
what do I stop I am from that
I've never seen so full of people!

I run into a house constructed so solid
At the door of the law we keep leaving hollows

Gee I havent done it justice, I just stopped when a sonnet was done, as is my wont lately, now I see the notebook things are full of good titles too, and be sure I'll use them, here near Concord. Ah, there's so many things to tell when I begin to try and tell them I feel there's no end to it like these poems that could be done "off of" your things, as I see the last words of your lines in "Glaze Spreads" make a funny sort of old-fashioned haiku!: I guess haiku is like the phony snow they make there on the mountain:

Myself Forgettal

Death to see how winds repeat
Glass spring
                        a woman
                                        skin touching
Skies hum

But alas it doesn't work! Too corny! I'm sure if I kept at it it would go but as Freud said only fatigue + hunger prevent me from going on.

I do feel like the baby will be born soon. We got 40 postcards of "The Flume" in Franconia N.H. [→ we cldnt possibly "know" 40 people (+ be so lonely) could we?] so when you see one in the mail, know it'll be baby news. (The insane woman at the Concord 5 + 10 rang up 10¢ 40 times!)

And do consider a visit sometime. [→ We may journey to "Berkshires" in May for me to read at B.C.C.]

LOVE, Bernadette (over 4 P.S.'s)

P.S. A return to NY is being discussed by us, partly based on this college's upheavals, + the needs for schools + friends. Will tell more later about that.

Wish me luck as "I am nature!"*

Quiz:

*Who said that?

P.P.S. Write back immed. if in yr poem you want "for P.O's Collected" to be printed at bottom (as in text but w.o. date).

MONDAY 21 JANUARY [1980]

Dear Bernadette,

With the baby's birth immediate I had thought to give you a pause (!) and not answer so quick, but here I seem to be proceeding anyway if only to answer your question re dedication of Forth Poem (yes, keep it in) or somehow to keep the issues of our talk in fairly close conjunction. I persist in thinking of these letters as "talk," though we both know they are also really writing. How many illusions one needs to keep on with correspondence! And how much I miss those all-night conversations we had here years ago, that seemed so perfectly germane (ha!) to the life of our thoughts and work then they seem to have been taken for granted. So hard to "accept loss forever" when you think that life itself will never stop. Kerouac must really have believed in death? How did I get so gloomy in this?! Sorry, I should be speaking of birth. But how can I write "one of our" letters without complaining somewhere? I'm feeling distracted today, so am wondering if I'm really going to get into the body of this to all the things I want to say here, though your managing a letter through all sorts of actual interruptions inspires me to try.

I must say that like you I'm pissed and depressed by almost all of the other letters I get. They don't seem to want or be able to talk about what I think to set in motion. So much of it seems keep-the-touch/take-the-temperature type correspondence, which it seems to me by nature can't be continued with any frequency. It becomes a kind of hysteria like walking again & again to the same door to see if it's locked. Then I wonder if people don't secretly just basically disagree with me, so they think what they're doing is politely declining to comment? This is presently precipitated by Bill B's dropping out just at the point when I thought we'd finally gotten something interesting going, so that when he finally does answer

I'll have forgotten just what we'd said. And Bill C pulling one of his patented numbers of dropping a card asking for a letter in return. And then Douglas Messerli sent me a copy of his book all inscribed and saying how much he was inspired by Own Face and again pestering me to send work for his mag so that I finally had to write and tell him what I thought of his magazine and why I wouldn't contribute to it. And finally (I wish it were!) I get this book-mss from a relative on Susan's Pasadena side of the family all about this guy's experience of becoming a father for the first time, titled (can you believe this?) From Here To Paternity. He of course wants my "professional opinion," is a nice enough person (I met him once a couple years ago) but the sort of writer that doesn't even pay enough attention to what he's written to see what it's actually saying. Some people come with signs pleading STOP ME BEFORE I WRITE MORE. This isn't the sort of letter I wanted to write you at all. Guess this cold I finally seem to be getting is up to its old thought-dissolving tricks.

Your question of why "questions of just the truth all the time," what an opening that is! Do we have the time? Vastness. If we mean certainty (Wittgensteinian) then I spose we have to admit that the eventuality is beyond us (practically a tautology). I find the root meaning says "faithful," which seems to posit at least some ignorance as a given. "Tell the truth" equals "Keep the faith"? My faith has been that if I mix in enough elements (themselves variables) what's true will eventually arise precipitant, but that multiplicity is a necessity. Then I keep hearing my old juniorhigh woodteacher madman's caroling "straight square and smooth" (only he said "smoof"), no doubt his highest value and version of the truth. But one soon learns it ain't so simple, a sort of sanity. Eventually this turns into ethics, which leads me into saying I think, in the process of our working at least, I see us as amoralists. Whatever else we are poses us problems once the work is done. We take on the creation itself, which includes devils. You can see how wide this door will open. And it's certainly(!) not a matter of agreement, as in "this is or is not the case." I figure it's the case if I can make it <u>be</u> the case. And I do set a lot of store by willfulness. I've always loved Melville for Ahab's saying "I'd smite the sun if it offended me!" It can get pretty active on these paper pages. We call up things, some of which end up in the old magic sense possessing us.

I guess

we have to talk about desire here as mainly transformational. Who was it talked about "the lineaments of gratified desire"? Ornamental phrase. And "lineaments" doesn't sound at all as surprising as those residues often are. When you say you'd want to write the truth of pregnancy I'm already itching to see what that desire would lead you to say. In Studying Hunger you kept putting it a way that's always stuck with me: "Can I say that?" Those four words perfectly hit at the whole problem range of truth in language. And I think you always "feel you've left the most important part out" since that feeling is post-partum (thank you!) desire left by the things you did write. This gets to be about a kind of momentum of thought you're dealing with in words. Duncan's always talking about "the tone-leading of vowels," but what about the thought-leading of words/sentences? Like, if I write quickly (thoughtlessly?) "the trees are slanted in wind," the word "slant" is peculiarly going to lead me into saying something I hadn't thought to say and I'm bound to follow that furtherance if I go on at all, at that pitch anyway. Of course, I see I've blocked that process here by including all that potentiality in such an observant sentence structure. I hope this sounds usefully basic and not just school-primer trivial. You know all this, etc. But to carry this point on, the problem seems not just whether that "slanted" came from out there or in here but that it arrives possessed of both the outside dry and the inside wet simultaneously. Agh, I feel like picking up my head and shaking it! Can't carry this any further right now, but anyway see what you get from it.

No, I didn't see the Kerouac piece in that Times Mag but I'm glad I didn't actually, I've gotten to the point I don't ever want to read a bad thing about him again, they tend to be the same bad thing over and over anyway, nothing rots like re-used wrongs. I got a gift book to go on the same shelf with your Julian Hawthorne, my folks found me a copy of the first edition of Jay Leyda's Melville Log (you know, that wonderful 2 vol. documentary of the life made of letters etc.), something I've wanted forever but it finally came to seem too expensive, so I'm a kid again with joy! Just finished Moldenhauer's vast biog of Anton Webern, a good and pretty readable research job. His death has got to be one of the world's great coincidental tragedies, just breaks your heart. Also reading The Brethren (another Xmas gift), lawyers again, written in those guys' faceless style. For pure trash read Trevanian's Shibumi, mostly 'cause the hero is a caver this time around (the detail is amazingly correct). Susan's reading Stephen King's The Stand, which sounds like good (long) trash too.

I'm trying to take a cue from your sense that Everything might be a clue to the eventual real title (re Memory). Somehow it too doesn't quite sit right, not that it's too vast, but . . . I dunno, I'm so familiar with this feeling of wrongness of titles, shit! I actually thought once of using "You, and I" as the title, but if for no other reason rejected it because I didn't want the title cropping up in the text in so (almost) underlined a position. You see, I seem to be able to find a way to reject just about any title! I still suspect that a long title might be best, at least one that could be abreviated (as it inevitably would be) to something that worked as well. That's almost like having to think of two titles, more work! Here's an odd story, apropos. The new LANGUAGE came (you probably have?) with a review of Own Face by Christopher Dewdney that I like pretty much, though I wish he could've done without some of that "referential methodology" terminology, which he never uses in his letters to me. But anyway, I get to the end of the review and dangling out there (the last two words) I find "the manifold," which has been typed up here above my desk for a month as a possible title for this prose I'm working on(!) I couldn't believe it, since I hadn't even seen that word anywhere for years (that I know of) and thought I'd gotten it fairly purely out of my own head. Now if I use it nobody will believe I didn't steal it from him! Actually though I think I'll probably use it anyway, what the fuck. But it did feel strange, practically a definition of coincidence.

As you can see, my electric typewriter is still "being repaired," three months now and they still tell me they can't get a part, just another thing I can't believe. I surely fucked up there, somehow had a feeling at the time I was committing a lemon but went ahead impulsively anyway. With a new ribbon and using only one side of the paper I can get by with this old clunker for a while (have to) anyway. Actually I wish I could get this one repaired, all it needs is a new platen and a good cleaning. But that's impossible around here and maybe anywhere by now, they probably quit making this size machine years ago. I've gotten fond of this machine, even to the color, and despite the fact that one's fingers tend to fall through the keys as you pointed out. Long familiarity and memory of the works written on it, I spose. I predict that this sort of hassle will become completely commonplace not too many years hence, so telling myself I better learn not to come all to pieces over it.

It's been so long now with bare ground that we've gotten carelessly used to it I'm afraid, so the inevitable white pounding will seem what? better or worse? Can't tell. I have more than a sneaking suspicion that this will be at any rate a totally strange winter throughout, but at least I don't have the premonition we'll need toescape far away like last year. ("toescape"!?) Susan and I are planning a long weekend at Martha's Vineyard in a few weeks, which is something we've wanted for years, sounds great and romantic, no matter the conditions. Sametime we're going to look over some houses to rent for a couple weeks in August. If this works out and the house proves big enough we could invite friends down too (sound good?). This is so far from sure I probably shoudn't even mention it yet.

I got Susan a baking stone for Xmas, so we've been treating ourselves to amazing 3-inch-thick pizzas. Celia's just made a great papier-mache landscape she's going to build a battle scene on for a school project (what?). It looks like it should have Lionel trains running through it. They're shooting a movie in Williamstown (Hollywood keeps following me around!), I watched Anthony Hopkins and Bo Derek talking outside a dorm the other day, surrounded by hundreds of seemingly superfluous grips etc. (whatever happened to the small-crew revolution ala Godard Truffaut early Sixties?) Took me 30 seconds at least to recognize Bo Derek, she's really incredibly ordinary looking. But the funny thing is, the movie's called A Change of Seasons (Hopkins' college prof married to Shirley MacLaine has affair with Bo D.) and they wanted snow but there obviously isn't any, which undoubtedly blows their big corny metaphor! Director is Noel Black, who shot Pretty Poison in Great Barrington (know anything more about him?).

Well, pretty trivial, but I wanted to write you quickly though I'd intended to be briefer. At further length next time, but for awhile all the real news will be from you!

Love to all,

Clark

[→ P.S.—re Forth Poem dedication: just put "for Peter O's Collected" at the bottom like it is in mss. Maybe underlined? However it looks good to you.]

[→ P.P.S.—Isn't it great how Flanders Rd got changed to Slanders Rd in LANGUAGE Own Face review!?]

3/2/80

Dear Clark—

I'm writing to you on my official "Max paper" in what is not an official letter to wish you a belated happy birthday this leap year! I wrote a poem the other day + wanted to call it that (leap year), but then saw I couldnt, it'd been done before, etc., but I wanted the title to also include the word "humility" or "humble" so here is your birthday conundrum—how to get

HUMILITY LEAP YEAR [(+ anything else that seems good)]

together as a title!

HAPPY BIRTHDAY!

Meanwhile we can compete with you "pumpers"—we've got frozen pipes and drains! + our landlord whose house has sheets of ice on the floor has disappeared + changed his phone no.!

Well let's see, I'm raising a glass of Jack Daniels to you now, my 2nd real drink since Max is born (the 1st a drink to Rosemary's birthday over the phone!). Max is a very nice baby who's fat + placid + lets us sleep + I feel so elated, almost crazily, since he's born, so much more than I expected, I mean these children + so beautiful + meditative they can be when one is not scared to death.

This paper is kind of small but I will use it to say this strange brown winter is rather blood-curdling isn't it? Dusty brown frozen ground blows around with the little dusty white snow under those crackling freezing blue zero degree skies, no wind, just to make us wonder how nothing will happen next + we do indeed live in a kind of desert where every day is the same bright sun. I lay in bed today staring at branches by blue sky in cold house trying to imagine convincingly that this sun was warm. And not only do I know spring will come but I'm preparing to write my annual, + what might turn out to be my last! of that genre, New England is . . . poem. I'm gathering the stuff—what shall it be this year? New England is ridiculous? insensate? deranged? lunatic? atavistic? recidivistic? lovely? Ah, another birthday conundrum!

One special indulgence I've granted myself since Max is born is to handwrite everything—I love it! I love to be so slow, knowing I'll get fast again soon enough. I often feel, in handwriting, that I am secretly imitating the style of all the people I know so that I can see in a random "a" or "g" Ed or Grace or Peggy or you or Susan—ah I am an elated madwoman tonight! Too many ah's.

Have you read Alice's new book? Very good I think, I envy her comprehension of forms + rhyme, again very "accessible" as Ted described it to me. I still have trouble with knowing her when I read her, as if I feel she wishes, (in life?) to be tougher (?). Well there's now a million things I would say but I've promised this not to be a "real" letter, just an indulgent congratulation + another letter will be following later in real answer when I'm again at my typewriter, which alas is dying so you may meet me again as an IBM!

Happiness, + this version of it I feel, is not easy, + I wonder what writing will learn from it, it's almost too subject to what is life, + it seems as if to be good at it you have to learn to be smarter, say as smart as Robt. Creeley or someone, as smart as history, memory being left behind among the unfeeling!

Thank Susan for the pictures, twice over. I watched the Olympics too to see if the skaters would make me weep but only 2 did. *Love,*

Bernadette

[→ Lewis sends big birthday greetings!]

3/25/80

Dear Clark,

I'm finally back at the typewriter though it's not my typewriter which went to the shop today for major repairs, so bad in fact I think the repairman did not understand the esteem in which I keep that 8-year-old machine which I remembered this afternoon Ed once threw on the floor because he knew it was the only thing that would make me mad! This flood of memory in the middle of hateful Concord full of just as vast an emptiness of light, I mean light's variety, on this spring day as ever. Now that's a funny way to begin. Louisville just won the championship, I guess I was rooting for UCLA. Lewis just said, "The teams I root for never win." Well that is true in poetry too. However we have what the midwife would call "a neat baby"—she even told me I had a "neat uterus" once! Max is great as his name might be implying and I have been unashamedly elated since he's been born. I've even been back at my desk fooling around a bit, I've been taking myself at my word that I have to re-learn how to write poetry and have not only been messing with various forms but actually really playing like I havent done in say 15 years! I got inspired by re-reading old notebooks I had kept when I was 20 or so in the hopes of finding in them a clue how to teach Lea, who's doing a directed study course with me, how to write alot without, as she requested, having to deal with her emotions at all. But the surprise of the day was when I noticed in all these old books which I'd thought I'd written as an adolescent with an intent to pure experimentation, endless references to all the blood, sperm, even gism and jasmine! and stuff, even monkeys! that Lea definitely did not want to deal with. But I also found alot of good lines and games and I was thinking of making some kind of gloss on these old books of mine but of course that's just the kind of thing I wont do at least right now. It's fascinating, when I sit down to work now, I have to be doing something new, I can't even bear to make a final copy of a poem, I have to write another one, I am so husbanding my time. And this now is my "vacation," we've a week off from school, what a blessing, and how I hate teaching! So much catering just to the egos of the students who feel since we're attending to their most intimate thoughts on paper, that this can somehow verify their entire existence! [→ Actually, I guess it does!] I know that sounds mean but what a blessing it is to have a student like Lea who says I dont want to write about myself, I just want to learn about writing. Meanwhile the whole question about writing about oneself has come to an interesting head with of course Lea's father! Russell with whom we've finally had some amazing conversations where Russell says he was never sincere or honest in anything he wrote & he asks why write about yourself, he doesnt understand say Lewis's instinct to do that and then Lewis and I both say, to write about one's self is one way to find something you can tell the truth about, followed by Russell's there can be no such thing, at least for him. We had one talk where he was saying I had what he called a narrative gift, which statement flattered me, and that I ought to write fiction, but that fiction to him is this irony! It's getting cold in here. **[Page break]**

. . . those three dots are meant to indicate the passage of time, Marie is always saying I want to do that the day before tomorrow, so now it's tomorrow in that sense, and today I heard my typewriter wasn't "worth fixing"!

well I've heard that before, how appropriate to be writing you in the midst of this drama, I really feel what they call a sense of loss! But back to the truth, oh shit. I guess my theory is that the mind knows what is the truth, just as it (the mind) knows the "meaning" of other words so that, just as when one declares one's intent (outloud, in words) to begin to remember one's dreams again after a bout of forgetting and nothing but the declaration itself seems to facilitate that's happening, the ability to remember, so the intention to truth, as a word, for whatever it's worth, will create same, force it. Which relates to what you were saying in the "slanted" sentence—I know I can read a book relatively unconsciously, or distractedly, and still know later what it said, its "meaning" has seeped in somewhere, gotten in, especially even a book I can't "understand"—do you like all these quote marks? very erudite! And also, more to the point of all the slantings we practice with in writing, when I write quickly (especially) I see that I've often carried through on, say, a perfect long metaphor without being "conscious" of it. So that the truth problem (tooth problem?) becomes it seems a question of the genuineness of one's intention, thus ethics, and also, to some extent, the personality—are you a liar by nature, that kind of thing. In fact, are you so devious (I dont mean you) you can kid yourself into believing what is not true for the sake of blah blah blah. Which is where, if you'll forgive me for trying to create the complete philosophy of poetry in less than a page, all the willfulness seems to work—I agree with you about that! For example I could say, I demand to continue to edge onto the truth even if that means I have to write gibberish, or, worse, even if my "confessionalism" evokes a hostile reaction.—(even in myself!). The willfulness relates too to all the selfishness requisite for attending to poetry, a state of things I feel most deeply now having these three children under 5. Now I feel like I'm leaving alot of loose ends here in the above (is that the truth!) but I've gotta go on to say, or reiterate actually, that writing (poetry) is always having to be that process of not knowing what you think, what you're going to say, and of finding out as you go along, something I just cannot teach to my students (teach should be in quotes too) and I've always assumed that [finding out involved questions of truth] [→ this is a noun in a way] which is why the mind must be empty, gertrude-stein-wise. Multiplicity too, that makes sense and also, I guess we have to include, the knowledge of millions of words so that the language really can do its work "by itself." Like I wrote a letter before where I noticed on reading it I had used the word "blessed" about four times in relation to all sorts of things, the weather, etc. but the one thing the letter was really about, a letter to Charlotte, was Max's birth and I never used the word in that relation—now, will she not notice it? But then I saw I hadnt wanted to say something (corny) like we were blessed with Max because Charlotte had just had a miscarriage so I was secretly? avoiding playing up Max as a blessing (in disguise? the miscarriage?)—perhaps a rather blatant example but to me it was interesting.

So what is the connection then between genuineness, as we speak of it, and desire? Is that then ethics? Ack! what have we done! When I said "can I say that" I was thinking most, am I allowed to say that, is it too _____ fill in blanks. So, tone of voice? I talked to Bill B. recently, and after having been amazed by James Schuyler's new book, I asked what he thought of it and he said, "too self-pitying." and then I said "how can you say that!" I had felt that the long title poem was like reading something I was literally dreaming had been written (hopefully by me)—it was the poem I would wish and as that every turn, every transition in it seemed "perfect," seemed like it ought to be that way, seemed like at the very least a reflection of the truth (but we cant get into Plato!). I've had that experience with some other books, epiphanies I guess they are, once in fact at the reading of The Maintains we did at the church where I suddenly leaped up (intellectually I guess) and started saying to myself, "language demands its form."

But when Russell tells us he's never been sincere, which is the word he used, in anything he wrote, then, much as I'm charmed by him as a person these days, I kind of pity him too and feel that that fiction he wants to encourage me to write is maybe the exact opposite of this finding out that fascinates me, though I know for someone like Hawthorne whom Russell is obsessed with too, that was not so. I mean when we are talking about the truth like this, daring to talk about it I guess (& the old can I say that might come up in this relation, I'm sure lots of people would make fun of us for this), isnt this something every poet understands as easily as drinking water when you're thirsty (I typed thirty), is it or not? I mean I know I'm gullible, in fact it's Russell and Bill C. who constantly enjoy putting me on. Well this could go on forever, I'm tempted to belabor this fiction question because it interests me, as us all, to try to write something like a novel. I think what happened with Russell is he finally read some prose of mine and saw I could write a good sentence, thus my narrative gift—not to belittle his instinct about me, I'm sure there's something to it but I feel it's rather egomaniacal to pursue it. And now I cant resist saying, aint it the truth. sorry.

Boy writing this letter is the most fun I've had since I've been back at the typewriter, but for a weird discursive thing I wrote as an exercise in which I gave myself the liberty of including lines like:

You hamper my putting on my halter by my halyard
So I get you in a hammerlock when you're in my hammock

—just like old times!

I will send you that work, you'll enjoy it, a tour de force I guess it is, I must apologize for my remissness (remission?) in not getting things xeroxed, it is just impossible here, the college which does school things for me for free, watches over what I submit like hackneyed hawks so I cant sneak things in but the first chance I get you're to get a copy of the whole (finished!) new book, 350 pages in all, and also that old manuscript of the outtakes from The Golden Book. So be patient as I'm always saying to Marie thinking she's me.

I've had a hard time reading these days, not only is it my last priority but I am often so hopped up I just have to go to the typewriter and cant recline. I thought at first after Max was born this great energy was an illusion and I was bound to come down or collapse or something in some great post-partum (desire!) decline but happily it hasnt happened so I am daring to make statements like I've never felt better, but the energy is rather frenetic and I read, except for Jimmy's book, kind of slowly in myriad places including of all things a Richard Yates novel called the good School (out of a kind of sentimentality, I read a book of his Revolutionary Road when I was in high school) and in Russell's Hamilton Stark which is interesting about this neighborhood and full of a kind of luxuriating in endless description—he's learned well from Hawthrone too how to write a pretty sentence. Russell by the way is regaling us with attentions in an attempt to keep us here next year, thus his being such a part of my consciousness, but

and this deserves a new paragraph (pariahs paragraphs are) there's some rumor I'm to be asked to run the poetry project, a hideous prospect to my mind and now that I think of it I'm sure you heard all about it while you were in NY for your reading which I heard all about from Peggy who not only attended but sent me her notebook notes taken during it! Needless to say (another rampart, I mean rampant high-school phrase) I heard the reading was great and Peggy quoted from your poems in her notes, only enough to make me wish to have been there. Am waiting to hear the rest.

So if called upon to serve, I think I might be hard put to say no (I think Tony Towle is my opponent!) because it would give us a way to exist in that place NY to which Lewis & Marie at least are determined to get. I said to Lewis the other day I wish we had hit upon a place outside NY where we felt good about staying and he said I dont think we ever could, said this without blinking! And then, well we spent three years in Lenox! For a metaphysical poet I think Lewis's sense of time is amazing! I would much rather he would run the poetry project! Just as I would rather teach grammar here, and he would prefer the poetry! What a mess. But no use discussing it till later, as we keep on discussing it.

I rarely worry about money but we did get stuck in the mud the other day, the whole giant car like a whale wedded to a belly of mud, the wheels could get out but the underside was grounded & what metaphor is that? No appreciable snow here at all this year, the sap is running in the trees and yesterday was spring and today winter again but what an insane winter, I'm glad I witnessed it, I feel like I can put together like a great wave memories, big impressions, of each country winter I've seen, like a farmer without dates. **[Page break]**

"The Manifold" is an almost perfect title, now then there's the problem too perfect, or maybe too erudite? I like it, the many fold, sweet many, sweet manifold, doubled together, from the Greek phlassein to form to mould (that's for fold), there must be a way to make it human-er. I still like it.

Well I gotta go wake up Max, sometimes after the furor of the day is over—too much for one as little as he in a noisy house like this—he sleeps so long I have to remind him he's hungry, otherwise late night wakings for us! I've got five more weeks of this teaching and then starting early May all my time's my own! till whatever happens next! we must be buxom I mean buddhistic about all this, I keep saying. I wonder if it's possible for me not to have time to work. I still have this image of living a white-trash sort of life in some inexpensive place in the south, no heat, being an ostensible lazy motherfucker & working like crazy, but this east coast life doesnt seem to want to let me do that. Despite this energy I feel I feel old having had my last baby, it's as if as soon as I got used to doing that and could feel the exuberance of it, I felt like it was also time to stop. Did I tell you Ted called us up & started saying, in some amazing one-sided ramblings, that he felt we ought to have nine children because then the older ones took care of the younger! Some nerve! Oh I'd give alot for a great long-winded face-to-face conversation among the Coolidges and Warshes/Mayers—perhaps it will happen yet! I gave Max my mater Mayer name, seeing him as the last child I'll have but I didnt want anyone to think I'd done that just because he's a boy—the girl child's name would've been even more formidable—the non-existent-now Theodora Malke Mayer Warsh! What a strange thought. now I see I forgot to talk to you about the fascinating "truth of pregnancy" question but when you finally do read what I wrote, you will see how close (I feel) that truth came to be, well what can I say but manifold! [→ Almost like nothing!]

Love,
Bernadette

—How's <u>your</u> typewriter?

TUESDAY 8 APRIL [1980]

Dear Bernadette,

I feel like I should start at the end of your letter with the Typewriter Question and then go on back and forth again. Just reread your letter (for the howmanyeth time) in my 8 A.M. (believe it or not—Susan has to leave the house at 7 on this early shift so we're all at breakfast by 6:30) blunked-out sleepy-eye period, so reading it almost like remembering a dream (or writing it down in half-awake state) and such a pleasure but so fully-packed I'm always nervous I'll leave out lots I want to answer. Then I remind myself that if we continue long enough (like writing itself anyway) everything will get said (ha!), and maybe that's as good an example of "faith" as I have these days. Actually I feel peeled this early in the morning, like the slightest touch could make me jump, and I wish this was more erotic (like removing silks or something) but it's more like having a secret top layer of skin removed and rubbing up against rough matters. Sounds like a good time for writing, as if I might say something really unconsidered, but I dunno . . . and of course I'm exaggerating, but. Maybe that's a whole "issue" too: the need to exaggerate just to get something said? The metaphor as hyperbole? This is getting pretty unconsidered! Anyway (log jam), the typewriter. I finally(that's no exaggeration) got the electric monster back after seven (count 'em) moths(months) of their presumably waiting for a part. I wondered which part but naturally the guy I talked to was so far removed (even physically: their North Adams office rather than the Bennington one I took it to) from the repair process there seemed no point in even asking him. Cost me $41 and in the middle of all this delay I realized clearly that I never had wanted the electric in the first place, just bought it on sheerest thoughtless impulse to "have a new machine." How dumb! I can't stand the thing now and just leave it in its big black plastic case on the floor in a corner I can't see from my desk. I'll try to sell it at first opportunity. Want it? It cost me (with the repairs) $341, so I'd try to get, say, $200. Is that fair? I'd feel horrible if you bought it and it instantly busted again (maybe it's a pure lemon?). What to do? What I really want is either, (a) get a new platen put on this one I'm so used to and have done so much work on despite fingers falling down between keys as you pointed out, but there seems no one in this area who can do such a job on a Hermes, or (b) buy a new manual of some kind. What kind? Any advice on a good new manual model? I feel stupid about all this, like a carpenter who realizes after half his life that he doesn't really know his own tools! Meanwhile I'll stagger along with this machine, which seems okay as long as I keep replacing ribbons far too often and never type on both sides of the page.

Enough of that. Makes me feel like a "real novelist" (ha!) taking all this space talking of machines. Aren't poets "supposed" to just scribble in notebooks and not have big dire relationships with typewriters? Maybe why all that big flap of Olson's in Projective Verse re playing the machine like an instrument, because poets never had considered such things before? Another exaggeration, but. Olson's proposal turns out to have been a big exaggeration (typewriter can't act in such a fine-grained way anyway) and now mostly forgotten about I suppose, except by dire LANGUAGE guys. "Guys" seems right in speaking of those guys, right? Now I feel like I'm fooling around as in goood-old-days manuscripts as you describe. I recall once looking back at old poems with the overlay-feeling that those were all structural primarily and, as you did, finding them all messy with sperm and sputum too! Was I focused on some sort of project or what? Somehow took the mind off what I was really saying for sure. The unconsidered rant has always seemed sexual to me, and I remember wishing I could get that same kind of flow going with different subject matter and think I did later in various errant works. But then there's the function of the mind in a sexual light casting anything in its guise. You could read a Burpee's Seed Catalog and get it hot? Or that time Ted did his number on Aram and me, interpreting just about every line of Dylan's Blond on Blond (or is it Blonde?) as proof he was a faggot, and me thinking later how interesting it is that you can do that (whether he did it intentionally as function of this or not. I spose he did actually) no matter the guise of the original metarial (material). But I do remember being disgusted at the limitation of my own vocabulary: why should poets be stuck with what "naturally" pops out of their head all the time. So leading to the dictionary (The Maintains) of course. And I think that's right, the more words you've felt of the better when you're writing along, to have it in there somewhere, fairly limitless, or at least have the impression that you're fully enough informed with words. Actually I still sometimes get hopelessly stuck for a word (horrors!) and spin around in place feeling like a gibbering idiot, as if the shape is there but one of its terms fell out along the way. Actually Duncan says something good about this somewhere, having the more words the better.

And I do prefer at this point willfulness to mindfulness (AG-word). As when I tried that breathing-meditation once I got so hung up on the extent of each breath I began to worry I'd eventually lose the autonomic circuit and have to remind myself to take each next breath for ever and ever. Anything that tensd(tends) to hitch you up in the going on, who needs it? I'll ride with will, desire, aggressive insistences, until something better comes along (and I doubt it will). I don't wanta feel like some Bill Berkson endlessly rereading ("practicing"?) his old poems to be sure they're "good"(!) As you say, I can't even type up things these days, much less think of making "a book," for the want of seeing what's next. Talking to Larry and others in NY I kept feeling that some kind of judgement is being practiced that I don't understand or certainly use. Everybody seemed hung up on some kind of "good poem" and it amazed me that they could be thinking that, I mean, I want to say, didn't we get beyond that? As if everybody's worried about The Ages or something eternally binding. Especially at "our" age!?!?! And this doesn't seem to have to do with truth but with, like, somebody wrote "better" poems last year than now and oughta shape up. Christ! So I'm overjoyed that you liked Jimmy's new book so much. All I heard in NY was how awful a "disappointment" it was(!), so I began to feel like I was the only one who'd liked it. I even said so in my workshop and, wow, the temperature in the room dropped below freezing instantly. It was incredible! As if they were all embarrased(never could spell that) and personally put-out that one of "their own" could "sink so low." But fuck all that. I love the book. Yes, it was one of those books (specialy the title poem) I was dreaming I had written as I was reading it, right! I think that there are always a few poets that don't interfere with you and feed you in a way so naturally on-going that you can't help feeling as if you'd written the work yourself. I've always felt that you and I work that way, and that's surely a blessing!

I'm gullible too. And I've always been easy to put on because I'll always take whatever as the truth, the first time through at least. There's something important about "surface" in this sense (truth), but I don't know how far I can get in discussing it right now. I had an argument with BB not long ago in letters about irony, and it might be interesting if I can reconstruct it. As I recall, he was saying that all language was ironic, and I said I couldn't see irony as any intrinsic part of language, just one of those terms that some professor will lay on and maybe you can then say yeah hmm I can see how you could think of it that way, but. A definite secondary overlay kind of gadget. Then Bill said (I can't believe he said this, but he did) language has no intrinsic nature since it's entirely new every time it pops out of my (Bill's) mouth. Then I said, gee, Bill, it would be nice (maybe) to be able to feel that way but I honestly can't, if only because there's too many other voices mixed up in it. Anyway, he did seem to be holding for a kind of "remove" as part of the writing process, "distancing" or whatever stands you aside. And then we got talking about roots and he said he thought all that was overrated and roots weren't all that useful (believe this?!?) and I finally had to drop the whole thing. Kind of thing makes me despair of ever talking to Bill seriously about writing. Makes me think I'm so gullible I always think there are certain things all poets hold true, then always get disappointed as it's proved again and again that's not so. At least in the way they talk about it (whole another level?). Secretly I suspect, with Bill anyway, he's trying these days to keep a distance personally from me, ever since I lambasted him in those letters last year (was it?). I was amazed when you told me on phone that Bill was reading in Bennington, since I had just talked with him a few days before and he hadn't mentioned that, Bennington being only an hour's drive from here. Shit, I guess I do understand all this, but to find oneself having to argue with a poet-friend that there is a language! makes me feel like I'm back down with the doodoo in the sandbox.

And then Corbett (this must be the Complaint portion of the letter!) writes me an actual whole letter (saints preserve us) which of course as usual doesn't have anything truly answerable in it just like his famous postcards, but he says, in telling me how much he enjoyed my poems in the last UA, the poems are "fresh and personal (dare I write this to the man who pronounced the personal poem a dead end?)." Holy shit, can't these guys read anymore!?!? Talk about a back-handed compliment! I read something like that and I just can't believe he knows anything about the process of writing. As if I should say, "Well, I'm sorry to have to tell you guys that the Personal Poem is not dead, in fact it's making a comeback"(!) Gee, sometimes it's fun to rant and rave! But, thank goodness for a few who come to your reading and modestly and briefly let you know that they received and enjoyed the poems (like Rudy), or like Peggy who somehow wonderfully was able to do the aforesaid and then retire, without making you feel you should have talked longer with them, understanding the difficult after-reading state. But that's rare. She's great.

"Language demands its form" is the perfect thing to say re The Maintains, and has a lot to do with all we've been discussing, my argument with BB et al. Not that that statement is an absolute or anything stopped, but that you can say that (!) means a secret about your relationship with the language. That you feel it as a power, that you feel it so inextricably a part of mind that you sometimes have use of it/it has use of you. This makes it possible to feel not only your own desire to make language (do something) but also to feel the language's desire to make you(ha!). Wait a minute, I really think there's something basic to this, hopefully without completely succumbing to the form of a form of a form of a form thing of using language to talk about language! I guess what I'm trying to say here is mainly that (after some point in the history of your own process in writing anyway) you can't maintain a distance from the language, for this passion-both-ways to be operating. It's a victim/victor thing, so hard to talk about. But, we've both felt the grip of the beast, and also the willfulness of our own grip to extend and possess. I feel like I spent so many years trying to possess the language (something I thought it interesting that a lame writer like Boer couldn't get close to grasping) (in that discussion Bertolette taped at Paul's house). And I didn't get any feel that I had possessed it until I got the shock that it had possessed me! See how this works? No doubt would sound pure nuts to many poets, but sure goes a long way toward describing how, say, the LANGUAGE guys continue to run up against dead walls since they see language as a blueprint to be anyway-tampered-with so have never gotten close enough to the language to allow it its power, thus will continue with dead batteries. And BB seems to think the power is all on his side, just wishes he had "more of it" (time, etc.).

I just can't stand the seeming fact that xeroxing costs so much or is even impossibly unavailable. I keep wanting it to be, feeling it really should be, free or at least just a few diddly pennies. Hard to accept that it cost me $100 to make three copies of my longwork, and that was by far the cheapest rate in SF. Seems like the more the financial hood lowers ominously the more "unrealistic" I become about that whole matter. I just can't consider it since money never has made brass tacks sense to me ever. We should have eachother's works simply by the need we have for them! I'll be sounding pious in a minute.

An odd thing is starting to heppn (!) happen to me with music; I find I'm avoiding listening to it for the first time in my life. All I seem to want to do is write and read. I've plucked out various factors that may make up a big reason for this effect. One is that my head has become so full of the musics going on all the time anyway, result of constant listening over the years, and actually playing the music way back there. I've always been able to "play" whole exact, say, Thelonious Monk solos in my mind, sometimes helplessly: I recall once taking a demerol pill and finding I couldn't stop a certain Coltrane solo from playing over and over again in my head, this went on for two or three hours till it finally wore me out (& the dope wore out too I spose) and I fell asleep where the solo continued for awhile more in a dream wherein I was playing the tenor, then finally stopped and got down off the bandstand. Another factor is that Hi-Fi-wise

I hear all the circuitry and stuff that's in between me and the music, which distorts the music itself into something more monstrous and harrying to hear. But, even more interestingly maybe, I think I'm finally beginning to figure out just what the differences are between Music-music and the so-called "music of language." This has always bothered me, like, when people make such an easy transposition between my musical experience (as musician) and my feel for sound in words and I think, yeah, but it's not so easy, you can't really make that jump without distorting qualities of both procedures. And then you have Pound, who had a fine ear for phrase-placement in words but evidently had a stone tin-ear for Music. And then Kerouac is interesting since obviously he did have a fine ear for music (I've heard him sing on a tape: almost perfect Sinatralike, or Chet Bakerlike, phrasing) that turned him on to a long line phrasing in words, but once you hear inside those lines you realize it's the music of the language taking over. He got the on-going rush of line from bebop, as did I, but I think that's still external to the route the language takes, or at least it's fascinating to try to find just how the language works with sound in a way (I swear) very different from pitched musics. So I've been trying to get sensitive to that, and now think I can hear it. Or at least I no longer feel the need to force a line/a sentence just for the sake of the sound. You can make the push using the other qualities of the language just as well, or maybe better? I dunno yet. Of course there are the many obvious examples of writers who never listened to music (Stein) or seemed actually to fear the sensual pull of it (Olson). Fascinating area, no? And should be discussed in lots more detail than I've been able to get here as an opener at least.

Here's another current (to me) deal, might be of interest. I've just had good evidence that I can actually forestall illness by insistence of will. Before I went to NYC I felt myself coming down with something and so kept repeating "I will not get this!" to myself (before going to sleep especially) since I knew I had to get through the trip, reading, etc. Then, the minute I got back up here with Larry and relaxed somewhat (though never can completely with L) I got a cold. Then, after he left, I knew I had to call you and did that, then immediately on hanging up the phone I took to my bed with fever and stomach flu that took me a week to get over! Resistance as a function of priorities? Seems proven to me anyway. **[Page break]**

I agree with you about THE MANIFOLD as title: it almost seems one of those that's carved in marble above the door to the tomb, but I like it anyway and will use it. One of those you find you have to use despite. It's just got so much other going for it despite that elder formality. It's all multiply what I mean and, damn it, I'm gonna make it mine!

Just read through first volume of Lew Welch letters and so don't want any of that eroded-psyche complaint tone to edge in here. That guy sure had a hard time trying to feel usefully okay about being anything, nevermind a poet. Makes me think how some of those beat guys seemed to feel they had to take whole nasty worlds on their public backs, a need thank god we don't have. Specially Welch, Snyder, Allen, and finally Kerouac I guess when his writing string wore thin he felt it all toomuch and wore out, though he never natively had that sort of adversary-advocate zealotry Allen, say, has. Poetry sure suffers from a personal responsibility for the wrongs of the tribe. Then I went and read in Desolation Angels to wash all that away. God, so pure a writer. I doubt we'll see a scribe of time of his kind again. Reading also (the endless succession): Cowper's The Task, that Jack Collom recommended as impulse for possible longpoem for him. A nice idea: to start with the sofa and then take walks and talk about mind, trouble is he's not a very good poet and the whole is spoiled by a helpless lecturing Christian piety. Also, reading in that neat Penguin Metaphysicals(!) anthology (know that great Traherne poem, Shadows in the Water?). Started Flaubert's Sentimental Education I've been meaning to read for years, figuring I should since I always did have a thing for older women(!) So far it's sorta boring but I figure I haven't read in it long enough to see, 60pp in, recent Baldick translation(also Penguin). I recall now your mentioning reading that Pound C to C anthology with pleasure(?) Right, it's terrific to just read through, without any thought of what he left out or might have included, just read the book as a book of the ages. I discovered Elizabeth Browning's Sonnets really for the first precise time in there, realizing they are incredible love poems, no? Actually I've yet to make my big Shakespeare push as I figured I probly wouldn't until the last minute (I always get caught in things like that). It's weird to promise to do something like this these days, well knowing how I'm going to have to follow all kinds of other reading/writing threads in the meantime. But I'll just immerse in

Shakespeare sea in June and that'll have to do, and have to hope I don't have some hot writing in the fire then (but how can I hope for that!??). One thing I thought would be great to do, but doubt I'll be able to, would be to go have a look at what Melville wrote in the margins of his Timon in Harvard Collection. It was one of his favorite S plays.

For the Newsy News Dept, not much. Celia discovered the other day that her armpits smell, so the house has been suffused with Secret Spray making her elders to sneeze. No doubt a bra will be next. And the constant hair-washing has begun unbidden. Her friend Guin washed her hair nine times the other day(!) and Celia had to be restrained. Today she goes in to have her first cavity drilled and is (rightfully) scared to jitters (I realized I'd been telling her horror stories about my drillings for years so much for parental wisdom!).

I'm going down to Providence tomorrow to see an old friend (& Master Lovecraftian) who just turned up down there again after many lost years, and will come back up here with my folks who'll stay the weekend. Then next weekend we go down to Princeton (what should I get from the P.U.Press?). I'm sure the summer will be upon us at this rate, like, immediately.

Love,

Clark

[→ P.S.—What is the date on the latest poem in that last batch I gave you? Let me know so I can think about typing up copies of the poems that follow so you have a complete set fairly up to date to read and choose for upcoming UAs.]

MAY 23 OR SO **[1980]**

Dear Clark,

Well it was great to see you, all of you, it's funny until we actually were face to face I hadnt realized how long it's been, I was expecting some of us might have even changed! & then the whole fact of your never having before been to a reading by me surely threw me? took me? for a loop. Actually if I'd thought of that before hand I think I might have given a much more what's the word? a less possible, no, a less popular reading??? A poet who cant find a word again. By the way, we never do feel free, as family of five now, to invite ourselves to invade anybody's house, thus our reticence—we werent being anti-social or nothing, as they say in Brooklyn. & thanks for that night, though I kept wishing I had your letter then to see what we were "up to." Family life, it seems, at least to me, lends itself better to letters or even phone calls than to face to face serious talking, except by accident. I guess I've always been a one-to-one (one on one?) type, even when BB was here, he wrote me afterwards complaining we hadnt gotten to talk, which we hadnt except here was this funny scene where both he & I (did I describe this to you?) were lulling Marie & Mose to sleep in the same room, in total silence, simply able to stare at each other & make faces! A terrific image, I was thinking, for a movie.

So by now I've given out my "marks" to students & cleared off **[of desk]** all the teaching paraphernalia of a myriad of kinds of papers & put them all in a big unsorted heap on the floor & for the last couple of days I've been writing letters (interspersed occasionally with attempts at poem) & I've even answered some letters older than yours! but I've saved yours for last, or actually third-last, now why am I saying all this? Just because these letters are such occasions! And to complete my introduction I have to fill you in on the rest of the typewriter saga from this end,—mine's got a new platen! It's quite spffy? spiffy in all ways & has all its parts—before I got it fixed it looked like I had been attempting to destroy it systematically with parts flying or falling off, pieces missing & the thing that holds the paper down would be falling into the space for the ribbon, etc. so now I feel quite "professional," no I dont. I guess I think our concern with typewriters is rather preternatural but like with other aspects of writing, it's nice to have something, anything, to hang on to. Let's see, where were we . . .

it's a nice

night **[Page break]**

I'm interested in that idea of a poet, your examples happily were you & me [+ Jimmy], feeding you naturally I think you put it so that you can feel you sort of wrote the thing yourself. I think this connects to what you were also saying about metaphor as exaggeration, that the stance (I cant think of better word) of the poet is a metaphor, that there is really no such thing as autobiography in poetry, & that the purpose of that metaphorical stance (yucky words!) is to sort of "not be a person" if I may say that. Or not be one person, but really, not be any person at all, I think I mean. [→ But to be in between language + "other people"—thus, "not everybody" can "write" "poetry"—ha!] When someone says to me, for instance, that my poems are, say, too cheerful!, my response is first to smile of course, but to think that that must be because the "person" I feel I have to be in poetry is not the self inevitably located in some recent moment of evolution (if I can say that too!) with all its small bigotries & concerns (thus the poet for instance cant be feminist exactly) but some kind of self that my person must figure has to be more cheerful [than "I" am]! In order to be larger & to allow for more, in order to transcend maybe my particular life or history—you know what I mean. When I ended my classes I made a speech to my poetry workshop about the poet as medium [→ like Godard, or even, for some, Dylan make people feel they almost are him]—do you find that idea fitting in to what we're talking about? I felt this instinct most strongly when I was writing Memory—that there the importance of the details of everything made it clear I could be no one, yet I did arrange the language, and very idiosyncratically—I chose the "occasion," I made the notations, etc. Ugh, I'm having trouble with words tonight. Maybe I could say, why I did it was so it could be done. Oh god, now you're going to laugh because I'm going to say, if metaphor is this exaggeration, then what is truth! And I have a tricky response—when I write a love poem, I am not "in love" journalistically, or the way you'd tell a friend. But I know the poem & circumstance together lead me sort of to a hope of love, at least the kind I'll be talking about, which . . . well I'll leave the rest to you. Maybe I should try & write about it! The thing is (really?) if you write poems, that doesnt mean that you necessarily believe in their perfectibility, right? I remember in the old days trying to find every possible way to derange that way the poem had of looking so cute & perfect on the page surrounded by all that precious space, etc. (Vito's ideas!). Thus I dreamt of him & Shakespeare at your house, but Vito in the dream was an old solider, worn out & haggard, back from the wars! & there was Shakespeare in his perfect robes talking to a rich man in robes even more golden & adorned than his own! I think actually the dream was all some peculiar analogy to what my unconscious makes of you & me but it'd take endless ages to figure it all out . . . anyway it was a pleasure to meet Shakespeare at your place. But where was I? Oh, so there's no such thing as a good poem in the sense that anybody in time knows about it which must mean, Wittgensteinianly, that no good poem exists. Tame tigers growl, & so on. Because even as a poet when you look at a poem, you're not in the act of writing! I'm a fucking purist. My theory became, during teaching this year, that every poem was good as long as the writer of it intended to "do poetry" & didnt confuse that with anything else in the cosmos. Thus I tried to put over on my class, who barely understood a word I said on this subject, the idea that I could not judge their works by any criteria at all & that the best thing to do was work existentially as a group to ferret out what each poem was demanding from the possibilities that the thing itself was allowing. But I must admit I've got no idea what BB means when he says "distancing"—what is that? If he believes in the "perfect poem" then maybe he can feel <u>HE</u> can control the world, thus his disappointment in (& also mere rewards from writing) poetry, but much more so, it seems to me, a big backlash in daily life. Well maybe I'm pushing that too far but just as I say I am not that person who's writing my poems exactly but I "Hope to be" another, I'll turn around & say that being a poet makes me expect to be exempt from all kinds of pettiness, but in a helpless way. Does that make any sense? I'm getting at something here which maybe you could express for me better. I dont mean money or stuff like that, I mean things like bickering, sexism, self-pity & even self-indulgence, though that gets tricky too. Oddly I've been feeling lately (my birthday!) that everything that's going on in the world at large is somehow more mine, it's also a function of having children obviously but too it has something to do with having put in more years in the world & having learned more about everything. I was thinking about that piece I wrote about Lewiston (did you ever read or hear it?) about all the chemicals, and now this Love Canal disaster. I cant imagine anyone living in that place for more than the time I was there which was one week without getting a sense they'd better get out of there fast because, for one thing, the sunsets were green. And then I think, historically, tritely, each of us people is just one, where am I & so on. Actually I've a whole new theory about triteness which I cant articulate. I feel trite lately (the word comes from the Latin, [→ <u>terere</u> I think] to rub or rub out, erase, wear away, etc.), I feel my ideas are trite in some ways, & my vocabulary inept & overused & hackneyed, I even wrote this poem in my notebook the other day, it went

<u>First Robin</u>
How come
it takes you
so long to come?

& I'm embarrassed but I'm telling you I dont know if that's as awful as it seems (i mean first of all the robins were around here all winter anyway) & of course maybe it's a function of too much teaching & reading of crap but I feel quite hilarious when I think about it. Alice & I are having a "bad poem" contest lately, to see which of us can come up with the worst/best!

Anyway

I'm certain I'm pushing to the limit, as always, what I've been doing & I'm trying to see not only how simple I can get but where is that funny boundary, like the boundaries of the person's flesh!, between awful simplicity & the conceivably sublime (if I can say that too!). I mean I know that poem about the robin has its funny aspects which I was not unaware of & I've been feeling quite funny, in the sense of laughing, about all of this because at the same time, as I told you, I am also daring myself to try & write total gibberish again, which is not easy (as it was?) & the whole experiment leaves me totally giddy with dismay at proving that a poet (if I'm one) can actually learn to forget what poetry is! Now I realize this part of the letter almost completely discredits my pretentious remarks in the beginning about things like "metaphorical stance"! but maybe not. I cant tell you how fascinating it is to me to watch the children go headlong into language—what they do all the time is take incredible chances, with syntax, with words themselves—the day before tomorrow, the day after yesterday—the inevitable logic of it all is so stunning! but with their chance-taking, in total imitation, they find out things & they, unlike "students," are so concerned with language's importance! Marie hears me say "citronella" & she says it the next day, mispronouncing it totally & then gives me the prideful eye—did I know what she meant? had she communicated what she wanted to do & at the same time shown off? All of that in one word. And ultimately, in relation to the Language guys (who recently asked me to "review" Lyn Hejinian's book because I'd expressed a liking for it—but "review"?), it's not the language that's a science but the grammar is. So I figure though you can denude the language of sense and grammar too, the one thing you absolutely have to leave is the language's own impulses (as you say) like the muscular impulse of a human to speak, & the power of the impulse to write, its lushness if you will, I mean the language's, & that is where, I think, they get confused about emotional matters. & that is where your poetry is so clear. Because that thing is heavily emotional & sexual & willful & all. & in among the language people's rules, they've ruled that one thing out as too personal because it is revealing but they've forgotten that we HAVE TO SPEAK. So their works dont survive at all. Am I being crazy? Am I right?

Well I need to find a title for my book of letters, but first I have to get it to you to read! Also all the stuff you said about music, I want to talk more about that but I must admit I cant express it, I too (like you said about Olson) fear music or else I'm lazy about it & dont bother to listen to it, I mean I see myself doing this & yet often & more often than not music makes me swoon & weep & so on, I cant bear it. But I used to write to it all the time when I was younger. Now I cant do it. And often in a line, I cant deny the musical end to it, as you say you've learned to do. Tell me more. I've got a week's freedom to write ahead of me & then we're journeying to NY to find an apartment & show Max his grandparents. I too am hoping to forestall all illnesses & yes I'm sure it can be done. Maybe I'll get my ms. xeroxed while I'm in NY, what a great idea! Also I've gotta get you my "gloss" on your big book soon, I was thinking of doing it on tape.

The new life is beginning to make more sense to me—I'm a "medium" in that way too! I'll have more news of that later, suffice it to say now I keep getting horrible letters with all kinds of complex responses to my new job/move & I mainly feel the complexity of it all should be left to me, yet I guess I'm flattered everyone actually is thinking about something I'm doing—the "public" world is weird, I've a long series of thoughts on being public in any way but they are so heavily psychoanalytic (& also trite!) I'd not want to put them on paper.

I'll check your poems & tell you the most recent date on them soon.

I'm surrounded by lilacs & an owl.

Love,

Bernadette

[→ P.S. Godard's new movie is called "Slow Motion" but actually it's called "Sauve Qui Peut La Vie" (Every Man for himself?)]

6/17/80 [→ I'M JUST GUESSING]

Dear Clark,

Just a note to ask I seem to remember you have a copy of Eliot Porter's book of photographs of Antarctica. Do You? I just saw an exhibition of some of his works in Southampton & got so inspired I knew I was right in my determination to use one of the Antarctica pix (if I can) as cover for Midwinter Day (which actually will come out sometime, probably 1981!) As we have a poor library here, I thought it easiest to write you to ask the publisher of the book and/or any idea you might have about reaching Porter himself. And also, which of the pix, if you do indeed have the book, you would recommend. I realized from a letter I got from Callahan that I had to quickly get my cover together otherwise, as he suggested, he would emboss a rose on it—I am not joking! I am not Franz Boas! I'd been thinking of one of the pictures of penguins (you have to picture this in black & white, I guess).

Meanwhile we did the deed & found a place to live in NY, so as of August 1st our address will be

172 E. 4th St. #9B NYC (I think the zip is 10009) which if it is makes a fortuitous combo of nos. It's a genteel apartment with big rooms with doors in a pre-war giant building in an enclave of the old more traditional neighborhood of Ukranian-Jewish-Italian (somewhat removed from the punk) extraction. I cant tell you what a horrific scene it was staying at Ted & Alice's apartment—I admire Alice (now why dont I also say Ted?) enormously for being able to do the work she's done in that place & with her kids, I cant believe it. One thing I'd like to be able to do, in our time in NY, is to help them to find another apartment, which scene is amazing—Lewis actually wound up sitting, at one point in our researches, at a big board table with a lower-east-side apartment=building mogul who was quite litterally (littorally?) slapping him on the back.

How are your Shakespeare researches going? Ah I wish so much we were still in contiguity so I could hear all about it! & I'm envious too (as I guess I've said before) at not being a part of that Shakes. enclave. (or exclave?).

Meanwhile^2 the situation at the church seems neat & intact & easy to hand over except perhaps for the great "The Record"! which I must admit I've no idea what to do about, but I will learn (hopefully from Ed). I made a most galling & fascinating grammar of the Poetry Project since I've been back which color-codes (as in emotions) all the readers & in the course of doing it I discovered a fiddelheaded etymological relation between & among the words grammar/gramary/glamour! (not grandma!), which titillates my something.

If you'll forgive me, as only you will, having a rather adolescent identity crisis at this moment, I'd like to say that in the last few weeks I've been able to identify myself as a contributor to BASE-BALL DIAMONDS, a person who wrote a poem in the shape of a volcano, an inhabitant of off-season (rather bombed-out) New Hampshire in "the only Henniker on earth," a participant at a luncheon at a fancy French NY restaurant (where I ate my first raspberries of the season) where Maureen Owen was present in a Mickey Mouse T-shirt, the new avid reader of Onions' Etymological Dictionary, the possessor of some (but dull maybe) secrets . . . but I do have a copy made of my new book which I will send you as soon as I read thru it once to make sure it's not full of neologisms that are just too blatant.

Write soon & send information/theories about Eliot Porter, Jack Collom (who sent us another book) & Shakespeare.

The most amazing thunderstorms have pelleted us both here & in NY with hail & rain & rainbows & we discovered a field of frais du bois yesterday & also a kind of wild violet I had never seen before.

I opened the Henniker equivalent to the Penny saver the other day & found in it everything I would need to stay here another year!

But I do not mean to bring that ambiguity into our correspondence (& to fate).

Love,
Bernadette

I just reopened the letter to realize I hadnt said anything about Philip Guston. I read about his death in NY (& about Henry Miller's there too) & I wrote about it as soon as I came back in a poem called "Lazuli Bunting" which is from a picture of a bird by Eliot Porter which if you like I'll send (the poem) on to you. Perhaps it would be good to have some sort of reading in Guston's honor, it would be good to do something, something mourning, let me know what you think. I've been plagued lately by dreams about my mother, perhaps it has to do with him. I keep faulting her, in my dreams, for not "being here"! As you like it.

WEDNESDAY 25 JUNE [1980]

Dear Bernadette,

I better write you before things get more out of hand and I additionally start actually moving around away from the desk. Shocked to realize that I won't have calm-of-desk to write (even letters) till late August, what with all this traveling and "appearing." The last few weeks has been most trying and unhinging in a lot of ways, so forgive if this letter is more scattered than usual. But I gotta make an attempt so's not to totally lose the threads of your last big letter (already over a month(!) old).

Of course I put off the Shakespeare research till the last possible moment(month), figuring that was the only way it'd still be fresh, wanting to ad-lib most of it off top of well-stocked S-Mind and not write it all out and just read it etc., plus knowing myself well enough by now to realize I'd inevitably put it off till close to deadline anyway (making profit of procrastination!). And then Philip dies right in the middle, which I'd been expecting for over a year (since he had his heart attacks) but of course that doesn't at all "prepare" you. Something strange: the night after he died (but I hadn't been told yet) I misheard the guy at the top of the 11 o'clock TV news say something about the death of a famous American "artist," so waited through all that crap (naturally they didn't mention it again till the end of the show) and then it was Henry Miller they meant (he died same day as Philip, an odd non-conjunction I guess) which I had already heard about but forgotten, so it felt like I got a kind of confused message through the warps of time and tube. It's hard for me to realize that he's dead still. Partly caused by the fact that we hadn't seen eachother (a few phonecalls & letters instead) for about a year, and even more due to the fact that I've so long had the habit of talking with him in my mind almost daily, which will continue, stealing from grief's share. Actually as I was telling Ted (he called from Boulder to "ascertain" his "own reality"), I mainly just feel blessed to have known Philip, feel that something generative has been passed on to me, which makes me more determined than ever. But I was amazed to realize, at the funeral, that I wanted some physical evidence of the death, making me see why earlier people wanted to display the body up on sticks or actually burn it in full view of crowds. I felt like there should be a thunderbolt, to put a period to the life, you know? There should be a clarity about ceasing to be, which was further muddled by the fact that, it being Jewish tradition, the burial had taken place almost a week before the service (before the next sundown), so all you got to see was a bunch of flowers on the ground and some guys getting up to say how great Philip was, etc. Ross Feld, David McKee & Morty Feldman (reading a ten-year-old aesthetic essay, which pissed me off as most inappropriate). The best was the saying of the Kaddish, to me anyway needing the presence of something ancient (if not cosmic). A small cloud passed over the sun at that moment with the sound of a tractor in the distance.

And of course there's the additional misery & confusion of the taxmen leaping over everybody to attach Philip's bank account and (can you believe this?) put a chain on the studio door so nobody (not even family) can get in till they've made their assay (at highest market value) of each picture (& he must have tens of thousands, counting all the drawings, in there, so the joke's on them in a small way considering all the work they'll have to do). Then, as the wheels of so-called law turn these days, they'll hit the family with a staggering tax bill forcing the sale of too many pictures at once. The first time I've felt the absolutely clear necessity of a crime, which actually isn't a crime at all: Back up a huge truck and steal away with as many pictures as possible. But it was too late for that.

[Page break]

Philip had never gotten around to changing his 1972 will, leaving everything to Musa. Almost a greater sense of loss, their rush to take all those pictures away from those few who knew them as generative. I wish I knew some way around this crime, but nobody seems to.

So, anyway, to answer your question about the Porter book: no, I don't have a copy, only saw the copy you took out of the Lenox library (?) Porter's things are so clearly color photographs that I wonder if they might lose a lot reproduced in black&white? But then, penguins are black&white(!?) Also, he seems so much a part of the market (I'm sure he gets big bucks for a cover photo) that I wonder if you'd get in trouble using one of his pictures? No doubt why you want to get in touch. I don't have an address, but I immediately think of Ron Padgett as a possibility because of his long relationship with Fairfield(?) Try him, if you haven't already. I think it's a good idea, and please don't allow Callahan to intrude with some foolish notion! A "rose"!?! !? Jesus . . .

The "Shakespeare Research" of course could go on forever, so in a way I'm glad to have an arbitrary stopping-point posited. The vastness of his range, emotional & every other way, does tend to shock & stymy. I read through 12 plays in a week at one point & realized that more than one a day is everyway too much. They do tend to rearrange your day and determine your thought, and I found myself weeping at them often. Lear (I must confess I'd never read entire before) had me feeling like I'd been run over by a pyramid. And I think I see why you (& Alice) like Twelfth Night so much(you should tell me in detail sometime though). It's the language that fascinates, naturally, so that I think I can make some teachable point of that. There is a kind of "rawness," re your thing about wanting to "derange perfectibility," as if layers of useage were being peeled away as you read, giving a view of origin of the language as we now know it. I was amazed & excited to discover that the Elizabethan period was the actual time when English was just starting to grow more sophisticated (in the sense of more complex syntactically, more multiple terms coming in, largely from the Latin of the Italian Renaissance influence) and Shakespeare was one of the main guys accomplishing this. A kind of bright raw density full of new possibility excitement. It gets a kind of three-dimensional flux reminding of that in-front-of/in-back-of feel of the horses legs and the spears in Uccello's battle pictures (and of course perspective itself was a new discovery then too). Then adding the crux of medieval magic still going on in country towns like Strafford with the Italian Hermetic magic (guys like Bruno, Ficino, Mirandola etc.) coming into London and you've got a most marvelous mix to jump with! Plus I agree with Kerouac that lots of Shakespeare's best stuff seems written in an inspired rush, almost unblotted (as he says), like in many of the Sonnets how the first two (or sometimes four) lines look like out-of-the-blue gift-shots that he later fills in and develops, rounds off to (amazing actually!) wholes.

And, yes, I

think you've put your finger on what's wrong with the Language Gang, exactly! That urge-to-speak/write is just the power-field they've locked themselves out of. Sort of amazing they don't realize it, but no doubt it's fear, right. If they push on long enough they'll inevitably wake to that, or not(or quit). And, talking about being not-just-a-personality when you write opens up maybe the vastest issue of this whole crazy art racket. Fascinating to talk of in terms of Masks (Philip & I used to alot, and of course Shakespeare, Melville . . .). Probably why I opened "your section" of my longwork with "Memory is a voice . . . of nobody." You're less yourself (in terms of that single personality you "recognize") and more other things, forces & voices. It all feels too vast for me to go on talking about here now, but hope to further later (remind me). As far as being a "medium," yes, I always feel when I'm reading some great writing and it's all I'm doing at that moment (no distractions) that I (almost?) am the mind that's putting things together that way. No "distance" then (hogwash, Bill!). If high matters are there and one is reading right deeply. I wanted to say something about insistence here too, will as such a prime in writing, but can't seem to catch it up at the moment. See anyway Shakespeare's crazy all-over-thelot "Will" Sonnets 135 & 136.

News of Godard's movie makes me crazy to see. The translation of title seems a peculiar mess in that the French has the feel of "panic" rather than "slow motion"(!?) I wonder if he titled the English release or what? Another Jean-Luc Joke?? I also heard it has a lot of "instant replays" in it.

Please do send the Lazuli Bunting poem. Actually if you felt like it, you could write me (within the next three weeks) c/o Hopkins/8300 Eastside Road/Healdsburg, Ca. 95448. It'd be great to get a letter from you there, and I could send you a Post-Boulder California Report back. No doubt I'll have sufficient farm-calm there to do so, and an IBM Selectric to boot. I can't wait to read your letter book too, hoping it comes in next few days so I can take it with me to read on the road. Hard to believe that next week today I'll be reading Timon to whoever at Naropa! Bob Rosenthal called, very thoughtfully, a few days ago asking if I could send some of my books (he said he'd get in touch with Lewis for copies of OWN FACE too) and offering to aid in any way he could with setting up housekeeping for us at ye olde Varsity Townhouses. Guess he'll be equivalent of T.A. to me and I'm glad of that.

Nice to have a friendly face at hand. Sounds like Naropa is on the skids, from what Bob reports. Only about 10 students have been attending the Shakespeare classes, attendance overall really down this year. So small in fact that classes are being held in one of the Townhouse rooms(!) Maybe we'll be in on the end? Oh well, it's only five days, whatever resultant.

By the way, re your idea about memorial reading for Philip at Church, Bill Berkson told me he had spoken to you about that and plans were already afoot for such in Fall. Good, count me in. David McKee also told me he's trying to set up a similar scene at the Whitney as intro to Philip's SF Show coming in there next Spring. Good I think to have a number of these events stretched over the year, keep the PG Spirit present.

Suddenly mid-summer here the last few days: temp in 90's and humid as hell. We have for the first time a pair of Baltimore Orioles in residence around the house. I think they must be building a nest somewhere close. Hope I can find just where as they're lovely things to see. Celia's glad to be out of school at last and really up for the trip. I think she'll miss seeing Gregory & Max, Allen&Peter next door (they have a house somewhere else now?), & other kids etc she remembers from last time. Actually it occurs to me we could be kinda lonely there this time. Even Larry said he'd be living somewhere else(?) God, it'll probably be more like living in a college dorm than ever!

Anyway, we go down to Providence on friday, then my folks will drive us to Bradley/Hartford on sunday for the flight to Denver. The following saturday we fly to California & the farm for two weeks (actually staying with the Palmers in town the first couple nights). Maybe get up to Yosemite for a few nights in there somewhere. Then back, and (me) to Bill's Southampton Seance July 24th. Then (then!) the Vineyard for the next two weeks. We probably won't be back here at all permanently till August 18th or so.
When do you move in at 4th St.?

Love to all,

Clark

JULY 5, 1980 SATURDAY

Dear Clark,

This is dreadful. I kept looking for your letter & I kept pulling out a letter from Susan Noel which for some strange reason began, "this is dreadful." But this is not dreadful at all, in fact there's nothing dreadful about it, I hope. Dreadful's an odd word.

I cant believe after enduring the dreadful holiday with the landlord & his "friend" fighting within our hearing incessantly, that tomorrow would still be Sunday, which means another fight for them! They are here so infrequently that even though they "own" the place, it seems like it is they invading our privacy, and it is. I am so irate (not to bore you with this) at having to listen to their bickering that not only am I going to tell them but I think we will leave here a week before we planned!

Every letter has to begin among complaining! I must admit I've gotten very self-conscious about my letter-writing style since re-writing my book of letters where I see myself weaving in & out of a kind of sloppiness which of course ("Of course" is just the kind of thing I mean) has to do with "talking" as David Antin might say. Though actually ("though actually" is even worse!) his new book by Sun & Moon is not so bad, compared to the pitfalls I am talking about. Well are your labors at Naropa ended?

I can picture so clearly your being about to leave the calm-of-the-desk, as you say in your letter. & you are worse off than I! Till late August! At least no matter what else I have to do, I have the calmofthedesk every night (except in NY I wont have Wednesdays). Then again I, like you, never was a good worker in the summer & at the moment I'm having a horrible time re-writing, if that's a word, my book of letters which I did have copied for you but then when I got back from NY & started working on it I saw that I was in such a turmoil about it & was toying with (& now doing) doing so much to it that to send it to you, raw, would be flagrant or presumptuous or something—suffice it to say I am immersed in it, now up to page 250 in the reworking & amazed at what I've learned about "conversation" vs. poetry. Also you are one of the main characters in the first [Lenox] half of the book! I've a thought to changing all the names, as I did in the final large version of Studying Hunger, it gives me some peculiar courage to do that. I'm expecting to be done with it in August, then I've got retyping to do—did you ever wish you had a secretary? & would you trust one? I've got so many things I want to show you, if only I could get them typed. Well be patient & you'll be the first person to read my finished version of this. Tell me, would you mind if I used an edited version of a letter I sent you as a part of the book? I'm not one to carbon my letters as you know but I did copy a few when I was writing this book & one of them's to you. The second half of the book contains "real" letters occasionally. If you have any reservations about it, you can let me know when you read the whole book, or beforehand. I must tell you I've had to edit out about a million things that might be offensive to one or another person. But, more later about this, talking like this only makes me wish you were here, the words are too many on paper.

What you say about Philip Guston's death is so simultaneously touching & astonishing to me, about needing proof of his death, I shouldnt say touching but moving. But it touches me as I've touched the dead & was always grateful though horrified at the age I was for that proof. But more the thing that horrified me always was that you couldnt give vent to grief at all, there was no formality for that, thus mourning occurs for us over a long period of time whereas a dance poem speech or even a momentary flailing about which is recognized is better. But then I did most of my mourning when I couldnt "speak." I've been working on a series of poems, which didnt originally relate to Guston's death at all, called "Two Haloed Mourners" from a picture Raphael Soyer sent me from his recent trip to Europe (by Aretino Spinello) & among that series is the Lazuli Bunting poem so I think I'll send you all of it. Meanwhile I'm going to write to Musa about the reading which everyone seems interested in doing, and I'll suggest November or December for it. I guess I didnt mention to you that when Clyfford Still died, just as Lewis was trying to tell me that from reading it in the paper, I saw an enormous snake in our pantry:

Moth like porphyry lights the town
Like a phratry against the city how many
Famous men die in a summer today it was
The painter Clyfford Still when he died
I opened the window in the pantry
To bring down the screen on the sill resting
Was a snake curled snakelike disturbed by me
It crawled back behind one of many of old
Cold New England's kitchen sinks, in childhood
A snake extracted from a pipe is preserved in a jar

In a plumber's window, in New York where I'll go back
Next week I was lucky to see Still's painting
Years ago I am abstract a poet I am not him for what
I forget is poetry compared—moth like porphyry.

A feeble attempt at a sonnet & I must say I'm totally engrossed, kind of belatedly in Shakespeare at this moment, I just read the Tempest & am astonished at its structure & now am in the middle of Twelfth Night again & before I say anything else I'll say how great to have Olivia, Viola & Malvolio be anagrams. I'm sure that's the first thing they say in Shakes. criticism but since I've never read it I feel quite pristine in this realization. Every group of characters in a Shakespeare play seems like a proliferation, true courses of the imagination, like pure imagination as in Hawthorne, like saying what can one mind create, summon up, well why not Juno & Ceres! etc. It all belongs to us. Did Shakespeare really invent the language as we use it? Surely he invented adjectives as far as I can see—well you say that in your letter, it's amazing to review it. You & I, and probably many others, can actually feel like Shakespeare now when we read him because we are so full of him. And surely, as you intimate, Shakespeare invented syntax (at least as it appears in, say, Frank O'Hara, you, me, & many others). I find in this re-reading that I am reading him as if it were a detective novel, I pick it up & am totally engrossed in the silly plots for the sake of the going-on quality it has. I love it, I am not only laughing in my boots at every word (reading comedies) but finding the language all alone to be like a summary of practically all of education. I was thinking of calling my book "drowned letters." Oh! Are you tired of thinking about Shakespeare?

The Will Sonnets—perhaps that is where we get all this stuff about will from! Why doesnt Bill "Will" Corbett take advantage of it? And Will Berkson too? Bill B's problem is that he is a Bill, a sealed document relating to goods or services, a list of things offered, as a menu or theater program, an entertainment, a handbill, a draft of a law (if you'll forgive me quoting my dictionary); the next time I write to Bill I'm going to say, Dear promissory note, . . . oh no I wont! & what of our names? Clark & Bernadette?--colorful in terms of Rimbaud. Clark like a stone, Bernadette

I'm distracted, Lewis &

I just caught a baby mouse in a box & liberated it outdoors, Bernadette Joseph's coat of many colors, actually did I ever show you my vision of the colors of your name

Ctan Lblue-gray Ared Rorange Kdark blue
Ctan Ogray Ogray Lblue-gray Igray Dblack Gbrown Egreen

Meanwhile let's see if I can summon up any "news" as normal people say: Russell seems to be abjuring our company now that he knows we are "going" & I'm mad about that, he told Bill C. I was depressed! When actually if he werent such a narcissist he'd see I was sad to leave a friend. Well as usual gossip makes no sense. Robt. Creeley writes to write that he cannot read at the church for less than $750 which is what his agent gets him, sort of, but he says he would read for free! Also Penelope's pregnant. A third family! Ted & Peter Orlovsky (wouldnt it be great if Ted's last name were Orlovsky?) have consented to give the first reading at the church. There's a long story I've got to tell you, in person, about Bill B. & "the record"—see now that I work at the P.P. I actually have tales to tell! Marie's got poison ivy, she's had it for a month, now resorting to cortisone ointments. Max can catapult himself practically out of his bassinet & can nearly sit up on his own, Sophia is obsessed with tales of some yellow house which none of us can identify the source of. New Hampshire is neither here nor there for us at this moment, our house is full of cartons, each of which I've decided to make stand for a word and from them I will assemble a poem called "Five to Seven" based on a mock-clock Lewis's father gave me to teach the children how to tell the time.

It's hot & I saw a hummingbird tonight about some milkweeds. Also a skunk walked up to me the other night & tried to make friends while I was out for my nighttime walk. A million giant frogs jump into the water when I jump into the pond & minnows bite at my feet, nibble I guess. Fireflies creep inside my window & light up. We should publish the cave collaboration again.

I'm dying to hear what you and Susan & Celia made of the Varsity Townhouses again, and of the Shakespeare reaction—& Yosemite? & all else. Do you think we'd be better off among the Renaissance?

Love,

Bernadette
as of July 27th (full moon) [→ the landlord wont let us stay past our appointed time, + is threatening us with repair-men.]: Ageloff Towers (who is Ageloff?)
172 E. 4th St. 9B
NYC 10009

MONDAY]4 JULY [1980]

Dear Bernadette,

Here sitting literally by the pool and the fuschias in California I hope this machine will allow me the power of a letter to you. It's a good old-enough IBMSelectric and should do but will I? So far so good, so clear. Wonderful to have your letter on the blue graph paper reminding me (you?) of <u>0 TO 9</u> days. The Palmers just left (here for weekend) and Michael left me with his new book mss (NOTES FOR ECHO LAKE) which is terrific and immediately inspired me to lots of writing in notebook at least so I have a phantom sensation of calm-of-the-desk if not the actual. In fact I'm starting to get the feeling of maybe being able to write anywhere, on the road on the run etc., making me glad I'm not a painter in regard to materials anyway. The fog is starting to lift, toward noon, as it seems to do efficiently everyday, those bright yellow hills coming clear. Susan and Celia left yesterday in a rented Toyota to visit the rest of the family, sisters Mary and Maggie, in Oregon and Washington, heading fearlessly up into that shaky country where quakes have been reported around Mount Hood and hears hoping!

(That's "here's") Naropa was quiet. Amazing contrast to last time, caused I spose partly by the smaller enrollment and Allen's no longer living in the Varsity Townhouses. Bob and Shelley next door this time and a great help, Bob actually having cleaned the whole apartment spotless before we came(except the sliding screendoor kept falling off). We took our morning swims around 8, the pool to ourselves. The classes were spaced oddly, one day at noon, the next day at 6 P.M. but I somehow managed to fall into the pattern. And get this: upon arrival they told me I had only <u>two</u> Shakespeare classes after previously telling me three, and before that two! A definite air of fuckup and collapse about the place. The Poetics School (no longer "Disembodied") seems to have little contact with the administration, in fact some active hassles with, sounds like maybe Trungpa feels he no longer needs the poetry to bring in students, few enough students overall anyway and little money, so in fact the poetics school feels more disembodied than ever! Which feels nice, more intimate, actually since the classes are all held in the Townhouses (you just go across the courtyard to another room like your own and teach) and most of the students live there too. More "Socratic," as Michael Brownstein said. The students are a tighter group, have been there together long enough to know eachother, more serious, none of the weekend gawkers I remember from last time, the whole scene is greatly condensed down. In fact, they say next summer will be the last summer session, they're going totally on winter semesters from then on, but I wonder if the school will even exist by that time. We didn't see as much of Allen and Peter, Allen was away at some "Sex Convention" the first two days we were there, but they did come to two of my classes (Allen adding a great Blake Urizen parallel to my Melecholia). (Melencolia!) Allen perhaps preoccupied with other matters, the Tom Clark scene seeming finally to be settling of its own crazy weight. Tom came to the Townhouses for a final meeting with Allen (he moved to Santa Barbara the following tuesday) one day just before my class, so I didn't even see him but Celia did and described him as "horrible looking" with his teeth all yellow and askew and dragging one foot, she hardly recognized him. Evidently he wanted to make some kind of "peace" with Allen before departing and proposed that Allen (or he and Allen) write a further book straightening out "the facts"(!) Can you believe it, now <u>he</u> wants to forget the whole thing! Sounds actively schizoid to me.

Anyway, not to belabor that foolishness, we had a very good time and I enjoyed the classes, few enough of them as there were. I read through practically the entirety of TIMON in one big session and actually got them to <u>hear</u> his language I think, quite a few told me so afterward anyway. Great to realize that one could actually read Shakespeare aloud as completely present language and not some worn version of Old Vic affectation etc. I'm just sorry I hadn't time to get to the Sonnets as I'd planned to read through quite a bit of that as well (too much preparation!). One magical moment: as a further S. connection in the introductory class I was reading the CANDLES chapter from Moby Dick and just as I finished with Ahab wiping the lightning from his harpoon one of those wild patented Colorado thunderstorms broke out all around the place, close bolts shivering everybody's timbers. The gods were with me, or were they?

What

to say of it all, teaching is a strange litmus? When I prepare to teach I always accumulate piles of dumb doubts, much like your wondering if those anagrams are the first thing they teach in academic Shakespeare, I have endless trouble relating my realizations to some more general "field" of humans, what do I know that I don't know they know they don't know, or something imponderable! Then what can you do (time pressures etc.) but go ahead and do it anyway, usually finding out (as I did, again) that none of this stuff ever occurred to them. Many of them were so demonstrably glad to hear him after getting endlessly hungup trying to understand him on the page. That Urge to Speak winning the day again, I guess. Though one woman student said she felt Timon was nothing but a worthless wimp, so I got to say it would be worth it to be such a wimp if one could get off such glorious raging speeches! Though of course nobody seemed to have read Melville Whitman Dante etc. and when I did a class on Guston very few had even heard of him, but I always take that as permission to just wail away. I was asked, by the way, if I would consider coming back to do a five-week in the winter sometime, and I had to go, unh . . . hmm. Of course it would depend on a few real external imponderables like will the school still be there and able to pay etc., but I still can't imagine staying energized enough to teach classes over that long a period. There would have to be days when I just felt stupid and couldn't get out of it. Short shots seem containable and cross-breedable with my daily writing work, but the long run? I really don't want to be a teacher and identify my only teaching value as coming at classes from the oblique angle of a thing very other (actual writing). Again, we'll see.

We

saw mostly Anne & Reed (Anne looking and acting very pregnant already), Larry (of course, though he was living in another townhouse a couple blocks away—Susan being still in Kentucky), Michael (we spent a nice afternoon and dinner before my reading up at his Wall Street place talking about how possible or impossible it was or is to write a novel), Bob & Shelley (Celia did a lot of hanging out with them and babysitting Max), and Sam Kashner (who was funny and great and always looked like he was leaning against something you couldn't see in the room). A couple of funny/serious talky dinners with Allen & Peter. Didn't see much of Dick at all, who was reputed to have a big motorcycle we didn't see so got the impression he was roaring around on that much of the time. Peter is teaching a big Compost Poetry Workshop in which, for instance, if somebody reads a poem with tapioca in it he then spends the whole rest of the class discussing how you make tapioca(!) And it was great being there the week Charlie Haden (Ornette Coleman's greatest bassplayer) was teaching, Larry and I both knowing old friends of his so we could have great sessions of bebop conversation and catch up on all the news of that scene. Charlie has triplet daughters who were there carrying tiny violin cases around and very serious about music. And of course the great Flatirons are still looming over all through that fascinatingly clear high air so close to the clouds, and I found a book called ROCK WISE by one of the local climbing heroes. Also made the great find finally of a copy of Melville's CLAREL in Brillig Works, there it was just sitting there on shelf calm and as if always there waiting for me as you please, a book I'd begun to think I'd never actually own, turned out there'd been a 1973 reprint I never knew about and only $9.50 in great-looking old-fashioned hard cover.

And lots of other bits of news I'm forgetting already. I understand perfectly your reworking the LetterBook and will anxiously await further. Though it would have been fun to compare the earlier version with what you finally do with it. Fine with me if you use whatever letter to me, sure. However and whatever goes best. Those colors of my name are amazing, I never did see and they do seem somehow "right," how did you do that? It's not the Rimbaud method is it? I never can remember his correspondences. The colors somehow amazingly remind me of my mother's family crest, but I'll have to check that. It would be easy to just sit here in this impossibly blue and yellow afternoon and describe all the species of bright flowers around, and then finally give up and succumb to jumping into that so-blue pool, as I will later. I found a beautiful blue-tail Skink lizard the other day and rescued him from the pool filter. And there are always these great black hawks circling over us, making me wonder what would happen if I started thrashing around as if drowning in the pool. Tomorrow my cousin (Fred the Biologist) arrives, so no doubt we'll have further animal adventures (does that sound unnatural?). California, this neck of it anyway, still seems very possible, if all those volcanos don't start popping in sequence like shirt buttons anyway. And this typewriter has been treating me so well maybe I'll now try out some poetry on it!

LOVE,

Clark
AUGUST 14, 1980

Dear Clark,

I find it hard to believe I havent written you since we've been in New York! First I must tell you it's been hot as hell for the whole time, so if I seem to be having lapses, either of typing, memory, remorse or logic, I'm afraid, as they say, anyone would feel that way. The devotedly dry (of rain) August summers are worse, to my mind—& I remember all too many of them—than the Boulder summers, of which of course I've only seen one, and the humidity, as in the banal phrase, "it's not the heat, . . ." etc. which I've always thought was the best example of a cliche (if you wanted to tell your writing class, for instance (not yours, but my old one),—hell this sentence is a miasma,), what I'm saying is that heavy moisture in the air creates in me a well-remembered (as everything seems to be in this city) heaviness in the chest which is not so much a nostalgic memory as it is a feeling of imminent death! No wonder Ted is so screwed up! Ah I wont begin to tell you all about that, suffice it to say we've been beleaguered, even in these two mere weeks where one might expect we'd be pitied for having just moved in—the problems of "getting settled" etc.—but of course in New York no such thing! beleaguered by requests for what they call loans so in our ingenuousness of course we gave two & in the ingenuousness of loaning of course never got them back & then the one person one might have felt inclined not only to loan but to give money to had to bear the brunt of our new-found cynicism. Oh dear, since we've been here I've been construing for myself the term nest of ninnies over & over again, & then again I find myself obsessed, not with some great poem that rings in my head but with the words from one of the children's books, that begins: "It's morning in the city, people are hurrying to work & to school; some stop to watch the construction sites . . ."

If you'll forgive me for beginning a new paragraph you'll probably also forgive me for saying or reiterating that, among the poets who live in New York (few of whom come from the city) the attitude to us is not a blatant & naive welcome that one could envision giving way to, but a kind of cynicism [→ ?] at "THE DIFFICULTIES"! which Lewis and I know too well! & my main reiteration is still at the fact (which I think I noticed for the first time when I was about twenty) that, to poets in New York, you can never say, oh look at that (tree, person, store) naively, else you must be immediately subject to a caustic remark (I always used to think I wasnt smart enough!). Now, interestingly, I find myself immune to some extent (though not immune enough not to mention it) and, en famille, I find myself feeling enough like superwoman, as they say, to even say to Ted, if you would only let me say two sentences you would see what I mean. However I dont mean to harp on him as he is feeling so put upon because his mother is sick, & so on.

Thank you for the great Naropa report. The thunderstorm in "class"—ah, I wish I'd been there. Here we'd had the most terrific storm a few days ago—& I had forgotten about NY storms & how violent & seeming to close one in from all directions they are—this island! I heard wonderful things about your teaching there & only wish I had been able to attend & be a part of the Shakespeare colloquium—is that the word?

It's noisy in the city, people are hurrying to work & to school . . . and to fires, disco dances, new malfunctioning buses, it's endless. There is a great old-fashioned wading pool in the park near our house where we've been spending an inordinate amount of time—I'm the only "grownup who gets wet." Meanwhile the children are having to adapt to sharing a room but they are doing well, and often outwit us in taking care of each other.

Did you get my Two Haloed Mourners? I developed a fear it'd been lost in the mails. The colors of your name come from some instinct I've always had, not the same as Rimbaud's as he only "colors" the vowels thus: A black, E white, I red, U green, O blue—all according to some accordance with alchemy as far as I can see.

A ruckous (?) in the children's room encourages me to finish later, as I'm also anxious to see what the Democrats have done today.

***It's later and reading over what I'd written already (ruckus, it's spelled) [→ from rumpus + ruction] I seem to wax rather hysterical in the early part of the letter, I dont feel that way exactly but Ted, who is in an altered & almost hostile state, does get to me. He & others in & out of town treat us like babies, who dont know what we've gotten ourselves into (not in relation to my job but NYC), Ted refers to our moving here as a disaster & when I told him we werent babies & had each lived 30 years in the city before he said, you guys have alot to learn about marriage, you dont know how to fight! Actually as the work of moving gets more & more finished—& it <u>is</u> finite!—we find we are living in this neighborhood very much the way we lived in Lenox, at least for the moment before school & work begin. And when I get angry I can go to the Polish butcher & have him pound some veal. I had a dream the other night that in order to distract people from noticing he'd parked his car illegally Ted pretended he was both moving & making a movie (zillions of movies being shot downtown this month), dropped two flowerpots & started escorting fancily dressed women in & out of his car—fairy tale cartoon characters. Ah the dream is a bit revealing. Ed was making a t.v. show last week & put Marie in it. I had another dream since we've been here that was quite startling or momentous or something. In life I had been listening to Harris one day talking desultorily of taking mescaline. Then I dreamt I had taken the drug & I was standing at the door of one of the rooms in the Henniker house. Pigeons started massing on my back & I realized I had to move just right to prevent them from scratching me. I immediately carefully shot through the roof along with Marie who became a sort of Roman candle (her temperament no doubt) in a First Communion dress. Then I saw that on the drug I could see & do no end of crazy things but I felt I'd had enough & decided to calm down. I've always enjoyed questions of choice in dreams. Remember the pigeons in our house in Lenox?

Enuf dreams? Cld go on forever, etc. I've been working on my book of photographs of buds but I dont quite know what to do with it. It'd be easy to fill it with poems, so far I have one long one, & just let the photos work on what I'm writing anyway. For some reason I've got a fascination with poem series but then when you do them, or I should say I, I always wind up having an instinct that something I'm writing doesnt belong in there, it's just something else. Maybe that's why I like it. I find New York makes me a bit long-winded so far—& I was that way already! Also I've been writing strange notations in a journal so I am scattered I guess. We walked yesterday to the older part of the Lower East Side, I dont know if you know that neighborhood, where the Essex St. Market & Orchard St. are & at the corner of Delancey & Essex Sts., which is a place much like a foreign country, say maybe Bolivia combined with Yugoslavia, I nearly collapsed with deja vus which were actually just memories as that was where I used to have to change trains to get to high school & often I would get off the awful [→ offal?] train with a friend of mine & wander around. It's almost busier there than it even is in midtown daytimes, endless higglers & busybodies & people of every imaginable type & nationality. Even the hotdog stands dont sell hotdogs there but some peculiar form of Jewish shishkebob. It's funny I think Lewis thought when we got to NY we wouldnt have to think so much about food & other things would preoccupy us more but the fact is, in this neighborhood, all the various foods are totally preoccupying to everyone. It's simple to walk a few blocks & have eaten a whole meal, if one gives way to it, and with the children, I often do. And a fine meal it is, some fruit, a miniature pizza rustica, an orzata, clams, a few knishes, and so on. Is this lost on you? Actually I should be telling Susan about it I guess! And I will.

There was something about the letters book I wanted to tell you & now I've forgotten, oh, it turns out as I finished the work on it that among real & "imaginary" (unsent) letters, there are many to you. My plan now is to retype the thing, much as I hate the idea but I saw it would cost $300 to farm the job out & that seems insane. My corrections were myriad but, I'm proud to say, only served to avoid insulting anyone or repeating myself which might sound odd but when you read it I hope you'll see I've left the good repetitions in. It's a fearsomely boring idea to have to type it all out again however I'll to it I hope first two weeks in September—oh god that means twenty pages a night! I'm also thinking of changing all the names, I found my "key" to the naming in Studying Hunger Journals & I'm studying it. I seem to have named Ed Max in that book! It really all becomes like families!

I cant remember if I told you how everyone described your reading at Southampton as being much like singing, both Bill & Ted were inspired by it. Ted also mentioned that you implied he was not "doing the work" & then he proceeded to tell me I only thought the works of myself, Clark & Alice were important. Well if I dont swear off quoting Ted, we'll not have much of a correspondence I'm afraid. Everyone seems to be reading the correspondences of Creeley & Olson though I havent seen the books yet—80 volumes it could be, someone said. However I dont feel able to compete at this time with those guys. One thing that one gets a sense of in New York—even with the few people here who are here, as most everyone has "escaped" for August—is the craziness of poets in a group or community. I mean each poet it seems like it would not be a total surprise to encounter in a place like Lenox or Henniker, living some life, but all together and all knowing each other! To me it becomes strange. I dont know exactly what I'm getting at, I guess what I'm getting at partly is the combination of knowledge of the work & knowledge of the person which is nearly unnatural and I suppose partly holy. Ha, when I say that it makes me wish we were conversing.

Write soon & send works for the magazine too,

Love,
Bernadette
(Children stole my good pen!)

THURSDAY 21 AUGUST [1980]

Dear Bernadette,

A day to hang out on the line. Whatever that means, one of those lines that pops out to stand for a time. And it's not even raining but probably soon will (these Berkshires!). I mean I got up late (for me these days, 11) and it was clear and full of a Fall light, energizing from the memory of all those Autumns when the work has a kind of steel zing, but by noon clouds crowded over everything and now it's all grey (though you feel that in stupid places like Albany the sun's still out and will be all day as we murk around here). Was feeling bad anyway, after fuckup of last night, and I feel complex and confused anyway coming finally "home" after whole winding summer of notebook haste but not really feeling home yet don't know what or where to start up again from well-known "calm of desk" (sounds like title of sweet reveries of some old fudge?). Oh dear, I see now this letter will be a muddle (or as I started my prose book last winter: "Perhaps this will be a big book of very little definition."), but perhaps letters should be sort of ponderable messes? Anyway (a word that sounds like typewriter carriage slamming back to the edge), last night we started out to see The Blues Brothers at new Cinema 1234567 (in that old BIG N opposite the MacDonalds on Housatonic), a movie I didn't really want to go see 'cause everybody says it's terrible and I can believe it but Celia wanted to and I started figuring ways how I could "enjoy" it or anyway pretend to for her sake, but we got there with five minutes to showtime and found long line at ticket window stalled by a girl who didn't know how to change money and I start figuring how we won't get in till 15 minutes after movie starts (hate that) at least and somebody's kid keeps running into me so finally I just see red and walk away feeling like (a movie in itself) the husband who keeps embarrassing the family by inexplicable acts in public, but I just couldn't stand it (random motions of indecisive people) and immediately felt bad about it (couldn't I have practiced patience?) and still do. No control, Clark, look out. Came down here and plunged into this crazy sorta interesting book about Sean Flynn & Dana Stone captured by the Viet Cong (TWO OF THE MISSING by Perry Deane Young) where on the 200th page the guy suddenly reveals that he's a homosexual as if he had to admit and explain feelings the reader had been getting but you realize you haven't had any(!) Gratuitous confession par excellence. But I'm pacing around down here with these scenes of guys' bodies jellied all over the pressroom and Young keeps saying things like "we had to come here," "biggest event of our lives" etc. and it sounds like what they've really managed to do is erect a big dormitoryroom or Lower EastSide goof-pad in midst of War, but it's all so senseless and scattered anyway why shouldn't they? And I even find myself wondering, Why didn't I do that? Go and have big outrageous adventures for very little reason. Nonsense, of course, when I think of it and what I was really doing in those years and how otherwise impossible, etc. But preoccupying for a night anyway. It is easy to feel distraught now though about spending the last ten years in a room half underground with a limited view of trees against sky. Shit, I hate alternatives (Don't ever give me options, said Guston) and always after the fact. Decisions. I love what you say about enjoying questions of choice in dreams, me too! Seems like those are the only REAL decisions you <u>can</u> make, they're so brusk and they immediately WORK (like deciding to wake up or knowing this is only a dream so I'll just relax and dig it, tho I must admit that has seldom happened to me). Decisions in waking are so mired in contingencies (current corporate word I actually hate) and alternate universes (do you know that physicists' trauma/fantasy about how when an experiment turns out a certain result all the other possible results do go on existing in parallel universes?). Oh shit. But, after ten years in this house on this tattered hillside I do feel like just picking up and going to live on Corfu or somewhere improbable but famous in charm. After coming back from Vineyard we were having dinner with my folks in one of those restaurants (in Providence) that are "okay steak and fish" places in refurbished old factory buildings with lotsa polished copper for businessmen's lunches and we commented on how this day was the tenth anniversary of both my folks' and our moves to new houses and I began thinking, Is ten years a graspable state of block-time would allow one to say Okay, Enough, Move on? Or is this just silly number-games (Decades, etc.)? But I have all this work to do, more plans thatway than ever actually, and should hold onto place of reasonable quiet/non-distraction(?) Well, this is perhaps the worst Complaint To Start Our Letters one of us has committed yet!

Yes, did get your TWO HALOED MOURNERS, many thanx, wonderful, don't worry, just before leaving for Island and read it quick once, not wanting to take chance of taking it along and having it get crushed into trunk of car along with all my folks' too many umbrellas and binoculars and cake-domes. Now back and reading again at more leisure, it feels like a vast work for its seemingly "brief" page length, something about the way it moves from densities out into the open and back again (I always wonder about studying out the geometry of written works: just now you might have sense of "vast" or size or scope or whatever space-defining terms of writing and how that all works(?)) I recall your saying some letters back about getting back into . . . what was the word? I don't wanta say "gibberish" (so of course that comes first to mind!) . . . obfuscated? Jesus, not "abstract" . . . anyway, you know (what I meant by dense), there really is no proper word for this yet I spose, and a good thing too, he said! How did you manage to do that?? (unanswerable question?) "Manage" is certainly wrong. This really is a scattered letter! Were you actually looking at the Spinello when writing it? Lots of visibles in there, reason I ask. And some terrific sestinas! I've never been able to crank those up to any satisfaction (did one last year and it came out with all the end words seeming like kids' cardboard flash-cards). I've always felt I should be able to do those but I can't. I like the weave, but sometimes feel it's pointing too obviously to the axles of those. I don't mean yours but the form itself . . . I dunno. Somehow always makes me feel I'm back in kindergarten. Anyway I'd love to hear you read this and almost can (especially the first three parts). Oh, just remembered I wrote a quick poem immediately on first-reading your work, I'll include with this. Maybe best reaction, rather than all these ramblings and questions, though I'm still wondering it (my poem) and its possible connections (both to your work and mine). Also reminds me of a set of 12 poems I wrote last winter and put away, called SOLUTION PASSAGE (I think!) I should send you since TWO HALOED MOURNERS plucked it out of the pile again. "Back" to a certain density in that one too actually. Trouble is I never could finish the last poem, ended up with this long string of "additional" (or "Where do they go?") pages at the end (not wanting to stop again?!), I maybe should end up just leaving there as "Addenda" to the last poem or something(?) I'll try and look again and type up and send you.

NYC sound messy. August the worst month to have to move in there I suppose. But friends could be a bit more sympathetic I think. I know well those smart-ass retorts at anything of a simple reaction you might say, yeah. But not being from there I could always say, oh that's just NewYork, just one port in the great world storm. Ted does sound in a dither (understandable I guess, his mother . . .) in ways he wasn't when I saw him in Southampton. Had a good time with him. Don't understand his reference to "not doing the work" (!!?!) Nothing I remember even implying. He must've pulled that out from way back somewhere (maybe from that Langton St booklet? if he saw that, and I usually get the feeling that Ted sees EVERYTHING, but I don't think I was thinking of him at that time especially, though who knows?, there certainly was that period a few years back when I wasn't seeing anything new out of Ted, but it's certainly nothing I would say to him now, in fact didn't . . . oh shit, how to deal with the far-ends of mistaken gossips? and I never did close that parenthesis.

Reading in Southampton was nice, do you know that room called "Ocean View Lounge"? Like Fraternity Lounge or semi-Holiday Inn Foyer but with amazing view over salt-bay sundown which is reflected entire in huge wall-mirrors behind you as you read making me think I was being upstaged by what only I could directly see(!) Tiny audience so felt I was reading for Ted & Bill alone, fairly relaxed in a room somewhere in the world. "Singing" reactions I spose come from great pleasure I feel in reading these new poems, having done it a few times now and still enjoying working out on the syllables. I get funny feelings sometimes these days, like "Maybe I am (just?) a poet!?" Then

I get anxious to get back into the long things.

Odd living out of Notebook these months, sometimes feels like just sketching along to keep going so you end up with page after page unfinishable strands, but in California find I actually wrote 30 or so POEMS (things I could just type right up), maybe because I feel it's a kind of "second home" now and also there's a "formality" in the housing: guest house away from the main building of everybody's business I can go to and write quiet. Vineyard mainly ramblings and dream data, though I did get one funny "Hulot at the Beach" poem I should save(I can't go to a beach these days without seeing Hulot setting up his collapsible chair!). Why can't I see PLAYTIME!!!

Realizing movies here past ten years SO disappointing. As if the whole heart's gone out of it, or have I (no doubt) just missed ALL the good ones? Now you'll be able to see and tell me about all the great Rivettes etc. down there (drat!). By the way, did you ever get to read that Rivette book? I'm getting to the point I'd like to reread it, if you can send it back or find another one down there or something. No hurry, but just to mention again so it don't get lost in the labyrinths of our endless (and almost collective!) libraries. I do have my MEMORIES of movies anyway, sometimes I think are almost better(?) As if MOVIES only existed for a brief while and we saw them all and now they've been replaced by some "Other" nobody cares about.

Been reading through Olson/Creeleys myself: they're so SERIOUS and up against something academic we weren't so much and nobody is now. Funny though (sad) to see them raging against rejections by miserable little mags like Golden Goose and Hearse etc. that hardly anybody even remembers now. Interesting though to see how much of an influence Creeley was on Olson, rather than the more commonly-taken other-way-around. Funny too to see Creeley pushing Bebop to Olson, not knowing he'll never be able to listen to it. That Music/Seduction Problem again.

Lotsa books here to read (feel that well-known avoidance/build-up-to-new-works principle at work again): a biography of Mabel Dodge Luhan(!), Marquez' Autumn of the Patriarch (ever read him? I still haven't 100 Years of Solitude everybody loves so much), The Zapping of America (microwave miseries), Mircea Eliades's No Souvenirs (Journals), Joyce's Letters . . . Ever read any of John Fowles? Somebody here pushing THE MAGUS on me. . . . Blah. Back to work, before I get handled by my fantasies and flip off to Bali or Mt St Helens or The Pyrenees or some flash improbable.

LOVE,

Clark

[**Page 113 →** Pardon a pickish mineralogical correction? Smithsonite is zinc carbonate, not silicate]

[**Page 115 →** re Ted Talky: I was thinking in Southampton how all the things I think to say to him usually get self-cancelled underneath his ongoing ramble so I end up in any intermittent spaces quiet. In fact he was saying in Tambourine Life lecture how he likes my reactions to his readings but I don't ever actually say much. No doubt!]

RUBBING THIS WORLD AND COMING UP WITH ONE

What could you say, the world got loused up by
brackish unattended burners? Lashed with
felt strapping all over the landscape?
I live by a wood-pulp chip-burner, like a vast
ash head or punk fleck, a thumb of incense
crystalled out large unavoidable as
mumps on a highway. Take a turn by to see it,
anyday it turned out would last enough to spy it
out. Poor threads of memory, it's right over
there. But what is the instant use of the large
and immoveable? I will name this great
imposition, name it Seemingly. And guard it
from notice with this poem. Never to be
gone as a century garden.
Or is in fact this one?

—30VII80

[after Two Haloed Mourners

—C.C.]

SEPTEMBER 2, 1981 OOOPS THE WADING POOL
WITH ALL ITS RAINBOWS HAS GOTTEN TO ME
1980

Dear Clark,

Yesterday was the day I had set to start typing my still untitled book of letters. Now I didnt start yesterday which was so-called Labor Day because we had a visitor, then Lewis & I decided no more night-time visitors! Then tonight Jack Collom came by (the trick is not to answer the phone at all!) & as there was no way we didnt want to talk to him (& Lewis claims he cannot tell a person, especially a person like Jack, not to come by, over the phone . . . !) so then the whole night of working was delayed and since it was, I have the opportunity to write you this letter! Meanwhile (*I've run out of nifty graph paper however I also know it was hard to read from) Jack told us a wonderful story about being caught in the hurricane (Allen) or on the edge of it in yucatan without even the means to evacuate & noticing that the local people were feeling quite cheerful about it, yet the ocean did rise or get closer by about 70 feet to Jack's cabaña. And he kept a journal of all of it & the local cafe owner told him to just "keep writing."

Perhaps this will be a big letter of very little definition (then). I cant imagine writing a little letter. It is so hot here you would what? Marie has taken to taking, during one of her myriad baths of the day, the hose in her hand, pretending it's a microphone (as she's been permitted to watch much t.v. to "beat the heat") and announcing "It's hot as hell in N.Y. today and the United States of America will be back after these messages"! Sophia doesnt take to the heat so easily or happily & wakes in the middle of the night with dreams caused by her being wrapped in a 100% wool blanket (so much for pure fabrics!) to which she is irremediably attached in the midst of this 100% humidity & heat. Max laughs at it all & even disdains the bottle of juice we offer him, thinking he is parched! He continues, willy-nilly, to attempt, not without enormous effort both physical and the other thing, to crawl forwards—something I as a grownup would save for the cooler weather if I were him however I still do pursue my studies of the epigram and find myself sweating just as much as Max while I am making notes on the Greek anthology & trying to figure out what Greek work they might have translated as "roguishly"! I find the epigrammatic form to be a bit more loose than I had originally, from earlier studies, thought,—some of the Greek forms are actually 10–12 lines long whereas the later English ones are predictably terse, witty & therefore short. I must admit I have no desire to be witty (maybe I do?!) but I do want to master this form—so I can write my Essay on Man? Man & Woman? Actually it's because I got obsessed with the word "epigram" (to write upon—the epiglottis!) However I'll surcease till I can figure out if there's anything to be done with it. Maybe it's just an excuse to make a briefer re-study of Greek! & Latin (Martial).

So you see, yes, letters are imponderable messes of all sorts. Ack! Like your leaving the movie—I assume Celia & Susan had to leave with you, though you didnt say—in one car, all of which reminded me, along with associations of Viet book of our coming here! You say: "Young keeps saying things like 'we had to come here,' 'biggest event of our lives' etc. & it sounds like what they've really managed to do is erect a big dormitoryroom or Lowereast Side goof-pad in the midst of War . . . but why shouldnt they?"

However my thought is these imponderable messes are what we are all in one way or the other, whether life is peaceful (as I had hoped it could be, yet I went ahead and succumbed to what Alice calls "whynotness" & had the 3 children) or whether it is not-peaceful yet apparently peaceful and still not peaceful. Now that may seem insane however to me NY is not-peaceful, Lenox was apparently peaceful and Henniker was "still not peaceful"—see the imponderableness of the mess? Because, all that time, if you'll forgive me, not only was love the same, but as Edwin might say, it keeps that name and it is not the same. Now please do tell me to get to the point which I think is here in NY I alternatively weep & shout for joy (I use "alternatively advisedly, I hate them too)—I would wish most in some way to be "stuck" in some place; I used to think I'd enjoy being in prison for that reason because I'd know there I could write, & probably that would be all. Ah what a mess we are all in, but the mess is all the same! I hope. And please dont mention to me, having just re-moved to NY, about parallel universes! That's enough to drive me nuts! I just wrote a blurb, requested for Helen Luster's book about that subject & of course that is Hannahs's territory too & both those guys have been able to somehow guess that

I am totally understanding of all their mishegos. [(I take that back)]

To tolerate chaos is something, I'm sure I've already told you, I learned from my children, but now here I am tolerating the chaos not only of the children, which seems minimal now, but also of the poetry community, the Project, the city, and . . . I cant remember the rest. To order yet another household is the way I had expressed to someone at some point the idea of working at St. Mark's.

Oh shit is right. "This tattered hillside" is certainly a wonderful phrase—have you been reading Hawthorne? Actually Clark why dont you & I create a scandal & run off to Corfu, as you say, what the hell? Now you see that New York (or most especially watching millions of late nite movies on t.v. might generate ideas like this! however ultimately without closing my parentheses at all, in a shameless way, I must say to you that I envy your position at the start of fall at the calm of the desk and I must reiterate to you (without any fooling around in it at all) that your work is worth all the peace that you must create to do it, whether it seems like peace or not, and it is only my sharing that sort of desire with you that not only makes me able to say this but also makes me able to create a peace for myself in the midst of what might seem to you to be the worst sort of chaos that a poet could endure. I get great pleasure from my children but I think all the exigencies of life are rather silly (please dont ever say I said this), mainly I think I mean the way poets behave, including myself and Lewis . . . I'll trail that off & continue to say (if you'll forgive me) that it's all the same to me, a great French phrase I've always loved (cela m'est egal, I think) . . . why am I saying all this? I think I hope your letter somehow provoked it, maybe . . . I saw myself proliferating in one sense and now, like in the past, there is something to be learned from that, I mean why are you up on that hill and I here doing what I'm doing? It makes no sense to me! Ah I've written myself into a corner again & I hope you arent offended by it, it's always been very easy for me to imagine myself another person. . . .

Now here I'll stop again, this letter as it seems might continue for days, otherwise it might not be accurate. Please don't ever worry that I will [→ not?] get my work done, it's not that I will get to be like Alice either, (whose name I always type "alive"), I'll never neglect my children (though I dont mean to say that she does, [→ dangerous area "slough of libel" or something] she is dutiful & she & Ted, I've learned are practically different from practically the whole rest of the world however they take care of what is their business—the thing I cant understand about them is their lack of hedonism, a whole other story), but in the midst of what is taking place on my own tattered island I know I can write and you know what? I've begun to think I'd better take advantage of all this kowtowing to me (being asked for readings all the time, etc, being flattered in ways) because (& now you might get mad at me) it may never happen again in my lifetime! I'm not being coy about that, I'm amazed & perhaps being horrible to state it but actually I could only state it to you.

Once when I lived in Great Barrington I put a suitcase full of things of mine in the woods, things I thought were somehow important. Well now tonight I find Lewis's father (which is not analogous) calls us up, and he is a man who has been adrift, on a momentary impulse that the heat might be bothering us. Oh shit I am just as stranded at the movies as you were!

Well let's get on with the rest of it, I did also want to say that do you think one's poems can develop too easy a facility? I feel I've mastered some language which I'd thought I'd gotten rid of but I see now it hard enough to try, why is it I want there always to be some risk: some horrible fortune, some residue beyond of the prolific! I get mad, someone says to me, did you write all those poems since you were in NY? & I think yes of course but I say no & wait to see if anyone knows if I'm telling the truth. Jack said he writes alot of dross & then sees if there's a turn of phrase in among it that might be useful somehow. With "two haloed mourners" I felt driven to exacerbate my style in the same way as I know Raphael Soyer always felt driven to exacerbate his contemporaries by being what they thought of as so ordinary, and yes I was looking at a postcard of the picture the whole time. I wanted to make trouble but at the sametime, which seems to me to be the problem now with whatever I do no one takes it as trouble & everyone is ready or unaware of what the poem actually looks like, if only you could see it! I thought of that work (the poem series) as some statement that (no not statement, what an awful word), some idea that quickly once can review the knowledge and the forms to date (to one's limited knowing of it all) & then write a message, like the ads on t.v.—this is all I can do up to this point. I dont mean it to be a tour de force though I know almost anything I do now is like that because I have, not meaning to sound self-adulating, a facility for certain kinds of prose & poetry. But I meant it to be a summary and also a dare—please, who's to tell me what to know next & how to know it & what to do? I should've said perhaps in one of the poems that I was seeking advice, perhaps I did.

Some of it's too easy; also I'm exhausted. What is it? Sorry, if we were in person, it wouldnt sound so bad.

Ted has recovered, to the extent that he can actually listen (new day new ribbon) to everyone & also todAY HE taught his first day which he said was awful, however the PATH strike ended on the very day he had to go to Hoboken. It's funny our "schedules" such as they are dont really coincide with Ted & Alice's (who are more or less free of their children for a good part of the day) so visiting them is still an occasion. Everybody in NY wants each of us (me & Lewis) to come & go separately; we keep being encouraged, nay, importuned to do so: "You never visit us alone!" I must admit I cant see the fun in it & Lewis & I are so accustomed to doing things together though in NY we've been forced for easiness to do chores separately, but social life we always assume is something we do together! So old-fashioned or something, I dont know. I feel it's not any fun in a way; maybe part of that is the New England car syndrome. anyway,

I will send the Rivette book back to you, I must admit I never got that engrossed in it, feeling so away from movies these last five years—Lewis & I have a plan to go on a date! to movies & the Orchidia! (where no one goes anymore, eschewing it for the Ukrainian National Home where I got thoroughly unconscionably drunk after our reading at this place called "Recherchez" a series set up by Will Bennet, an odd summer series for which we were all also thoroughly paid & I read my new New York poems (did I tell you this yesterday? I guess I implied it anyway). I enjoyed very much giving such a "quick" reading of all new works with a few, as a sort of transition, to make a story, from Henniker. Though the place was so hot it seemed like a burden to read longer than 20 minutes, which I didnt, and Lewis thought I was weeping because I was wiping sweat away from my face & drops of it had been falling on my manuscripts!

I did read the French Lieutenants Wife once but I found it to be the most desultory of trash books. Recently I read Mary Oppen's Autobiography which is notable at least for a great narrative technique she has which is to tell of meeting someone, tell the first thing they said to her, then start a new paragraph which continues the narrative of her life chronologically but with no transition from the set scene. It is very wonderful in that way.

Your poem "Rubbing This World . . ." is terrific like a sort of cross between John Bunyan and John Ashbery plus some great visual artist like maybe Stan Brakhage, this is what I see. Actually perhaps I've never said this to you about your works—if you'll forgive me for being the literary critic for a while, a temerity which is perhaps a result of living in this tough town, as they say—but many of your poems, and in the prose often there is, have such a striking admixture of the formal-to-the-extent-of-the-sublime with the colloquial, like in this case "got loused up" or something like that, then plus the word accumulations "wood-pulp chip-burner" etc. which conglomeration is often what I'm thinking of when I think of a work having or containing or whatever the word is, everything. Does that make sense? Then again you are secretly also rapidly getting to be very good at so much direct address, so there is drama.

Listen, answer me this question—do you think it is possible to read a poet's works, one whom you dont know I guess, or even one you do (at least you know what he or she looks like & more or less what they're like)—to read the works and judge, make a judgement as to whether they are "good" or "bad"? I am asking this in relation to the idea of selecting readers when it happens that I am not familiar with the history of those people's writings. I find it an impossible task. My instinct is to find a book by the person, read it & see what I think. But often I cannot know what I think, and either I think everything is good or perhaps admissible or defensible (after all, it's written by a person), or else I think all is "bad." What I'm asking I suppose is what state of mind do you think is most conducive to this sort of attempt at making a judgment or decision which is necessarily hasty? It seems important to be fair but not to the point where it takes an enormous amount of time—is that too unfair to say? I asked Ted about this poet named Roy Fisher, thinking since Fisher is British, that Ted might have got familiar with his work at past times & Ted announced that he didnt feel it politic to say anything—I (& who am I?!) ought to read the works and decide! I was pissed off! I feel very strongly that advice from the so-called community is even more valuable than my own less than selfless judgments (Only one person, etc.). What do you think?

Well, if I am ever to type out my book, I must end. I wish I could envision seeing you soon. Perhaps I will actually. I have a plan to hire Bill B. to emcee the Philip Guston reading, to give him an excuse for a trip to NY, and then hopefully you would come down for that too? Yes? Sometime in December is the thought at the moment. Bill was so sad to be leaving in a way, though he is nothing if not—what? Objective? at a distance? Enigmatic! Do you think asking him to do it is a good idea?

Do you want to hear some gossip which has nothing to do with NY? (Sworm! to secrecy you are!): Corbett is doing some peculiar no. where he writes me all the time & never writes Lewis! & Lewis gets a bit hurt (as Lewis is dutiful in corresponding with him) & then we realized that what it has to do with is that, out of a desire for continuity in my life, I had written at some length to Russell & Bill C. got jealous! I think.

This letter is getting outlandishly long &, I'm afraid, outlandishly self-indulgent! However I wont not finish a story! This whole situation makes me mad because Bill's not writing Lewis causes me problems, as Lewis sees Bill's letters to me & so on, and, recently I've become afraid it might even have something to do with Poetry Project! As Bill wrote for a reading. I think it is somewhat inadvertent, forgetful, & so on on Bill's part, however in all this time in NY I've gotten 3 letters from him, never having written one, & Lewis who wrote him has gotten no answer! Meanwhile I'm all the more mad because I need a Greek book that only can be got in Cambridge & I dont feel free to request it.

Now it's gotten cooler, actually since I began this letter to you, which is a great relief and all of a sudden the children act like normal people. It's funny, I often shout at them that if they dont act like people I will . . . then of course I cant think what to say.

The magazine is in the works, half-typed & waiting on more supplies (In NY you can get everything delivered so easily!) & we've yet to turn on the mimeo machine in this apartment which is a thought that scares me though I think we have enough amps or whatever they are. It seems like a startling issue, and in which I'm going to do more letters, so that that book doesnt just disappear forever.

There's a myriad of things to tell I guess but now I cant remember any of them. I am writing alot of what I keep thinking of as humorous works but they are awfully sloppy to my mind. Then no one else thinks that, but then, when did I ever have anyone else to have an opinion before? I see I am in too much of a hurry, as always, and must be more patient about what, in writing, New York brings—I hope it's just the same old thing, new thing. I have a craving for a project (apart from The Project) & I have what they call a sneaking suspicion that it will resemble Pope's Essay on Man. Am I getting boring just because I'm getting old? Now that opens up a whole other series of thoughts which I absolutely will not get into!

Much love,
Bernadette

MONDAY 8 SEPTEMBER [1980]

Dear Bernadette,

This big cool bright green and blue morning, and being monday as well, makes me want to get right down to business. Ha, I actually just spent the last hour or so looking hopelessly for passages in books I had thought of in half-sleep and looking up words, but, double-ha, who's gonna tell me that just those pursuits aren't the writer's business? And sometimes that's my vision of old age: fussing endlessly with dictionaries. Reading your letter I keep trying to come up with some real useful solution to your problem of trying to judge other poets (be a friend and come up with some answers, Clark!) but . . . it's irremediable (doubt I've ever used that word before!). Or at least "answers" is right 'cause there's no one that'll do. I think I suffer from always being taught to expect there'll be just one "best" solution to any problem, so have to keep reminding myself that there are cases (probly all the hardest problems, most important anyway) where that's never true. How's that for helping you out!? And so I tend to get lost along the way of all those penurious alternatives (how's that for an itchy oxymoron?).

Perhaps no "parallel universes" then but how about all the nonparallel friends and aquaintances? (Eleanor of Aquitane?) (Sometimes even the names are a problem?) So seriously as I can get it. I too find myself having a horrible time (& getting horribler) deciding on other poets, no doubt one of the reasons why my vision of your new job is so terrifying. I mean it's easy enough to reason out in terms of growing more toward the center of your work, any judgements then having to proceed outward from there you become less&less Fair? So I tell myself. As we've discussed before it becomes harder to read other (specially young, living, etc.) poets anyway, in fact the poetry scene seems in such a knotted mess right now I can't deal with it except as a Mess. Fairness never a portion of the solitary writing mind, right? Art not Democratic, etc. But (for sure) once you're put in the position of choosing for other people (just who will read etc.) then some kind of Fairness is the first wall you run into. So you have to stretch . . . I keep thinking somebody else should have those jobs, some enlightened non-artist we always seem to be looking for, like a Jean Paulhan for our scene and time? Okay, that personage doesn't exist and perhaps never did in such a pure selfless way. But for a working artist it does seem to me deucedly extracurricular. Pulling you ten ways when none'll do, etc. I'm of Two Minds (strange phrase) at least. One: you try to be fair, take advice, allow anybody who (as you say) seems defensible, has a body of work (even if you haven't or can't read it), end up with a pleasant enough scatter, and/or include as many as possible of the young who haven't had readings (as I think Ron tried). But, making the darkest possible opposition, would you give Richard Kostelanetz a reading? I must say, I would devilishly enjoy keeping him quiet if only for an evening(!) And I can imagine a real dilemma with, say, Diane Wakoski, who seems to be "well regarded" by lots but whose work I can't tolerate, so would have to take much flak for Xing her out. And this points inexorably to the Second Mind, which is being an utter martinet about the matter and picking only according to secret central writing mind, fuck Fairness. Which, in the best light, would surely produce an interesting series (products of the single interested mind) and one unlike the fairly lame "pleasant" scatter of recent Po Proj years. Though it would certainly limit the Field of Choose, you'd no doubt have to forget about double-readings everyweek, might even shorten the season. Unless you extended to other "fields" (philosophy, psychology, whatever), which wouldn't be a bad idea(?) Are you duty-bound to commonly-accepted "poets"?

Doubt this is very helpful. As you can see I'd have a harder time with the job than you're having. Also, I didn't mean to make it seem a strict matter of This-or-That-ism, just define the problem as I see it(shit, horrid phrase! maybe I'm just erecting walls?). But what a (hopefully?) needless worry this judgement business! I tend to personify it as Larry (prime practitioner in my life of Judgement of Poets and all other nerves of opinion and NYC businesses you were speaking of), how his crusty urge to rate everybody always seemed to me rather a need to build a system of external justification for whatever he felt about poets/painters/etc minute to minute (and it <u>does</u> change) but couldn't say <u>except</u> in the framework of Opinion. Convolution City! But you see what I'm getting at? What the writing-mind "thinks" about some other artist is perhaps too swiftly precocious or swoopingly arrogant, or just too tottering in any World of Discourse ('cause whatever it is it <u>ain't</u> Discourse!), to be accepted except in the form of an Opnion (Onion) Opinion(which has its own strict and to-the-side form). As I think we've discussed, whenever you see great poem/movie/painting you often can't say anything articulate but feel your secret mind moving along new circuits, being modified, changing, right?, I mean if it doesn't change you (as told of old) . . . ? and if you're in midst of change (mind) what could you use to say anything that would be taken as solid language? I guess what I'm saying here also is that Opinion is Avoidance (of what's really going on in mind-exposed), is like a stone shied through a window (tossed with a curt to-the-side motion). So Judgements are useless, or used up at such a rate they're no longer seen as Judgement (which word always means a rain-dark moment to me). Larry never seemed to be speaking from what I could understand as Need of a Writer. I mean, so what, so you end up with this parade of statues. But then, he does seem to have to keep changing his hierarchies, so (shit) maybe it's just another form of the same thing I just can't selfly identify?!?! Whatta mess! Who does understand the other person? I can imagine 'em plenty, but then that's mine. Maybe there is something interesting though back there about opinion?

My attempt to help you out seems to have turned into a big essay about Doubt! A danger of close-up mind-process letters. Picking poets sounds like work in an active hallucination (that everyday outside mind we spend so much otherwise time/energy working away from). Judge seems to root-mean "to say the Law," but in art's case just what is the Law? You might as well say the Mystery, or a shifting tundra. Ah, but I can hear you saying, Yeah, great, but what am I gonna do? I got this stack of letters pleading for readings . . . I'd say don't worry about deciding according to your prejudices (inevitable anyway with anybody?), they come from an interesting place. And I wouldn't spend too much time reading works of people you don't know, unless you figure this as an excuse to be doing something you wanted to do sometime anyway but couldn't otherwise find the time for. If you ask for too many people's opinions (!) that'll get more confusing. Alternatives dull the point. And go after the people you really want (see if they'd be available, etc.). You know. I hate giving advice, but I know you want it (but I know you know it!). And maybe some Projects? Like, it occurred to me awhile back that it'd be great to have another Stein Marathon, now that everybody seems to have forgotten her again. I have real fond memories of the original one. Or Kerouac? Anybody you could get going on with. The Guston Memorial. And yeah, I think, ask Bill B, right. He's the obvious choice and I'm sure would do predictable good job as MC. Of course there is the problem of friends & acquaintances who think they've got an "in" with you in the job. Corbett, I'm sure that's on his mind, besides whatever else you know to be the case (recall his chronic Gotham Gloire notions). But then that seems more handleable than the other (above). What a task! Feel free to ask, whatever. If you want the advice of a person who basically feels himself incapable of performing said task. But then, I never thought I would be able to teach either.

You say, "Don't worry that I will not get my work done." I never did worry about that. But, knowing you would always take care to do that I worried you would take on too much other and so end up driven nuts by attempting coordination of too many tasks at once. To understand my worry I spose you have to know the part of my story where (I probably told you this?) years ago I tried for most of three years to carry on the picky (& ultimately boring) task of working 8-hours a day in a library while also (& mainly) trying to write fulltime (all night plus sneaking to the john with notebook while at library ducking the boss & sneaky coworkers) in midst of collapsing (anyway, impossible) young marriage, all of which finally (naturally) caused mind (&body) breakdown, truly horrible, couldn't get out of bed one day, couldn't move, couldn't think even, totally smashed against several unbreachable walls. Of course at this precise time, I now realize looking back in old notebooks, I was desperately trying to write millions of pages so to break through into my work, which I was only able to do after I got out of this intolerable scene and took instruction from it that the writing had to come first of all "jobs," no matter what contortions I had to go through to keep it there. Actually the writing itself pulled me through the marriage-breakup wreckage, a minimum of pounding head against walls, etc. So, I identify that as source of whatever worries I might have expressed to you about you. But I do believe you when you say you feel yourself able to take on extra tasks(just let me have a little worry of my own anyway!). How can I feel right about judging(!) somebody else's energies when I've done such a sorry job of predicting my own? And, sure, I know I'm better at this than I used to be, about myself anyway. You know I'm with you, whatever the task, hope that goes without saying.

"It's all the same to me" is a wonderful phrase, and so right it should have come from some French character. C'est la Vie, etc. And with that great weight-of-world shrug and half-grin(same grin I saw on the face of Godard when he told young audience of BayArea filmmakers "no hard feelings" as they asked his opinion of their work). And, yeah, I dig very much that "trouble" you wanted to make in Mourners. Reminds me partly of Valery's famous (to me anyway) statement re "they had mistaken as liberties what we thought of as problems" (even though I spose Valery was sort of a hincty prick who thought he could write a poem anytime on strength of technique amassment?). And even more so, though it opens another big area entire, Guston's amazing (for 1958 especially, when everybody seems to have instantly forgotten it or actively hidden it away and then forgotten where it was) remark: "I do not see why the loss of faith in the known image and symbol in our time should be celebrated as a freedom. It is a loss from which we suffer, and this pathos motivates modern painting and poetry at its heart." It seems like I've had to live centuries until I can begin to see the truth in that. From the end of WWII till now does seem a much longer time than its years. Packed lifetimes. And somewhere the other day I came on the shocking fact that the period of cave art we see in places like Lascaux & Altamira went on uninterrupted for 25,000 years! Some substrate. But, to get back to the "trouble," and maybe beyond busting one's own facility (which, yeah, I'm always trying to do but it gets tougher), I wonder if the scarcity in writers of the desire to include big regions of disturbance in their work means that there are so few who even conceive of their work as large enough in scope to take the stress of these kinds of areas? Not to just pat ourselves on the back, but, yeah, why not? We often speak of the desire for "Everything" etc., no? I mean, I've long wanted to call a long work of mine THE WORLD, if only that didn't have such obvious and local diminishing combinations. And that phrase (of yours), "some residue beyond (of) the prolific" is wondrous! Lotta hope for the future locked in that one! But sometimes I wish I could have no ideas about my work, so I could see what it would then be. To come unawares on a vastness (! lots of childhood in that one). Or, as Haggard in King Solomon's Mines, "And now, said Sir Henry, trek." (plus being best poise of that word I've ever seen) Grandiose? But juicy. I know you see how silly and necessary all this is. And writing is a life, in deeper ways than one. Who sees these things? It scares me sometimes these days when I think I really don't know what other people know. I mean, what haven't they even ever considered? How to know that? Have I all this time been assuming . . . etc. It's a shock, the realization that nobody knows. How's that for a sentence? And "Whynotism" is a beautiful term (thanks, Alice!) Whoops, I mean Whynotness! Is that what in the Existential old days (for us, Fifties) they used to call "gratuitous"? This is wandering. While on the Vineyard I read through (I somehow love that business of the books you read in a place like that, whatever they are, because they're the only ones you can get at the moment and for no other reason, you're forced . . . like being in prison in a way?) all of Elizabeth Bishop's poems and frankly I can't see what's supposed to be so great about her, why people like Bill B and Ashbery and jesus even Jimmy (who's so much better at that kind of "landscape" poem it's unbelievable) think she's grand. It's a depressive tone in her work that damages all the objects et al. in it in one direction only. Down cast. And jimmy always puts everything out there so clear, tangible and with so much more wit. Bill dragged me to hear her read at the Gugg years ago and I can't recall a single word she spoke. I just remember Robert Lowell clearing his throat introducing her, and Marianne Moore being supported by her man in livery down the aisle. It cracks me up, too, that Liz Bishop is that sportscaster on Albany TV!

Various: Is that

Elspeth Huxley book on Scott of the Antarctic any good? I recall you reading it once in Lenox and now it's a cheap remainder. Biog of Mabel Dodge didn't turn out all that interesting, though hard to say if it's Emily Hahn's fault or Mabel's(?) Somehow I'd still like to take a look at MD's endless books of memoirs (now that they're long unavailable?), there must have been something happening at the end there in Taos with her Indian husband & Lawrence et al.? Still hung up on biographies, got one here on Monet I'm starting(Charles Merrill Mount's). I guess it's the business of imagining another life, which I seem more&more able to do at the drop of a stick. What's <u>that</u> about? Sometimes I've thought it'd be fun to write an imaginary biography of somebody. I mean, don't look up <u>any</u> facts and just write it. Projects and Days . . . I even sometimes think these days, Why <u>am</u> I a poet? (the route to) Because lines like "birds and rosettes on a tan settee" come helplessly to mind whenever? That's one from pre-sleep lastnight and doesn't sound like much and I usually throw most of these instantly away. Or at least I could never save 'em up for years and then make a poem of them (as Phil Whalen seems to do). I put something in a notebook like that, it's gone (usually). Reminds me of that little "birds come early" poem of yours. I have millions of those too, but usually nothing comes of them, no use. Or, more truly, I don't know what to do with them.

Oh, on that Greek book you need from Cambridge? Tell me what it is and I'll tell my mother, who goes up there fairly frequently and I know would be pleased to help you out. Really. She loves "hunts" like that.

Watching that US Open Men's Tennis Final was amazing yesterday, like a life (too). In fact McEnroe gave a spasm (like death) at the end, supposedly of "victory." Borg is mystifying, the way he's able to turn long defeat-lengths finally into real arrow weapons. Like Zen accuracy turn of mind? I'd like to ask him the right questions, but he probly couldn't (or wouldn't?) answer.

First chilly (but bright) Fall day, when you have to decide whether to leave doors open or not. Autumn makes me think of Tanguy. Yesterday the oil tanks of Albany blew up and I thought maybe (secretly hoped) the whole city would go. Hope I didn't answer this time too quick?

LOVE,

Clark

SEPTEMBER 21 1980

Dear Clark,

I keep wanting to begin my letter by saying exactly what you said to begin yours, this big cool bright green and blue morning . . . but I guess I have to begin by saying this big hot bright purple night behind the Empire State building, and being Sunday as well, makes me want to get down to business before I get involved in that silly old school-week again! work week, what a silly idea! though I guess you have that too in a sense, specific days each week to do certain things, isn't that as if a joke's being played on us? I don't mean to wax too beatnik or something however I just cannot get used to it and I find myself balking at telling Marie (who wants to know!) yes tomorrow's Monday and that means school, etc. I guess it's all no worse than saying, I'll meet you a year from Monday, as has always been everyone's wont.

Many thanks for your ruminations on doubt and judgment. Ha, I doubt I could've gotten the kind of conversation going that I needed with anybody but you—does it have to do with morals?—and I appreciate your responding at length to what might've seemed like a boring question. I must admit I think it's probably all to the good that it's not a non-artist doing the choosing, and in the midst of my ruminations I seem to have come up with a kind of sketch which runs like this: if somebody asks for a reading (like logic) then I have to think of them twice, meanwhile I schedule some according to my own desire to hear them and make my own life interesting, meanwhile I listen attentively to what others say about others and try to process it all as if I were a computer. It's interesting actually to go about town without ever having to make conversation, if I don't choose to, except about this. I mean I can simply say to almost anybody, oh who would you like to have read? And then ensues the rest of the talk, and there's no doubt everybody has ideas. I must admit what I dont like is letting another's opinions influence the choice and then finding out later, it's been a great mistake! As I'm afraid already happened in the case of Rose Lesniak whom I had scheduled to read with helen Adam in October, and then I gave a reading with Rose at the Ear Inn and she was awful! It was like a soap opera transformed into "performance work" or something. Her case also having much to do with what Lewis refers to as "the young people not doing their homework" which means they don't read, and don't write poetry they write something about politics and shout it out well and that's supposed to suffice—just the opposite, in a way, of the Language idea. (Actually that only relates to a group of women, while Lewis is finding fault with a group of men too). It was funny when I gave this reading I got into alot of trouble with the feminists there (Rose, Barbara Barg, Eileen Myles, Jane DeLynn). I read "Two Haloed Mourners" and in the midst of reading it I took off, I was as if flying and I think it was a good reading, however that didn't matter, it was only the fact (to them) that I had made some remarks about not wanting them to schedule me to read with strictly feminist prose writers, and I had asked to read with a poet. Now all this is information, I hope; Alice and others keep saying, oh you had your first encounter with the feminists! I must admit I think I am the most ardent feminist of all time, however in the course of this argument someone said to me, oh you think we don't like you because you have children! & I thought to myself, gosh (or fuck this!) I never thought of that idea, I thought they'd like me because I had children! (Turns out I'm not supposed to have a husband, or at least one I like!).

So much for gossip (I said to Ron apropos this, you mean I can't say whatever I want just because I'm the "Director" and he said "No," then I told him I would always remember this clipped "no" of his)

My instinct with writing I'm not familiar with is to dismiss it until I get some further word (as if from the stars or something), so that is a problem. I also feel that discovering some great new writer or whomever (as you are sort of saying) has to happen in its own time, so it is not as if I can find out about many more great writers in the next few months! right? Your beautiful descriptions of opinion are inspiring to me and make me see that chance mixed with blessing mixed with instinctual kind of insight—just as in the structuring of a long prose work—is or are the only way of doing this work, and probably will work just as well for Poetry Project as it did, for, say, MEMORY. Ah how daring I sound!

Speaking of monuments to judgment, we all went to the Statue of Liberty today just like tourists. Marie had had a great desire to see this sculpture up close and what a hilarious time we had doing it! The ferry to Liberty Island only takes about ten minutes but you get on it with about a million other people, many of them with families (in fact it is just about the most family-oriented trip in NY City!) of all the nationalities imaginable and then everyone is huddling their bodies up these stairs, well it is the most fantastic idea, I kept thinking about wondering in the midst of it why is it that the human wants so much to go forward, even the desire or the impulse (as in an infant) to speak is a desire to move into the future—the word gets spewed out and after all the word and the letters of that word put together in that way already meant what they mean as a word before the word was even formed, maybe just a few moments before, but humans move forward always whether it's through the use of feet or cars or travel bureaus, just the way the crowds were going through the gates and up the stairs in a rush and filling in the spaces between, it is people's bent and the monument's rangers couldn't plan it any other way, so I began thinking then what is the meditative instinct, it is the instinct to do the exact opposite to what humans generally want to do, to speak to not speak, to move to sit still, and thereby to get the knowledge that nobody else has. Perhaps it's corny to tell one's thoughts about these things but later I asked Marie why she thought children were different from grownups and she said, they are little people but they are also peaches because they eat so many more peaches than grownups. What I'm trying to say is that what I say probably makes as much sense as what she says, and is certainly as well-considered.

Again I must reiterate, before I let the subject of opinion fall down the drain where it then will spew up hideous gases and fumes to poison us all, that if I study the writings of anyone for a while I can easily see something good or interesting about them, and then, when in answer to the question what is it, I say it is just that they are human, I see it is not only a mess but a morass very similar to the idea of mud.

Out of which, my sister tells me, some interesting sculptures might be made.

Meanwhile—questions of more doubt!—I am about 1/3rd of the way through re-working this manuscript which I thought I was just re-typing but inevitably I am making a whole new thing of, and in another meanwhile, realizing I never sent you my gloss on your BIG MANUSCRIPT (tenettively titled, ha! no, SOMETHING, no, SOMETHING ELSE, no . . . wait a second what should I call mine, can you believe I almost entertained the idea of INTERCOURSE (which still doesn't seem too bad, in a way, oh god)) which I will send you in the midst of this because the projects seem related to me, but what I started out to say was it's taking me approximately twice as much time as I thought it would, so that is an axiom I'm sure I can apply in the future. the funny thing is there's hardly anything to do at the Poetry Project, what with two other people working with me, that cannot get done rather painlessly, though I know in the future I will eat those words too. Mental anguish, I once said (how awful to quote self) is middle English. Baby cries.

Guston's remark that you mention is breathtaking and not only that the idea of the 25,000 years of uninterrupted artwork is quite overtaking my brain. How great, I have often thought, it would be, to be the artist or shaman in the primitive community I can so easily picture myself a member of,—where you actually have something to do!!! "The World" (not the magazine) will forgive us that instinct or desire, I know, just as the world makes it necessary to have so many fucking doubts, these days for me wondering if I've somehow "sold out" by not saying enough (each word could or ought to be in quotes, alas) (Marie asked me the other day what alas means) in the book I'm working on, which like all books while I'm finishing it, seems trivial and poor, and makes me feel like a masturbator or lunatic (full moon in three days and atavistic Rosemary will have a party for it on her roof!), just the usual.

In NY the grandiose ideas sometimes seem shameful however then you just do not answer the telephone and doorbell. It's easy to keep the clock ticking if it's not electric, forgive me. Oh god, what do other people know? I'd always answered everything, but often now I don't say that to myself. Is that, as you say, old age? I read this fascinating story in the Sunday Times today about Hemingway's granddaughter, one of them, who caught a 400-lb. marlin (there was much in the story about how much beer she drank), and the story was in fact exploitative and bad (she wrote it), however it made me feel unconscionably old and wise to read it, I don't know how to explain that but to say I expended much time trying to explain my fascination with it to Marie and to no avail. I think I feel much like Liz Bishop (the one from Albany), she is so funny looking in her macho way.

The Elspeth Husley book on Scott is great, or at least good enough, I must admit I found it wonderful and needed it. There's a new biography of Hawthorne by Mellow, the same guy who wrote CHARMED CIRCLE, so there is one person in the world, besides me, who is obsessed with Stein and Hawthorne at the same time (havent got it yet—$20! like every book, though we invested in Laura Riding's Collected at the same price). I'm reading Huncke's autobiography which is such a bad job of typewriting I mean typesetting I can barely read it, however a fine gift to my nights.

I wish I could say I think I'm a poet because you are, however nowadays that might be true but in the days when I was trying to figure out why I was a poet I didn't know you. But I can't think of another good answer, I think it's because, yes, those lines occur, or, I cannot go forward into the present-future without it like the way people say oh I have to jog to feel good, no I don't mean that, but Ron said something like that the other day and I was quite surprised. I do know I have to write something down and I've always been enamored, in a kind of masochistic way, of seeing how long I can leave it without making something of it, as if it might get better (as it gets more condensed? no!) the longer it waits, like a fucking stew. It's desire though too like to get the meal done (so you can go to bed!), oh fuck images of food. Thank you Gertrude.

The lines that occur, I make a list of them and I hope I can get them all on my desk on pieces of paper, and then when something else is happening, I need them (am I inarticulate or what?)

What I need in Greek is the Loeb Classics edition (in Greek and facing (trot) English) of THE GREEK ANTHOLOGY. I need two of them, one for me and one for Rosemary and enclosed is a check blank, no wait a minute, I'll send that to your mother, it can only be gotten as far as I know, from the Harvard bookstore (is it 88 Meeting St. Providence? yes?) I've looked all over NY and can't find it.

Autumn makes me think of Picasso whose show we went to see and it makes me think he does in fact inhabit Saturn, as I predicted he would, and he is doing as fine as a warhead, thrown to the ground in some spatial accident—what a wreck he was! I often thought of Bob Dylan while I was watching Picasso's pictures and all I can say is Picasso was terrific in his stubborn unwillingness to abdicate a day-to-day relation, and certainly he was famous and it's odd to see how famous he was and how much "influence" there was, it's like a roll over that has some momentum, it's good and observable and at some point it's too much for the eyes, it's generous too which is the best part, and all the paint slapped on is so much more real than one would expect, and much of it is so much more old than you'd expect too (many of the observers took Max's "raspberries" as a (to them) welcome condemnation of the abstractions!). The most fascinating part was the prolific nature of it all and the imitations of the old masters (all put in the "last" room, as they ordered it for us), and the myriad of people in front of all the paintings, preventing us from studying them, and looking so interesting. I kept saying to Lewis "where are the rest of his works!"! I wanted to see all the dross. So many millions of ideas all so lost! Something wrong, I don't know what. If I did, I might actually know something. **[Page break]**

So we are as if tourists, yesterday the Picasso show, today the statue of Liberty! Not bad in the sense of learning something.

Visually startling in terms of all the varieties of people at each place, especially the deformed and handicapped that one forgets completely about in New England, it's amazing how frequently on the Lower East Side a man or woman without a hand walks by! and as amazing to me is that the children never comment on it.

Oh fuck it I wish I could see you, it would be so much easier to mention things, much less to get a take on what each of us looked like.

Lewis and Marie are doing great and seem thriving, Sophia who has her reservations is slowly accommodating in a very nice way, Max of course is just astonishing everyone by crawling and standing before his time and I am wondering how it is I can remember so much about New York and at the same time have an entirely different life here than I ever had!

We had some pristine fall days here, the kind I was expecting when I was trying to envision what it would be like in September in New York, but today I'm afraid it got hot again and on the Statue of Liberty ferry I heard some Englishmen quoting a tourists' flyer about the NY seasons and laughing up their sleeves, meanwhile bumping us with their bulky camera equipment. I must admit I too took some pictures on this excursion, one of Marie below a giant backside of the female statue!

There is so much more to tell, my thoughts get lost on little pieces of paper, all of which I always hope to retrieve at some point, not to speak of the ones that don't make it to the paper yet—suffice it to say we haven't worked out a real schedule yet but soon I'd assume I'll have a pen by me at all times. Though would I want to? A whole other story.

LOVE among the castabout
warheads,
Bernadette

Addendum one: Having just read "Two Haloed" I must admit I'm sorry (I must admit I have to stop saying I must admit) there were so many typos in it; I did type it in a rush in N.H. but I hope they weren't too awful. I have such a problem, as I am having now re-typing the letters book, with not being able to re-read clean copies for errors, I mentioned this to Alice today and we had an interesting talk about the investment, so-called, in one's works, and all the time it takes to type a long work out, which is a risk (not writing any new works during that time!) and so, for fear of feeling like a fool, one abhors the last step, the dullest proofreading! Oh if only we didn't have typewriters at all! What alot of work it would save.

Thanks for the carbonate/silicate distinction, it seems like the smithsonite equation with "calamine" has something to do with being British, though I've only got my dictionary to go on, however I was able to incorporate your change before the reading.

Addendum two: Marie, who keeps running through the room on various errands approached me now carrying a gallon of milk!—she is much concerned with doing everything by herself these days, but perhaps this is too much!

a gallon of love (is that how images were born?)
(born?),
B^2

p.s. our bell's just rung as it frequently does and we have to elect to work!

funny lie, fiddelheaded life.

MONDAY 6 OCTOBER [1980]

Dear Bernadette,

Being monday, as it says above, why not start with that business of days of the week you bring up. I agree, and I think always have, even during school days when it made more "sense"(?), that specific and repeating day-desigations(nations) are silly. I always want each day to be like a prime number, divisible by nothing but itself and one. Start again and again fresh even if there is a repetition as Gertrude said. Reminds me somehow of that old Fugs song, "Monday nothing, Tuesday nothing . . ." etcetc. Sundays used to piss me off mainly 'cause my folks wouldn't let me see my friends on that day, leaving me with some vague idea that "religion" was the order but of course I didn't have (being "Congregational"!) any clear notion (are there <u>clear</u> notions?) what that meant I was supposed to occupy myself with, my folks never having told me how to meditate or contemplate or otherwise use that unoccupied space. So of course I daydreamed, appropriately enough. "But you're imagining things." "Right, that's exactly what I am doing." Probably this has something also to do with that "moving forward" you were talking about. After all, it's never truly "monday again." And days don't go in and come out the other end of anything.

This is one of those days (ha!) when I feel kinda moodily contemplative, feeling like I know all my works at a glance and even the future ones, so why bother? As if I were faced with a wall with all my works hanging on it at once, and if I move a little further down the hall there I'll see ones I haven't even written yet. Luckily I know this sort of inertial illusion for what it is. Is that as wise to myself as I can ever expect to get? Practically enough maybe. Moving forward and never (a vow to never) wave to anybody who's not moving also. Momentum is not only a big question, besides being maybe a central principle?, but a big love of mine. And now I've said that I immediately have to say Stillness is equally. After all I like to think we are the Polar Explorers! Why are we writers? Luckily questions are by nature unstable. I sometimes like to entertain the notion (image of the writer doing a headstand wiggling maracas between his/her teeth in front of what to anybody else looks like mere empty space) that by putting words together, even if just two words at a time, I've got something that at that precise moment anyway doesn't exist for anybody else anywhere on earth. That's maybe childish but basic and why not? Unrepeatability and tiny genius! Plus I'm getting the bonus of a new arrangement of the mix. Actually I just thought of that and can't be really sure if I've ever entertained it. This must be a poet's sidebar. Everything we say about writing must be to the side or in between? I'm going to win the all-time doubt-in-motion award! The trouble probly is that we ('re taught?) expect all the work to amount up to something? Impossible for me to see it in large (where's that phrase come from? Sounds like a biz term). I was amazed but not surprised to find this in a letter Phil Whalen wrote to Lew Welch in 1969: (re ON BEAR'S HEAD) "I wish that the book amounted to something—& after all, it just don't, not really." We all know the feeling, but it made me feel terribly sad for a moment. What I'm sure it does amount to, which of course he can't know not being for a moment any of the other people reading it at whatever other moments, is a big continuation of the urge to write (& read) poetry. Which arrives nowhere, amount not being a transitive verb(especially for poets?), and inspiration having no scale. Actually I have an old book of poems (once almost published by Follett) titled AMOUNT and I recall being fascinated with the Latin root: to the mountain. The peak of course never being reached, and so the book not published(!)

I've been following through that three-parter on present state of the Book Biz in NewYorker and it's stuff we somehow already know even if not exactly but still horribly depressing stark down in fact and future fact. Conglomerate ownership, print media divisions, going for the big commerciality, loss of the friendly neighborhood bookseller, etc. blahblahblah. The kind of piece that Larry is going to later insist we all must read (like that Pauline Kael Hoooywood Biz piece he was assigning to his class at Naropa!) even though we all have read it and don't even want to discuss it anymore. One thing that got me: how these huge suburban shoppingcenter bookchains like Waldenbooks which are taking over everything and even determining by computerized sales "projections" just which manuscripts will be accepted by the publishers(!) are being purposely designed to look like supermarkets so that nobody will feel intimidated or embarrassed to walk in. Shit, not only am I intimidated to walk into a supermarket but I honestly can't ever remember feeling intimidated by walking into a book store. Amazing. They'd claim that makes me an elite snob I spose. Maybe we will end up members of terrorist cells planning to place plastique behind the racks. Either that or a state of out-of-work shamanism, right.

Subject matter, fume and clatter. What are you doing about sending out mss these days? I must admit (I'll use that one for awhile) I can't do it at all these days. The chances are so awful. Especially the ones where the copy of the magazine comes with a sincere-young-letter folded in. Did you get THE DIFFICULTIES? That guy's really after me. Two copies, letters, etc. I don't even like the title. But the worst is that stupid cart&horse piece by Paul, STUPID being just the word and no doubt the reason why I can't seem to call and invite them over for dinner. Susan keeps saying, Should we invite the Metcalfs over for dinner this weekend, and I say, uhhh . . . Sell this letter to Bob Wilson immediately! Or better still publish it so I'll have to put up or shut up on such literary friendship opinions. Gossip as a factor of rehash, or the Case of the Ineradicable Spot. (Wonder is Castang's City any good? I think my heart went out of most of that scene when Wahloo died)

This letter is even more of a mess than usual. I can't seem to continue a thought today. Milarepa here I come, eh Allen? Heart Beat has finally hit the Pissoir Palace on North Street for a week and I wish I didn't feel somehow "duty-bound" to go see it. Roll of typing-paper carefully draped over the mirror just won't be funny enough (as George Peppard's Subterraneans somehow is in retrospect, or at least more innocently fucked). Every time I see Godard's new movie mentioned somewhere I practically weep. The high point of last week was reading through script of Pierrot Le Fou and looking at the pictures (color ones in the English edition I have). Nobody but you & Ed will ever understand why Godard stills seem the most beautiful & meditatable pictures in the world to me. They all happened out of the corners of my eyes as I walked down the streets in our time. Now I'm in Pittsfield and the streets are all out of focus. The projectionists gone hunting on their bicycles . . .

Perfectly what I think too when you say at the Picasso show "I wanted to see all the dross." There's a mystery here I was trying to get at in my PICASSO DEAD piece now lost in old Worlds, something [about] his pictures being the spaces between his acts. Secrets that get lost going on <u>in</u> between. How to say this and outwit the varnish. Sometimes I read through my old works and remember where they came from shockingly complete, amazed, and at how little of it I was able to keep in the work. Reminds me of your idea to make a shorthand to catch every twist and turn (fist and yearn). Everything, indeed! Maybe I should use that title for the big work(?) I think I would in a minute if I wasn't afraid people'd think I'm kidding.

The leaves today are just at that point midway between yellow and green they look golden.

I got my doubts that guy Mellow's book on Hawthorne can be much good if Charmed Circle was any indication. Ever read it? He's some sort of art critic who had no sympathy for and in fact seemed to hate her writing, really pissed me off (again). Almost made you wish she had never known any painters. **[Page break]**

(the next day) I realized with some sinking sensations last night before falling asleep that I truly haven't any idea why I write. In fact I can clearly recall days as a kid when writing was no part of my program. Long hours alone staring at and handling crystals on shelves, stumbling around slushy quarries in winter twilight my father reading a newspaper in the car. Lots of pressure, even by junior highschool, to "choose a career" in those days. I did think of being a musician, that's always been my other guise. Why did I "choose" Geology I'm sure I had no clear image of as a job. Probably just succumbed somewhere along the way to the Career Plan Handbook. Actually I was just wandering around in a daze, my father always used to accuse me of. Are we all variants of unconscious hybrids? Trying to think of the first poems I was aware of . . . Probably the songs in A.A. Milne, and I remember my mother singing me that song about "shadows of the evening steal across the sky" (I always visualized a great steel shutter closing over). Sci-Fi reveries. Old Geology texts. DownBeat magazine. Donald Duck and later E.C. horror comics. Early movies: They Were Expendable, and that England WWII blitz movie with the weird dome-shaped hills cracking open into airplane hangers in the night of bombs and a kid shinnying down a vine-covered wall to wobble away down a lane on his bicycle and get killed (I think). Important to discover just what movie this was, but I've never been able to (it's wasn't Mrs. Minniver). No doubt about it, On the Road gave me my first image of not only what to write about (which wouldn't be believed by Language types?) but of myself actually doing that: I could actually see myself sitting down and writing words, at a typewriter even though

I had never used one. And it's funny to realize that this was in the midst of a big dorm season of reading Camus and Sartre and Colin Wilson's Outsider and Hesse, sitting up many late nights hearing about Wittgenstein from a guy named Ed Pincus who became a documentary film maker and the second man on the hit list of the guy who shot Al Lowenstein. Sometimes I think I should publish my earliest poems (no matter how terrible), just to show how this all began.

A little unintentional autobiography there. What would a geometry of the strings in these our various letters form? Not to mention the forms of the writing that makes up the strings. A little something left over from time I thought I'd be a scientist. Mapping things out. Although (unlike you?) I never did enjoy diagramming sentences, something always askew about that to me. Though I'm sure I had a rotten teacher. Reading Michael Palmer's marvelous new mss (Notes for Echo Lake) and thereby being drawn back into Rimbaud (trying decipher with a French dictionary and very little knowledge of the structure), I began to wish to learn French (at least enough to read it) again. No doubt I'll get over it, but do you know if there's a "better" (easier) French textbook I might putter around with? It often seems just ridiculous to me that I can't read French, I'm so drawn to French writers. It's never too late to learn the clarinet? Probably I should stick to the mysteries of English . . .

I was thinking it might be fun to write imaginary travel letters to each other. This wasn't inspired by Ted & Ron's Big Travel Dialogs, I don't know what it was inspired by, maybe the impossible landscapes that have always been at least as interesting to me as the people I meet in my dreams, and also by the way these places keep intruding in the new prose mss I'm working on (with the stories). These letters would be more connected to the <u>places</u> we'd be visiting by imagination. What really inspires this is my current wish to actually be walking through some faraway city and describing to you all I see there. "Here today in the Medina, tinkle tinkle . . ." Perhaps this has something to do with your Letters Book too? Ah, always avoiding by more the too much to do I already have.

I know what you mean about leaving things stew, but those little pieces of paper usually remain useless pieces of paper if I leave them alone too long. Ditto with lines in notebooks, they stay that way, usually. I'm not a very good fabricator(which has nothing to do with true lies). I seem to have to get a mass going every time, which might generate spin-off lines that I'll use usually later in the same work if not at the same sitting. Sometimes I get an actual taste of how scrap-lines actually are fragmented and "lost" as if "intended" to be just that, nothing to be done about it. Just what can one do with broken glass? Some people make collages I spose, but I always want to follow the ones that carry on. Something to do here with what you once said about the transformation process of writing down dreams. The famous "lapses" are I suppose something else again, intelligent hinges within the fabric of a matter moving. Shit, I can't believe I'm sitting here making "definitions"? Saying things like the above in these letters makes me feel like we've just met, which I guess is somehow true if we can keep saying here all those things we never get to say in conversation?

Actually (that's one word I've got to stop using!) I love giving myself lots of distractions (like reading all the time off-the-wall books etc.) so I'll always later have the pleasure of discovering the amazing continuities I find in works written over a long period. At least the systematic mind seems to work best in writing when it's covered up in process. Ah, lovely chaos, show me your roots! Etc.

This might be a good idea: the next movie you see, no matter what it is, write down right away everything you can remember and think about it and send it to me and I'll do the same. I did this once with Louis Malle's Black Moon, I told myself only this: write down whatever you remember about it and the pages have gotten more interesting over the years (to me anyway, and this is maybe a good example as any of a "secret work"). Ha, as if you needed another project!

We've been having a lot of power outages lately, interruptions in the Study of Fluids. Something I could easily get outraged about. I've been trying this Godel Escher Bach book Michael Brownstein said was interesting but I get all hopelessly bogged down in the math and the guy's pedantic tone (he's a computer teacher). Which all caused me to write down the following lines:

I like numbers, but I don't like mathematics.
I like painting, but I don't like colors.

How strange to find something true and <u>then</u> to try and discover yourself in it! Here's something interesting that Bertrand Russell (of all people) said in 1918: "I <u>must</u>, before I die, find <u>some</u> way to say the essential thing that is in me, that I have never said yet—a thing that is not love or hate or pity or scorn, but the very breath of life, fierce and coming from far away, bringing into human life the vastness and the fearful passionless force of non-human things." (Wonder if he ever read Melville?)

Better leave you for now and something for later. The cat's asleep. The projects are waiting.

All Love,
Clark

P.S.—Can you believe 1st class letters are going up to 20¢ March 1st!??
Maybe we'll be forced back to our phonecalls?

NOVEMBER 22, 1980

Dear Clark,

What an amazing rash? of events seem to be taking place lately—for a while it was mostly birthday celebrations, all the scorpios, as they say, both within and without the family—then it was what I've come to think of as what other people think of as <u>de rigeur</u> events in new york, so that this past week I wound up going out 3 nights in a row! After we do such things, Lewis always has a sort of hangover caused by not being able to work and he and I agree, like people reforming from drink in the morning, never ever either to go out again or to let anyone in! I must admit though that I often find it quite alot of fun. These three nights I'm talking of were Harris reading at the poetry project, to attend which of course is my "job" (& he was very good, he had a kind of clarity which was happily deficient in the cowboys, sexist remarks & recherche hippie-ism of some of his past works, in fact I'm beginning to have the theory that Harris turns out to be a poet who benefits from his "middle age" because he is no longer posing and what he thinks perhaps is lost as it were with youth is well rid of; he read with Tom Weatherly who was desultory and has obviously not been writing much); then the next night the inevitable

Lita Hornicks party which made me angry because I kept being "told" "I" "had to" go, however I began to think that I actually did "have to" etc. so I went and managed to propose marriage to John Ashbery who answered by making a series of quick puns on the word "bridge" so wittily as to make me think such a marriage might actually be enjoyable, otherwise the party was quite dull (except for Larry and Susan's costumes!), in fact it was literally full of businessmen who kept coming on to one in such a way as I dont think I've seen in 15 years; and last night Alice & I read our collaboration together, a reading which had been scheduled for the previous night until we learned that nearly half our expected audience would prefer to attend the Hornick shindig! I found reading the work with Alice very illuminating, I'd never really done anything like it before, it was amazing to really have another voice almost. We read for an hour and twenty minutes and I made a tape which I would love for you to hear. I guess I can't say much more about it because I cant seem to be articulate but I learned alot and eventually will be able to say it. I guess I didnt start out to describe these events to you but I began talking about them in order to tell you that in the course of the last few nights Lewis told me he'd had two conversations in a row with poets who seem to think they have some choice about being poets, as if they could be other "things" and sort of throw it all up for some more well-paying work! Then—more of the secret knowledge of having so much input as they used to call it—people keep saying things like, well who is going to publish that, and I always do expect everyone who is a poet not to make the assumption about published work. And further, and this is all in relation to that part of your letter, so articulate it is about the poet's sidebar on through AMOUNT, there is an almost continuous argument going on at poetry project between me and everybody else in which they say we must drum up audiences and I say no not necessarily it's only the work which is important. And then there's a sideline to this argument where I'm often expected to attend 3 or 4 readings a week and I say no I've gotta do my work, so the sum of what I'm saying is that a whole lotta people seem to have lost their perspective about why (or what) are we writers. Re supermarkets (ha!) I am phobic of them and I've begun to realize in my own middle-age that most of my remaining phobias are actually quite sensible, I think it simply is that in one's youth (how come I keep saying things like this?) one doesnt have the nerve or the corroboration to know not doing what everyone else can do is sanity. I sound like Polonius or somebody!

And not to go on with this, but supermarkets, subways, publishing conglomerates, banks, who in his or her right mind would want to walk in to those? Well it's more than obvious I know but I've always been a dimwit in the sense that I really do not understand why, for instance, there is such a thing as MacDonalds or something. Nor do I have any greater understanding how anyone can be a poet and write poetry without apprehending the almost absolutist conditions or givens of it. So here we are, two purists, just swinging our arms around in each other's vicinities. I must admit (oh sorry I keep saying that!) that nothing "in life" is ever what I expect it to be and what I mean is (am I being interminably simple-minded and corny in this letter?) I've learned now that I don't think I would in fact be able to do the work at the poetry project if it weren't for having the children too because my relationship with them is so radically sane and permits me to see more clearly what is my work, self, life, etc. and what is something else, extraneous, or overblown. Interestingly then too, there is also the political. When Robert Creeley came to do his workshop he talked wonderfully about that, maybe I wrote you about it in my short letter? I can't remember! Oh and Godard's movie fits into this too, and it is shocking. It is just and as always the most real idea of the present culture you can see, plus full of autobiography. And the last shot, which is long, is the most beautiful thing I've ever seen in a movie. (Now this is what I get for not answering more promptly—I'm either repeating myself, or not saying enough!).

I don't send any mss out these days either, though I sent part of my new book to The World for the prose issue—did you send anything? Otherwise there don't seem to be no place to send cept UNITED ARTISTS and how about some more poems for us? I get some weird requests like from Turkey Buzzard Review and Galloping Dog Press, but I dont answer. MIDWINTER DAY will come out sometime when it's about 2½ years old, which I guess I shouldnt complain about, in a small edition because Callahan doesnt see it as one of his big "sellers," fuck it. I'd like to publish a book of my own again but I cant even figure if it should be a new one or an old one. And maybe tuumba will do a short thing of mine, that's it. nobody's breaking down the doors here. In fact I've been trying to get a chance to read from the letters book which is tentatively titled—are you ready?—THE DESIRES OF MOTHERS TO PLEASE OTHERS IN LETTERS—but with all my "power" I can't find a reading to read by myself! I got a review copy of the Mellow Hawthorne book to do for the newsletter and my plan is to review it with SCOTT & AMUNDSEN, so I can get to read these fancy hardcovers. The Mellow is not too bad, it's got some information which isn't anywhere else but I'll never forgive the guy for being so fucking wordy, after all it was Henry James who did it right.

Last night after the reading to which three high-school friends of mine came, we sat around reciting all the first poems we had had to memorize, and singing the amazing catholic tunes we all knew by heart (Lewis and others bored and perhaps embarrassed!). I dont think anybody writes for any known reason, thus all the fascination with a poet's autobiography—because there's no clue! It'd be as easy to say I write because of "when dry leaves that before the hurricane fly/when they meet with an obstacle mount to the sky" as for any other reason. Or maybe, "Ode" by Arthur O'Shaughnessy: "We are the movers and shakers, and we are the dreamers of dreams, wandering by lone sea breakers and sitting by desolate streams . . ." Or Milton's Sonnet on his blindness or even "The Man with the Hoe"! or the speeches i had to memorize from "Julius Ceasar"! When I was 14 I had a job working weekends at St. Vincents Hospital and I used to go and stand at what I knew was e.e. cummings' door on Patchin Place, however I'd no idea why I was standing there, or whether it was any more important than the fact that I also loved to look at the strange leather beatnik shoulder bags in the stores in Greenwich village. What was your "first" poem?

About French, better to read it simply with an enormous dictionary I would guess. I learned French in school among the very worst textbooks and the exigencies of having to do things like say the Hail Mary in French every day and the pledge allegiance: "Je jure . . ." However any knowledge of French that I got was never enough to be able to read French poetry, at least without a securely gigantic dictionary. At the moment actually I'm much more interested in studying Greek again, & the Greek Anthology is on its way to me and next I'm going to get a bigger dictionary, and I found a great text in Books & co. about Greek & Latin meters, but I never mean to be able to read those languages exactly but just to steal from them their dead knowledge & do something with it. I guess that's why I've never been interested in translating anything at all (cf.

"Mayer" translations in new Rocky Ledge! in which by the way your poems were wonderful, especially all of them, especially "Women" and "Ode yet a Moment").

Ah, imaginary travel letters, yes! I had a dream last night I was in England going to an interesting museum in a slum and everyone was speaking English though I kept expecting them not to because it's Not-London as well as London. I saw a beautiful dark red housing project and when I saw it in the dream I realized it was a place I'd see some day, I knew it was a real place, strange-looking as it was. Perhaps I thought it was a place that didnt even exist yet! Up till I saw it I was as if following the directions in a travel book in dream, I was getting on the right bus, going to the right museum, noticing that the museum, though it had good things inside it, was ridiculous from the outside, not like a museum at all, with none of the accepted attendant dignity, rather more like a flophouse—just like poetry! Then I wondered if I'd noticed how I came there, so I could get back. I knew I'd have to ask directions and then I'd learn what the language really was. What a great dream it was! I never saw the inside of the museum.

yes let's write some, but how shall we begin? Do you read the travel section of the Sunday Times ever? I could make a cut-up perhaps to begin, or write a "What's doing in. . . ."

One thing that's been happening to me lately, when I'm pressed for time to dally at the typewriter and just fool around, is that it becomes obvious which poem is which, which has to be written, which is just flying about, which is nothing, but then when I write one there's always two or three more waiting around. Instead of reading I'm having people and their psychologies, if one can still say that, and my own too because I can study it without having to be polite. I only wish all the chores of life were done by somebody else for me so I could really have <u>all</u> my time. And I dare to say that I find little good in doing laundry, cooking and cleaning, though I do learn much from taking care of children, shopping and working at the mesmerized and rather-located-in-time poetry project. The thing I think I hate most in the world of doing is what they call sorting clothes and folding them. However the entire thing makes sense to me and I dont know how to explain it—what I mean is what I'm learning from what I'm doing makes sense to my work and it is, for practically the first time for me, an exhilarating feeling which I often think has to do with my age . . . oh shit but I can't go on with that otherwise I'll wind up saying things so corny as you will never write me again!

That Bertrand Russell quote you quoted me about non-human things is so astonishing I dont even know if I know what he means except when I read it over and over I feel like I am falling into some abyss over some precipice where there are a million words all of which I know, with my bad memory, I can remember by HEART!

Oh dear **[Page break]**

O shit or o voice, how I hate too having a voice!

Nevertheless the sloppy style of the New York weather makes it be spring again tomorrow & the only thing you have to worry about is the winds on 4th street where there are a number of housing projects between which the winds whip and blow the children down. So the rest of the city was right to shelter the aisles of the avenues with windowless brick. I hardly ever get to see the moon.

I'm glad you're coming to the Philip Guston reading and I hope we can find some time to talk in among that trip, and will you be staying long enough to see any movies? Lewis and I barely get the chance to & have only seen Godard and something else, forgettable.

Our goldfish, [Ringo], died and we have a gerbil! Name of Gretchen, a gift from a friend who found she couldnt shelter gerbils and cats in the same place. Gretchen likes to gnaw on and reprocess the cardboard tubes from toilet-paper and paper-towel rolls and otherwise is an abstemious animal who is not shy.

Did you have a foot of snow as I read?

Too many things to talk about now, I'm getting scattered, I'm tempted to just pick up the phone!

Marie is having some sort of adolescence and she broods instead of getting mad when we insist that she do or not do something. Sophia's riding high on turning three and seems most compatible and her eyes are getting nearly as dark as mine. Max leaps up out of his high chair and tries to sit on the top of it, and he rehearses for walking along the edge of the couch. All three went to a poetry reading at the Ear Inn today, and they were not "good." Since Marie & Sophia have been in schools, Sophia often says to me, "bernadette, are you good or bad?!"

Now what is the sublime?

Love,
Bernadette

[Typed on the back of a Public Theater flyer for Jacques Rivette's *L'Amour Fou*.]

12/13/80

Dear Clark,

I'm writing you this note, I guess it wont reach you before you leave for New York, I wanted to write you on the back of this, I went and saw L'Amour Fou again! & was going to encourage you to try & come in time to see it but then I saw it was closing too soon alas. It was amazing to see it again, it is one movie I, with all my bad memory, remembered every scene of, in fact before I took lewis to see it I think I told him everything about it! Then when we sat down, after the first half hour or so I had this sinking feeling that lewis might wind up hating it, however of course he didnt, but the funny thing was my fear was mostly that he wouldnt want to stay for the whole thing, and not that we'd have to have an aesthetic argument! Suffice it to say lewis was most inspired and I now feel free to say, having seen the movie at 8=year intervals, that it's my second favorite movie of all time (do I sound like Larry?).

Nice golden rod paper this too? I'm listening to a wonderful Dave Van Ronk album: "chicken is nice with palm butter and rice . . ." it's amazing how quickly you can fill up your mind in NY especially if you've got a little cash.

Now I see I havent mentioned the whole John lennon thing yet either which I guess I dont know what to say about except I found myself rather angrily saying to someone in the Poetry Project office that day that I'd always felt I could be a great poet if I had some other culture to exist in, that is, I dont like hating my culture (which I guess I do) & it's mostly thoughts of the American culture, in the sense of the disparity between rich, poor etc. and famous, not famous & hero, not hero, etc. that has been the stuff of my thoughts since lennon's murder, not even to mention the astonishing fact that Marie and I, on our way to school that morning, witnessed the aftermath of another murder!, a cop shot a man who was trying to shoot his wife, and we saw some of that, then a few steps later I saw the headlines in the paper, it seemed pitiful all around to have to weep for john lennon and to have to weep for the man who was trying to shoot his wife too and to have to listen to so many people's descriptions of both the murders, and, amazingly, Michael Halberstam's murder too, which was much written about in the Times, and then to hear Reagan saying it wasnt the fault of any handgun laws and then to hear Reagan's advisers give their opinions about the NEA, which were very interesting, they think there should be a distinction made between high art, serious art, and "Popular" art, by which they mean any art that has to do with a community, a lower=class group, or black etc. people. 1981 here we come I guess. Not that it seems much different, except that it does. Well forgive me for going on, I only mean t to write you a note about L'Amour Fou, appropriately enough, oh dear, see you soon.

Love, Bernadette

[→ If you do happen to get this before you come down, please call me as soon as you get here, I've no idea of your schedule. I'll be at the Poetry office on Tuesday till quarter to 3, then after that, by 3:30 I'll be home (2545308) & we'll be having a birthday party for Marie which it would be wonderful if you could come to.]

WEDNESDAY 7 JANUARY **[1981]**

Dear Bernadette,

I better get started answering you somehow before whatelse causes noise and disturbance here. Starting from nowhere but trouble . . . ha! could be opening of a terrible detective novel? We're having our, I guess, usual winter season pipe clog miseries: main drain backing up sewage into basement so afraid to flush toilets you sit around hoping you don't have to take a shit and then you do anyway and the stink . . . Whole scatological novels could be written. Spent whole of yesterday sitting here waiting for plumber to drive up and thinking I couldn't get started doing anything, but then end of day and the guy hadn't showed up (natch) and I found I'd written five or six poems anyway, what I love about this job(!) actually surprise yourself at your own elbow. And it's funny, after years of this winter pipe flipflop and hassle I feel even worse about it all but simultaneously more calm overall (see how impossible to write about experience?) and I finally know my mind works at all different levels all the time. Which one is dominant? None for long. Then I wonder, Where is the world, right now, this second? Certainly not at the end of a stuck pipe (my mind). Sometimes I think what is native to me is not meditation but a continual overreaching. Better to have it all pouring in (even through a window) than be stuck on a point. What do I know about limitation (might be a possible motto?). And sometimes I get (shore up with) a great kind of ultimacy kick, like what does it matter what anyone says, or does not do, about writing, it's still there! Kerouac. Yesterday too I was reading through here&there McNally's book all about K's horrible binges etc. and it didn't make me sad finally. One could say, well, I know all that. Stare at his picture and sometimes think, I don't know this guy at all. Brodey told me he has a great blowup of that photo of Jack and his cat on his wall. You just stare at his picture like at people in a Godard movie, who are they? Watch what they're doing, maybe with no ideas of "finding out" anything? I keep thinking about what you said (NYC) about "coldhearted." You should go on with that, write me more, feel there's a secret there(?) I wonder, and the counter turns up: Is that amazing shot of Karina at the window with Eluard's book in reflection space coldhearted? Naturally one can think of differences. To stand and hold forth beauty is certainly to deny loss. Why those academic guys are mucked from the start? Gets me back to sorts of will. Shit, this is muddled and I bridle.

Guess I'm a little sad today and still waiting for the fucking plumber who probably won't come today either, five inches of new snow last night and so far unplowed. Celia came home with stomach cramps last night and I instantly thought, Some other kind of cramps? But Susan says she figures not for another year, basing the timing on herself. But today Celia's down the hill sledding with gangs of whoops. No-school joy. Sad to think of spending just a short time with you guys in city, what a great silly time we had with "Machu Picchu," so much so I'll probably get there and just fall down laughing to the annoyance of tourists. What's so goddam funny in this City of the Hooy Incas?!?

(Hooey is right) And that's "Knowledge" for you, that I probably will do just that. Why does life keep doing all these horrid severing things to all us good friends? Shit, I better bring a bottle down here and have an actual reason for all this melancholia! Tune myself up into syrupy snarls and scream with laughter and kick the cat. Having myself a wonderful reading of your duo book (though I'm afraid the title will always remind me how I missed that movie again) and thinking it's great you're able to keep turning out all these publications! You <u>should</u> do more of your <u>own</u> things! Don't wait, while you have the means. Total approval by me, though you really don't need anybody's, just self impetus and what the fuck. Nobody else is lining up, etc. Mind if I complain? People who publish us seem such lame quantities, mostly, no? Their reasons . . . Who knows or wants to know their reasons. Or that they gotta have any particularly. **[Page break]**

I just got M. Wolfe (I can't even call him "Michael" since it's some actual person's name) reply to my Ultimatum. He's all big apologies and promises to do my book "in two more months." Agh. Well, ok. Once again into the revolver. I do love that book, so probably have made bigger efforts at repressing all feeling about it. So much for your "Ultimacy," Clark. I told him I want the cover to be sky-blue with white writing, cursive (title). Kind of a goof but I think appropriately nice. I decided I couldn't use anything more illustrative than that since almost anything pictured would limit the spread of "Ones" in the title too much. Someday, I swear, I am going to put a full-face photo of me on a cover, but I'll have to find the write [(!)] photo (haven't seen it yet) (maybe you should do it?). And I'm wondering if I should buy a decent camera, for travel etc. Got any suggestions? What are those Canon or Olympus or whatever Japanese ones I keep seeing advertised like? What's the one you picked out? I realize this can be a big technical headache blitz like Hi-Fi. Saw my cousin's slides of Hawaii the other night he took with (I think) a Canon: great bite to the details. Or maybe it was this amazing Swiss projector we borrowed from the Barrs, which even made the shoddy slides we'd made with our Instamatic look like ultimate still movies. Thinking, too, that's all I need right now to get all involved with taking pictures! But then comes rushing in, Why shouldn't I do everything?!?!?

Why shouldn't I have a beer. Here. At elbow. Have one with me? I'm watching this strange yellowish cloud rapidly advance down the valley, trees start to twicth(twiTch) with the winds they blow, now it's snowing like a fit. Winter. (yellow?) Loved your paragraph on Lyn Hejinian's MY LIFE. That's just what I think too. Being the medium. And writing about a picture is what SHIT, the carriage just knocked over my beer bottle completely ruining new pome on pad! Some writer!(wrong elbow?). Now I've had to stop and sponge it all up and the whole place smells like brew (not too bad actually, working in a beer cave). Maybe this'll make the snow stop. Anyway, I was going to say writing about a picture is what I've always done (lots, anyway), inspired by (recall?) Kerouac's saying (in Introduction to The Americans); "what poems can be written about this book of pictures some day by some young new writer high by candlelight bending over them describing every gray mysterious detail." And I've done it actually, like a project almost, with your MEMORY slabs, Godard stills, old 1870's survey glassplate vistas by Watkins & O'Sullivan & Jackson. And postcards of paintings from museums, like I just did with a Saint Jerome by Joos van Cleve the Elder, 1521, Bill Corbett gave me card of. Got a perty (pretty) good poem out of that to add to my meditations on Jerome world mind and chamber. No project actually, at the moment of doing, just looking at it and line follows line, you never know (I almost said, How can you tell?). The snow stopped.

Celia made a great remark othernite at dinner, everybody else talking fooey and hooey and suddenly a silence and she says, Did you ever notice how when you see something that happened going on in your mind it's always a still picture? Immediately of course everybody started to disagree with this, but it's a thought I had months ago and I think it got into MINE somewhere. or someplace written. Yeah, right, it was in that section of MINE that's actually a continuation of a passage about the angel coming through his ceiling in Kafka's Diaries. Sometimes I think I could spend the rest of my life looking at galleries of Renaissance pictures, just peering inside there and writing up that whole world. Ever read Foucault's The Order of Things where he talks about how at one time words were felt to be secret signs carved into the world like cracks in rocks? Then immediately came the period of language as commentary (like on Bible), hermeneutics, etc. Natural enough a drag? But we certainly proceed off a glimmer of that earlier feeling, right? I better stop and type up that beer-poem before it's totally lost to the smear.

Got it, and the beer is finished too (it didn't all spill). It's been amazingly cold here lately, 27 below zero on Xmas day. 15 below the other night. Have to leave the water trickling in the sink nights so the pipes don't freeze. A new arctic being erected here? Time to reread ALONE I guess. There should only be some inspiring auroras to go along with the lack of temperature (lack of temp?!). Pattern of this winter is just about set. The only time it warms up is when it snows. At least there's been no ice glaze so far (knock wood). "No ice" looks like "noise" with an unnatural space. It's funny to have nothing to say. Ha! Lots of pretty good writing comes from nothing on the mind, as we well know. I could never be a lawyer, I could hardly get up in school to give a floortalk. A floortalk could also be a chalktalk? How fast all these things I remember like yesterday became archaic. What if you instituted a series of floortalks at the Poetry Project? Finger to lips making rapid blublublu motions. As the Pythons would say, It started all right but now it's got too silly.

Later. The road somehow actually did get plowed while I typed. And the plumber did arrive. Snaked out the drain again but said that isn't the problem. Seems we'll have to have the septic tank dug up, investigated, something blocked or frozen in there. Oh woe. Oh snore. Is this the kind of thing "outside yourself" that one is supposed to get interested in to avoid going nuts?!? I wish it would all just go away and me go back to work. I got my own practicality, like development of indentations on a page. (What an idea!) But then Barry W wrote me he got poisoned(!) Yes, he moved into a new house in Oakland and the landlord hired some incompetent exterminator to remove the termites and ended up fumigating the household. Barry had to put all his books clothes in storage and undergo some "detoxification" process, worrying about "longterm effects" on health, etc. Some problems. Sunny Cal. But he should learn a lesson about limitations (am I being coldhearted?), the ones he puts in his own way. Those guys (I can't avoid the grouping even though I know the differences of person) oughta found a School, so we could refuse to attend. Is what it feels like after all: writing is this or that. I don't wanta know. I want my pipes to be fixed and go away.

Now it's night, eight degrees of mercury and I ran out of beer after the one bottle (Some drinker!). This letter contains no ideas. It's almost like one of those "personal letters" they tried to drum into my head in grammarschool; this happened, then that, etc. But I don't see how you could possibly be at all intrigued by all these so yawn problems of pipes and all assorted backups. Problems must be a way of going on after all. Sounds of tractor in the night. He must be neatening up. Wish I could see your collaboration (that word shouldn't take so long to type, somehow) with Alice. How goes it? Hope it won't have as many hiati (sp?) as our cave thing. And I'm still dying to see your Letter work (oops, forgot your great title!). Guess I'm not the only one with Xeroxing problems. I think I remember Lewis talking about a Journals-issue of UA? So was reading through this summer's Vineyard notebook yesterday and think it might interest you for that project. Give me a deadline, preferably a long one so I can start right now to take forever getting it copied. I don't know why it just isn't easier to show people things. This letter contains more complaints than ever. Oh, and don't feel you have to put THIN PLACES in your already fully-packed issue upcoming. Enough's enough. Later's fine. Celia's dutifully practicing her scales upstairs. After half a dozen listen-throughs of the new BluesBrothers lp (terrific band they've got, actually). At dinner she said, "I saw this issue of PEOPLE magazine with Yoko on the cover, all about how she's coping. God . . ." I told her Yoko probably had absolutely nothing to do with it. Anyway.

This is the "Anyway" Letter. Write soon and ask me questions or something so I can get back on the track. I should have answered your last right away, I now see. When is McPhee coming? Was Michael McClure boring? All my thanks for great gift of yourselves in the city. I had a great time! and should visit more, you're right.

Love to all

(& machu picchu) Clark

JANUARY 12 1981

Dear Clark,

It's funny I have all kinds of practical? things to say as a result of your stuck-pipe dilemma, that is, not to be stuck on a point. What with all the limitless work I seem to have to do, and what I mean by that is I dont have to do it exactly, but I always have more to do than I can finish. Combination of endless Poetry Project letter-writing, which I sort of dig (though I dont like the carbons) and the impossibility of ever "finishing" one's own work anyway, so anyway, (another anyway letter) I find the following Polonius=like assertions to be true: ha ha. One, trying to keep everything in order is a useless waste of time, best method is to indeed overreach (the limitations) and simply begin, then in a few minutes it becomes apparent that there is either more or less to do, if quantity is one's care. . . . Two, I forget what two was supposed to be, oh, an entropy seems to set in for me in this life where I actually DESIRE to waste time contemplating my activities rather than doing them, I think this is self-serving though because I believe in the end efficiency is not a desireable (it doesnt make one desireable!) human trait. Three, (is this getting funny) there is always the seeking after pleasure in one's days, which is why I deride ambition. Does that make sense? Well all this set off by your "Limitations Lecture." Which set off such anality in me, oh shit.

I cant remember what I said about being coldhearted which I'm sure means there is a secret there. Your mentioning Karina is interesting, Godard to my mind always presented her as coldhearted, or more nearly, vacant (not in any bad sense of that word), not silly or vacuous but simply vacant, empty, eyes as holes, mirror to etc., she is another. You must illuminate me though about what this conversation is about because it's fascinating nonetheless. Speaking of coldheartedness, how about forgetfulness? Could they be the same thing? My mind edits so dramatically in the city and I find that my old dictum, I leave out the most important part, takes funny turns for me, and that while one is editing for one's self (just survival or even pleasure) you still leave the vacancy, if you'll allow me, for all things equal, so as to be (oh no not again) the medium, I almost said the fucking medium. But I didnt.

I've been wanting to write you since your visit to tell you what a pleasure it was and how great your reading was and how it stays in my mind & I wish we were in the same city or country again, but in some place where we could hear each other read all the time. I mean why didnt we ever turn those Wednesday afternoons in Lenox into little readings? Too corny I guess, but now as Poetry Project director, a term I hate, I'm allowed to have all kinds of corny ideas for "events." Surely I'll get to hear you read more often now that I'm in New York I hope. I've committed myself, quite bravely I think, to give four readings in two months, and I'm dying to do it too! One at a Monday night at the project, Feb. 9th with a poet I dont know at all, or a prose writer I think, named Susan McConnell, next at the New School on Feb. 20th, then early in March sometime with Hannah at the Anthology Film Archives unless the guy who's setting it up decides to adhere to his rule that a man must read with a woman, and vice versa, in which case (he'd wanted me to read with Sillyman) I wont read because I only wanted to read with Hannah, and then later in March at some weird cafe on 18th st. I've planned different things to read at each reading and only hope my audience, such as it might be, doesnt get impatient at such gadabout tendencies, but after all those years of so few readings, and now listening to so many, I've a tremendous desire to read my work. At the New School so far I plan to do something I've never done before and that you might find shameful, I'm going to read a mixture of old and new works, a sort of at best hodgepodge at worst my favorite tunes, I wonder what that might be like, it's as if pretending that i am really one person, which I dont like to think that I am, instead of the 3 or 4 I'd be hoping to be, at least while writing.

Now Peggy has just called and has regaled me with things I said in letters to her and our old friend Mary in 1965 and even before that! Amazing things about men and women and their relations and then we got involved in discussing exactly how Xmas was celebrated in our respective homes as kids (goats?) &nthen we talked about how difficult it is for any human being to change, or to emerge, say, from a kind of upbringing that portends this or that (a kind of girlhood . . .) into this actual life where, I hope, I (or she, Peggy) is perceiving things accurately (is that A REAlistic hope?) and with one's ability to love others still intact. How much do you think we are still today, at our ages, influenced by circumstance? Do you know what I mean? If one can talk about distorted perceptions—don't we see things as they are? Or not? For instance—this may sound silly but I think it's sort of apt—why do I still have long hair, when, if I were 10 years younger I might likely look like a so-called punk? I must admit I dont really care what I look like but that's not the point I'm making, question I'm asking (is it too silly? I do like to wear certain kinds of clothes like cotton & woolen ones, and I wouldnt want to get dressed in nylon stockings and high heels for any known reason so it is a kind of choice, based on past preoccupations, and also based on a fixation at a point in time). This is getting foggy.

Apropos publishing

I'm dying to do 3 books by myself: my new letters book (which as soon as I incorporate Peggy's proofreading corrections into manuscript, I'll send to you, promise, sorry, I dont seem to want to deal with it so I've been putting it off), and an old prose book which would include a series of short pieces (like a book of short stories), including Ferenczi, & We plow the roads & Problem solving dream & others, and a new book of poems. But I dont dare do three! It's taken Callahan more than two years to get Midwinter Day together (if it is) & when it is he's going to want me to be interviewed at B. Dalton's, and Annabel writes to say she's still "thinking" of doing a book by me. However I wont complain. Then there's also the Cave Book and the complete Studying Hunger . . . I wont go on. Hannah asked me today what she should ever think of doing with all her journals, then she yelled at me for ever being responsible for her writing so many much? journals. She's in the process of excerpting 60 pages for a book from 1,000 pages! Well like the nurse in the hospital who told me I couldnt nurse Marie without professional help, I told Hannah that people had been writing journals for millions of years, whether the functions of the words have changed or not (all this quick type), and it wasnt me.

The camera I got is an Olympus-M-1 and it's very good, it costs about $300. But if you can afford it, try and find yourself a Leica M-1 (which isnt being made anymore but you can still get them), or another kind of Leica, it's the best kind of camera but they cost new about $800 or a thousand. I would envy you severely if you had one. This reminds me of the old typewriter talk, there's much to say. I got a camera with a light meter that I can use when and if I want it, that is, turn it on and off. Dont get a camera that is so automatic you cannot turn off the light meter, as many are these days. Because then you cant make the kind of exposures you want, desire. Canons are o.k. Dont get Minoltas. Nikons are good but overpriced. The Olympus (just this particular one) is good as a cheap one & the Leicas as expensive ones, and that is all I know about that (after colluding with Ed for about a year before I got mine).

Your attempt to enjoy a beer (& now I've got one) is very funny, I cant tell you how many beers I've knocked over with my carriage (not a bad title?): every gray mysterious detail, yes! I envy your life because you can look so much; my life now is all psychology which is o.k. for a while but I crave the leisure to look. Watching Sophia learn to draw makes me see how a portrait of me, for instance, by her, tends to turn into steps and windows and all the things she's mastered so far, a few H's, lots of O's or snowballs, my hands coming out of where my ears might be, I look like a space person, I'm inspired by watching the progression of it, she's only recently learned to even make a face with mouth and eyes, now a whole portrait, with fingers, for a moment it looked like a Philip Guston work, then it got too busy, but the pleasure in my watching was seeing her proceed from one thing to the next, it seemed so right while I was watching it, though the portrait came out looking what you might call crazy, then she says to me, this is a portrait of you my mommy because I love her. So then there is also the emotional investment on top of or after or into or within the work which can be spoken too, and I thought (& this was before! I'd got your letter, or actually after I'd gotten it but before I'd been able to read it!) words as signs come after the impulse to move and be, just as I'd always known, now that's nothing new, but it was new at that moment, I thought you move, one moves, and out the top of the head or out the ears come the hands come the words, oh these children's pictures always have such big heads! If we were farmers do you think the children would see all our bodies as larger? [→Today at P. Project received a "proposal" from Alan Davies to do a lecture called "Abuttal" wherein he professes he will prove that language has no relation to reality nor does writing with experience (his words, natch)! Meanwhile Bob Rosenthal is mad at Lewis for smoking a cigarette in the Parish Hall + thus setting a bad example (this is a big thing).] So then so many words, so much stuff as you and I create, well that I think is our only (one & only) fault, sometimes. A fault of the times, just like what I was asking—is there something we do that is not quite accurate, that is a little bit off? And the only answer I can think of (but maybe you have another) is that indeed we do write too much & just like you told me Philip Guston said that great thing which I cant quote exactly about abstract expressionism being not something you would exactly be wanting to do, and admitting to that, so this proliferation, which seems so necessary to me (do you agree?) is all a function of the times I think, and of the culture of course too. It's not just that to get something good you have to produce so much more, but perhaps the drag of the whole history, so much stuff, so then to go back and review nonsense is cutting it all a bit shorter, isnt it? Kerouac started it, there's no doubt about it in my mind, the great word accumulations, you can say anything, big cold Creeley January fungi Shakespeare's Sonnets type of day it is. But time goes too slowly I feel so often for us to learn our lessons, thus my impatience with being one person, and even greater my impatience at being a woman which I've often thought (back to my conversation with Peggy) slowed me down alot because of the way I was brought up.

I'm out of beer, now truly Kerouacian, I've poured myself a glass of sweet wine Simon Pettet brought over as a gift, alas. It's also been cold in NY, cold for NY, but not so cold as up there, here it's 9 in the daytime, 0 at night, everybody's shocked but me & Lewis who are only grateful we dont have to drive around in alot of snow, and our union suits are in fine condition, and we have plenty of indoor heat, in fact too much, but Ted & Alice, and others have transient heating & many in the city dont get enough heat when it's this cold. I've got our heat half on, and everyone who visits considers it cool in here but I find it overwhelming & stuffy and am only deferring to the rest of my family. Ny though is very slippery lately, there's been some snow, and when I walk about with Max in the backpack I am constantly fearing falling due to my lack of balance with him, he's over 25 lbs in the pack and with another child on one hand I'm off balance. I do love though walking everywhere and stepping fearlessly in the slush of NY with all my country apparatus to keep me warm and dry.

I keep wanting to start a very serious studious series of discussions among poets in NY so that there will be a time, wet aside, I mean set aside, when all the petty grievances & mishegoss & boring social things wont be the subject of the conversation but that poetry will be. The only people who talk really about poetry to me, besides Lewis, are Alice and Jack Collom, and, if I can get him to shut up, Ted. And Peggy too. Others just make conversation which is o.k. but it misses much. I keep wanting to make people get together and discuss the subject of, say, "All I thought while I was writing my last poem, and all I did." However I doubt this will ever come to pass due to cynicism. Maybe in the summer I was thinking, when everybody is desperate?

I feel like we've been talking now for long enough that I should have been able to summon you up & we can join in conversation in person, however you arent here yet. And before you get here I'll have to to my bed to be sprightly for tomorrow morning's braving of the zero degrees with Marie and on to the Poetry Project for whatever it's worth, often I learn things.

THIN PLACES will be in the next issue if the staples will staple it, if not in the one after that. The first journal issue (of which there will be two) will most likely take place in April or May so that could be a deadline, and what is dead about it, you could think about (there'll be another issue in between). My collaboration with Alice looks awful on the page, we never have typed it out clean, but if you want and with Alice's permission I'll send you what we have, just **[copies of]** our original copies sort of. We all need some secretaries! Helpers!

Michael McClure was indeed boring but I think he was probably less boring than he's ever been, but he is so supercilious really where does he get off? He points with his fingers while he's reading a poem as if to show (audience) where each word is situated (well as I say that it doesnt sound so bad but suffice it to say I found it offensive), he is prideful, what is the word. But he and Jerome Rothenberg had, after each read, a sort of duel of the poems where they took turns kind of trying to top each other, rifling through various of their books and manuscripts and really making quite a scene of it, topping each other, but in a nice way, making tacit comments by their next choices of poems—oh is that a male thing? I found it quite inspiring to see, and McClure recited the beginning of the Canterbury Tales very wonderfully, though cattily, in the sense of the "effect." What a world it is.

I'm in the midst of MINE which is so fine, I cant believe it's not a part of the giant work, the chapter on the self. But I'll save the rest of my thoughts till I'm finished.

But wait, I cant save them all, what an amazing writing it is, all those thoughts, every time I read a sentence of it I get this feeling that it's an instinct of my own. What a pleasure, I read it slowly, I cant have favorite parts, I feel like I'm standing in my dreams at the town pump having the conversation with a fellow worker that I'm dreaming I'm having, and everything is perfect, if you'll forgive me bringing up perfection again. I say yes all the time. now Max is waking up, I'll continue tomorrow.
Well rather I think I'll send this off quickly. I've got a new plan to do a week's diary at Poetry Project (it's tomorrow + I cant remember if I already told you

this), + you know, if I do it, it will make Everybody mad (I'm having too much fun!). Today it was 7°. Enclosed is the picture I was telling about (forgive its being splattered a bit with sauce). Poor old life.

Mucho picchu (Elevated Love),
Bernadette

THURSDAY 22 JANUARY [1981]

Dear Bernadette,

Overcast morning, but not to snow, certain peach sectors. I'm always nervous beginning, hate to begin. May have something to with . . . do with that childhood influence of circumstance, parental or just facts of day, you questioned. Mysterious. I'll get back to that. Or that's the problem: that you can never precisely recover those influential moments? Anyway, I always have to wake up a few moments, maybe after I have in fact started somehow()!)(?) (can't type, again) (& will my old faulty typer hold up for a few more?), wake up and say, this is interesting, what I am now in the midst of having started. Speaking of morning and starts, I just wrote down in a work called RESEARCH (which is now threatening to stretch beyond that funny 20-page "limit"), the lines: "Everything has to be reinvented, including the morning/You could have, say, coffee, or two shots." You can tell I'm thinking about Godard, like mad lately. Looking through all the books on him I have here, filmscripts, etc. Mostly the stills. That Richard Roud paperback is one of the greatest PictureBooks ever invented, though the text is silly, stupid I now realize, and he's supposed to be one of the big Godard experts, ha! (Somebody once dubbed him "the High Priest of Godard") Celia's home (all week) with horrid flu, wandering around upstairs watching stupid daytime TV (but also doing something mysterious with her tape recorder), feverish and bored. Daily life, or as Godard would say: in other words, Eternity. Ever notice how he's always saying "in other words . . ."? Spent tuesday sprawled in front of RayGun Ignoruration TV, babies in RedCross hats lying in grass of Mall. All those California millionaires dropping their furcoats at their feet on the grandstand and just walking away, the day they began to own the world. I'm suspicious we're in for some bad to worser years. Or is that what poets always say? That night I watched long boring/interesting satellite shots of Algiers airport, all blurs of primary blue and red light, like in Godard's Anticipation, waiting for the hostages. Then I wrote down in notebook: If only the hostages were sexy. Or could someone find racist marines erotic? What do I know about politics, or more precisely, about the thoughts of those who practice politician? **[BM: *P + Phil*]** I imagine they are people who have no time to look, or as Godard said, "to take a look of it." Lost in the Universe of Discourse. And here the chickadees settle for cracked corn. Or actually mainly reject it in favor of what mysterious flecks in the snow? You're right, of course I want to say, that we write too much. That's how we find out who we are. Or, as Godard said when somebody asked him, If people are as nauseating as you say, why keep making pictures for them?, "It's my life. Stendhal used to say that the role of the animal is to sit in an attic and write novels." And then I'm haunted by Godard saying on Cavett: "to create you have to go out of your room." Next I'm back in my other primary mode of monk-in-cell, words pressed out of paper by pressure of extreme interiority (an "interiority complex"?). Otherwise you can go to the backlands of Whereeverland and walk a road. Dialectics. Which is what this mountain of info leads directly to?

The Coald-hearted (Cold) thing seems lost. It was something you toched(touched) on in NYC that I'd hoped you'd remember. We could sure all use lessons in seizing the moment of these things that might have been spun out interestingly, readings to eachother in Lenox long ago or whatever now gone forever. But, you're right about Karina. I was first going to disagree but by the time (short time!) it took to get to the end of that (your) sentence I agreed. Perfectly the outside surface of the other, which is a certain beauty (especially if from a male view?). I do appreciate such justice (Godard word from now on). Where one starts from. No razzmatazz of false overlay "emotion." And maybe forgetfulness does play a part: to say, with camera, say, What do I see? Your eyes, your mouth, etc. Your look. And his theory of syntax: to cut on a glance. Looking through all his old scripts etc. I kept realizing how all-of-a-piece it is, all there right at the beginning, full of amazing confluences (it'd be wonderful to see Breathless again right now for these reasons). And I found this exchange in A Woman Is A Woman, so interesting in light of the new movie: Alfred (Belmondo) & Angela (Karina) in a cafe, she's trying to experiment to find out if he really means it when he says he loves her.

Angela: What if it's not true?

Alfred: It is.

Angela: I don't know . . . Yes, I suppose I do . . . I don't know what's the matter. I'm always making mistakes. But one can't ever be sure. (She plays with her hair) Let's try . . . Tell me a lie.

Alfred (looking out of the window): It's raining!

Angela: Now, tell me the truth.

Alfred: It's sunny.

Angela: Ahh!

Alfred: What's the matter?

Angela: Your face doesn't change at all.

Alfred: So what?

Angela (pensively) Well, there ought to be a difference, because there's a difference between the truth and a lie!

Alfred (reaching for a cigar): I don't think it matters . . . You just have to be able to tell! (He lights the cigar)

Angela: Well, <u>you</u> know what you mean, but other people aren't obliged to believe you . . . And it's a pity . . . because it means that **[BM: →]** it's every man for himself.

(It's so cold down here my nose is starting to drip) Maybe it helps to see from that "mineral point of view" ? We have to get ourselves into funny positions! **[BM: ?]** Maybe what we mean is "coldblooded"? To proceed, no matter, and let the chips fall, etc.? Or were you actually thinking of Godard's view of women? Rivette once commented, Did you ever notice how he never uses a woman over 25? I think Marina Vlady must be over 25 (Two or Three Things), but this was before that. This is getting confusing, but in the proper way? Apropos, your "my mind edits so dramatically." But what does carry over into this "overreaching"? Some kind of Ghosts of Structure? I hate using that word "structure," but what would be more exact? And it should be more exact! I look at your face and I see . . .

This is getting to the edge of something good, but I haven't the battery this morning. **[BM: →]** And I do envy your discussion with Peggy re girlhood etc. How long have you know eachother? I have no touch anymore with anybody I was close to before highschool. Except my cousin, but he's five years younger and wasn't around much of the time. The trouble is the memory of all those growing-up things now fit so neatly into a schemata learned later. Takes the form usually of recalling how your parents wanted you to do something and you knew even then they were crazy so rejected it. Doesn't help in thinking of it all now. Can't think of it all now, the problem. [**BM: *self-port.***] I do have those strange moments of looking at my face and my father's face and seeing how I'm looking more like him. And there was this strange moment lately when my mother brought out a photo of my father, taken when he was seventeen standing with amazingly shining dark hair combed and with his violin in hand, I thought it looked amazing, almost dashing and a little cruel in ways I'd never thought of him being, and he turned and violently objected to it, hated the picture as if he couldn't stand such an image of himself now, and I asked why but he couldn't say at all why. My mother said later it was because he didn't like the way his ears stuck out too much (they didn't), but I'm sure it wasn't that. He just didn't recognize himself. But it was certainly violent.

I think we probably do lose the sense of surface (re your wondering why you have long hair), whether because of increased interiority or what, I don't know, probably? I often have the feeling that I have no idea what I look like, and haven't cared much about appearance/clothes in years anyway. I should start looking at myself in the mirror more, again. [**BM: *miss something? (punk)***] I do remember doing that a lot when a teenager. Do you think you could point at an exact time when this got fixed (as you say), [**BM: $ *one fling***] or you stopped carrying around instant images of yourself, or what? I remember having a Kerouac slouch-hat period, when the idea was sort of to not have the image of "everybody else," which was actually a fairly exact image in itself you tried to aspire to: beatup old clothes, which was probably chino pants with a striped shirt of too many washings, nondescript zipper jacket. [**BM: *black leotights***] I remember McClure once trying to describe a kind of "Beat Dandy" style, which was probably pre-hippie, just before the colors brightened again. I know, the clothes aren't important but I'm thinking maybe that's the point at which I got "fixed" and at least stopped thinking about inventing an exterior. I got interior-oriented pretty quick at that point I suppose. Clothes became these strange objects. Doors to all kinds of other worlds slamming shut. About "seeing things accurately": that's odd because it makes me think how the "things" are always changing, so? Or is that just what you mean, another example of <u>not</u> seeing things accurately? I guess I'd have to say that the most accurate delineation of things I can get to is in my work, the multiplicity of which always confuses people. We've had to develop a speed . . . **[BM: *if I just glance . . .*]** I'm stuck on the Fifties as this period where, either everything started coming in or I began to realize that this whole huge mess was there and what did one do with it, in it, starting to think as an artist. And it seems then immediately this glut/flux took a mighty Hegelian dialectical turn: the Yes,But scene. One seems the product of the other? Leading both to increased randomness procedures and intenser interior personal crazy bite of the thing. **[BM: *Charles pro-pers.*]** Pretty present tense, whatever. And I always had all these other things besides writing (room solitude) going, like walking around looking at pictures, watching movies (very present), playing jazz in bands (a lot of fighting with other exteriors), driving across country looking, the caves, the climbing, etcetcetc. (which is maybe why I clue into Godard so easily: he's got no barriers between poetry movies painting music, it's all being alive and making a difference) But there was that point at which I decided I knew it was writing I should be pointing at (it was when I split up with my first wife actually), and even Godard said at some equal point: I dropped everything else and specialized on movies.

I'm getting off . . .

And maybe this is a good example 'cause when I spin way off on one thing I get to a point where that thing gets so all-involving it's harder to make the connections(!?) Principles of Poetry, Chapter 127465432? Well, we really <u>should</u> talk about all these things, and at length, but if you really did it (re your idea for a discussion series) some pretty strange people would start to come out. Who writes this stuff is always interesting, even if it finally has nothing to do with secrets. **[BM: →]** It's good you're going to do all these readings now, 'cause maybe you'll find like me you enjoy it more, not having to worry about who you seem to be in terms of programs of writing or whatever. Bill (B) told me I'm starting to sit up straight (!) more now when I read. Which is probably about the only time I do! But I just thought with great fondness of that Paula Cooper Maintains reading where you wrote the while and people thought you rude(!) A truly bright memory.

To other and

more commercial matters: Is that Olympus you recommended The OM-<u>10</u>

(you typed OM-1) I've seen advertised recently in an unwatchably stupid Cheryl Tiegs spot on tv? **[BM: *whales*]** Or was there actually an OM-1 that's maybe not available anymore (been "superseded"?)? **[BM: *prose-poems*]** I had a dream the other night of coming out of a camera shop with an Olympus in hand realizing though I'd forgotten to find out if one could turn off the automatic light-meter. So maybe I actually am about to purchase one of these gizmos(?) Trouble is, I know I'd want to take endless pictures and the expense of developing? What kind of film is best? **[Page break]**

By the way, Stuck Pipe Dilemma is over, turned out we needed our septic tank drained (fairly quick simple procedure, which cost $75). You're supposed to do that at least every 5 years and it's been 10. Now if only that funny rattle in the rearend of our car would stop . . .

What is Problem Solving Dream? **[BM: →]** And has it been printed somewhere? I feel stupid, like I've got it around here somewhere but forgot where exactly. That's a wonderful idea for short prose (shirt pose?) book. There are lots of great things I'd love to see collected. **[BM: *NYSCA Levitt*]** Don't forget, Dear Reader, & Attempt To Write A Love Poem! Wishing I had made xeroxes of all your things as they appeared in magazines and put them together in a binder for reading access. And thinking on my stuff, most of it's so scattered (in magazines) it'll probably never be collected. I'm not really interested to at the moment anyway (so when?). Watching stack of new poems rise here on desk and dreaming of a big book of those!

Did you ever read Michel Foucault's books, find anything interesting in there? Dunno if I ever talked with you about that. I see he has recent sex books. Why hasn't anyone written a GREAT sex book?!?!? Ha. And thinking of Godard, it seems like all the great new French poets became movie makers (in Fifties). Reading Eluard's Capital of Pain and realizing how those poems are the script for Alphaville, all kinds of connections, not simply "quotes," etc. I wonder what it would cost to buy prints of his movies thesedays? Lots of them in 16mm I imagine. Probably there are people who own them and show them in their houses, like that weird MURIEL Society Larry told me about. But where and who are they??!? I keep imagining that Ed would own them and I can see us all going over to his house for great screenings and talk. **[BM: →]** Why hasn't this happened?

Yeha, (wha?) YEAH, maybe MINE is the Chapter (Longwork) on the Self. Great idea! I've been thinking of it very differently and separately, being "oof" the . . . (maybe I should leave all my mistakes as is?), er, off the longwork the past year or so. But I'm beginning to think maybe MINE goes there. **[BM: →]** I can't believe how "philosophical" I've gotten. If that's the word (?) At least I've gotten less scared of seeing "ideas" written out in works. A lot of potential for just that seems to have been built up over all the years of more wordy stuff. This RESEARCH thing I'm on, I don't know what it is, it certainly isn't a poem. Also I started writing a dialog too, which RESEARCH sort of is here and there. Is there even more strangeness ahead, I hadn't counted on?

Another reason I love Godard: he's another "failed novelist."

Your diary of a week's Poetry Project is a great idea. I wish I had better handwriting, especially at the speeds necessary for such projects. I intend to give such a go on Galapagos/Peru trip. Fullest documentation possible, inner and outer. Hope I don't end up with just an indecipherable scrawl running from plane to ship to land!

We love Sophia's portrait and put it right up on the livingroom wall. Makes me nostalgic for the period when Celia was just starting things like that. My first pictures were all fighterplanes and battleships spewing bloody crayon of the war (my mother saved them). My first drawing of a human was probably a Japanese pilot being blown to bits. No, actually it was a drawing of the Buddha in the RISD museum: looks like a big red spider.

Anne wrote and asked me to type up transcript of the Godard/Cavett shows, which I did. Hope you're not mad. I figure they'll be able to get it out quicker anyway, upcoming UAs sounding fully-packed already. Still, wish it had been you that asked!

Soon. Love,

Clark

FEBRUARY NO! MARCH 1 1981

Dear Clark,

Marching on, I'd better start at the beginning, where is it?

Sophia's got into the habit of lovingly screwing up my typewriter ribbon every morning when she sneaks out of her room! Other wonderful thing she does is sit on the radiator in front of the window wrapped head to toe in her precious blanket meditating on upcoming morning over city and schoolyard, then slowly Marie awakens and the two of them join to "watch the boys play hockey" or stand on their heads as is their wont at 7 a.m. in the great muralled? yard.

Anyway Happy Birthday! Dont know if you'll get this or your present first. I tried to call you that day but no luck, now I'm looking for another excuse to call, if only I could conscion a Poetry Project call! Perhaps I need some advice from you or something (this is what they used to call situational ethics in college (Catholic) theology class.

So now I've begun (it seems like last night I mean last time I answered too fast and this time too slow, I hope you didnt go to macchu picchu yet, aw I just wanted to say it again) & I'll follow your letter frommorning/beginning to politics, indeed it does "feel" different in America since you watched the IN-Agloomeration of the Reagent President (know what a reagent is? just another chemical I guess). One way the years will be worser is fer joints like the Poetry project et al., 50% off your already paltry honorarium, sirs. Seriously ahem I'd just made out all these ambitious budgets (& much work it was!) to try & pay poets $250 each (did I tell you this?) next year & was really beginning to believe the money could be raised & getting excited about how poets deserve it, etc. when, woke up one morning, read the Times, ugh. If the cuts go through there's no telling exactly what it'll mean specifically but what I didnt realize was the Pres. had the power to affect next year's money, that is, this coming October's. I thought we were assured one more year of largesses. Neverthelesses, I've a million notions about what to do about that & it's not the Poe.Proj. that'll suffer worst but smaller newer places & ones that are mostly involved with black people, believe it or not. The most irksome thing is that now I've gotta take up my time playing politician, or rather organizer, & go ahead and spearhead (ha!) a letter-writing campaign, well I guess I dont have to but it's sorta my job. Actually Ron has been doing alot of that work for me—he writes millions of letters to congressmen etc. all the time anyway & has already gotten me involved in politics before. Everybody wants to use Poeproj stationery, like to write the judge about Amiri Baraka, etc. Long stories. Well, if it's not too boring I'll just add to this rhetorical mess that govt. money is 5/7th of poetproject budget, so you can figure what all this might turn out to mean. It would be interesting to have to go back to one's own devices plus rich people, like in old days. Charge giant admission fees, make the readings seem practically exclusive—maybe more people would come? or, every reading a benefit, I dont know, dont ask me. But I have had to think and even talk quite alot about it. At reading at the New School, part of "conversations with writers" series, I had to give a veritable lecture on the subject, found it quite easy too, after consuming entire sixpack. But I'll tell you this, it's an odd feeling to be an erstwhile? politician (I meant a once-in-a-while). I even have to do a certain amount of what they call wheeling & dealing over the telephone. & now I've reassembled the Friends Committee, previously a group of rich and influential (?) people, now to include some genuinely friendly ones, for what purpose I'll never know, but I've got Peggy committed to make them all a dinner in the Parish Hall, which'll make it all alot of fun. What usually happens is they, the Friends, sit around trying to figure how to raise money for the poetry project & then, failing that, some make donations. Ah, what am I doing spending all this time telling you about my affairs? Here's more: last week I had to yell at the pseudo-hippie entrepreneur of a lousy pseudo-rock newspaper in New Jersey because he'd published a lie about the poetry project! Then the "journalist" involved called me up & said he was attracted to me ("so right out of the 60's" he said, "I'd look like that too if I didnt have this high-powered job"!) (it was Bob Rosenthal who got me involved in all this, Ted described Bob's behaviour as that of a shopkeeper obsessed with his store, and indeed he has become my nemesis, he is constantly saying things to me like: what is your policy on this?!).

"To take a look of it" is what I am most interested in, in my life and work. When I talk about seeing things accurately I guess what I'm saying is if I just glance & dont see "right" or just "gloss" an emotional set-up & dont have time to think about it or dont have a way to see all, or all at once, then what? It's just this obsession with the idea of everything which may do us in in the end, no? Speed, yes; in NY I seem to write too fast, if that's possible, in fact I've been seeming to be growing a new form, like a new limb? which is a faster than light prose poem which I think is a poem but the lines get so long & then while I'm writing it I forget completely about the lines and just end them when the page isnt wide enough anymore & go on to the next all the while remembering, or seeming to remember everything about poetry & still assuming I'm doing that but not doing it either in any defensible way (afterwards, if you know what I mean). Then I never re-type them but (to make them look "food" or "better," I meant "good"!) & when I read them they sound fine but they never look "good." Then the guy at the New School reading, who doesnt really know anything about poetry, referred to some of them as prose. I dont care, but all I can say is I get lost in them & they are very often about trying to visualize the city or be in it, and I realized I'm still getting used to it & whatever I have to do to do that, it's not the worst thing, I cant fathom I've only been here six months, I cannot not be involved or fused or mediumistic or whatever it is about my surroundings anymore, I think I used to be able to be, at least when I was awakening from some great adolescence in writing, but anyway, how did that start? Oh, your reference to the Universe of Discourse. Indeed! I still want to be another, I still am not settled with myself, is that permanent? What a funny set of words. Meanwhile, discoursably, there've been going on here these Poetry & Philosophy workshops which've been disappointing to me in many ways: partly I think I was expecting my two favorite subjects to yield some great new thoughts and illuminating abstruse ideas up, but the level of the discussions was pretty low and the philosopher, Edmund Leites, who, along with Charles Bernstein, did them, always kind of stuck to one point, as if it were new & never got beyond it, like he would spend a whole night saying that one-dimensional, or logical, philosophical language was no good & there were better ways of doing it. Also, he liked to stir up controversy, thinking it had a value in itself, so he'd make remarks about poetry, knowing there would be objections, like equating a poem of Eileen Myles with one of Mark Strand's, a cheap trick. Also he made sexist remarks, which I wont belabor you with. Anyway it was not heady to my mind. I did get a few ideas from the language that was used & that was the most fun. But I cant fathom why someone would discourse on a subject and not say the greatest, rather than the lowliest, things about it. Charles managed to say something interesting in defense of writing about or based on the person as a political gesture. Then I said well what is political about that, if it is simply what it is necessary that one does. Then, horribly, awful Bruce Andrews (& this whole thing had turned into rather a language gathering) said oh, every response to the environment is political. & then I said well if that's your answer I wont argue that. But it was interesting for Charles to defend so strongly the personal; he relates all his talk of styles of writing to political meanings, and I guess you probably know, I didnt really know that from not reading Language magazine. I was trying to think of that wonderful quote of Philip Guston's you wrote me in a letter a while ago about abstract expressionism, & that one does it & there was something kind of sad or anguished about it—can you remember it? Do I have it wrong? I was also thinking of what you said in your letter about randomness and "intenser interior personal crazy bite of the thing." I must tell you that after these workshops were over Edmund Leites came up to me and said he found my remarks during them to be anti-intellectual, while he put his arm around my waist & gave me a kiss, an embrace from which I politely extricated myself & shouted: "I am shocked! How could anyone consider me anti-intellectual!" I was told later that his sexist wont permits this kind of mishegoss. It was funny, even Ron expressed to me the feeling that these guys were trying to present very old ideas, ones he said he had had years ago, as if they had no history, were completely new. Charles said that is the way one must teach but I dont believe it, I think you rather over-rate your audience, and too with so many poets in the audience one could really get higher. I had to attend these things, as part of my job, and took the chance to say a few things I dont get to say in regular conversation with the poets around here, and I wound up being completely contradictory, I'd defend the "personal poem," then I'd defend "gibberish" without shame, coal-hearted as I am.

Surely it's cold-blooded what we do. I remember Vito (not that I'll defend him exactly!) communicating that to me when I was 15 years old, in the form of the work-first ethic, but the kind of "observation" we are always talking about, combined with the instinct to poetry is a nearly impossible self-toppling, and if you put with that too the ideas about experimentation & randomness, etc. plus the stuff about the necessarily personal, or even, the observation of the self, then you wind up having practically more than any human could what? Not to speak of all the books that need to be read! So let's stand on our heads again but keep our good humor, or not keep it, what the hell, it's every man for himself! No, not exactly, but in relation to the truth and a lie it is. I read so much "new" poetry these days I cant tell who is posing except I can but I dont want to admit that there is so much posing going on. I think keeping one's instincts intact could probably be written about in a kind of book like Adelle Davis's, you know, what are they called, Let's Eat Right to Keep Fit & Let's Have Healthy Children, etc. (David Rubinfine once told me Adelle Davis was a secret drinker & smoker).

[→ typewriter fucking up]

This is fun, I could go on forever, I forget what I was going to say. My thoughts about writing lately are in a complete upheaval and mess, sometimes I even succumb to thinking I'm too old to make the kind of changes I want in my own work! That's when I'm feeling exhausted. Now I've got a plan to write another prose book the only idea of which is that it will begin to tell a story by having the longest sentences I can feel free to put to paper (interruption: Lewis just came in to read me a poem he'd written about Israel & Palestine! quite an amazing pro-Palestinian work which he was worried about, having recently read all about it in various books, wondering if he could feel free to say these things, it's a great work about living in a backward country (this one) & while he was reading it I was realizing that the Reagan (like the Regent too!) ideas are actually feudal & maybe we'll all be dealing with some sort of slavery again! Lewis has been writing amazingly, he finished his novel, did I tell you, called AGES & SALLY (I mean AGNES)) . . . I was saying about this prose book, it would begin like Henry James, only I would steal a plot from somewhere, but no, now that I hear myself saying it I realize it wont work, though it might turn into something else, I wanted to steal a plot & make part of it take place in ancient Greece! Oh I'm still thinking about this poem of Lewis's. Where am I? Balmy NY, one day last week it was 69°, then we had all the rain everyone was hoping for, what an easy winter it has been, it's always 40 or even warmer, we never know what the children should wear. Did I tell you Marie has learned to read? The most amazing occurrence, it just happened, she just simply decided to read and now she does, I am almost tempted to say after five years of work! When I would tell people about it my eyes (I almost wrote my ears) would fill with tears, now she reads everything. She's also getting her first permanent teeth, only trouble is the old ones dont seem to want to come out? I dont know quite what to do but assume nature knows about it too. Sophia is a strange person—still the hedonist, I saw her the other day reclining with a bunch of grapes! still the mediator, now she is even both those things in relation to words and can spill forth such a stream of language about her whole life and memories and present experience and theories and all mixed in with associations and going on forever that only I and Lewis can even begin to interpret it, she often says the opposite of what she means, in a way, like she will say, oh I've never tasted beets, when what she means is I've never tasted them this minute! She is a great mystery and Max never makes noise! I'm convinced he is so confounded and amused by all the noise of his sisters that he doesnt need to & sometimes after playing with them for a long time, if he's very tired, he'll make new sounds for me, but otherwise all he says so far is ma'am-ma'am-ma'am, or mom-mom-mom & for the rest of the time grins wittingly & if you put him down on the floor before he feels he's got his fill of either food or love he puts his head down sadly to the carpet & then looks to see what you will do about it—not a dull-witted boy by any means!

I wanted to tell you this story, I cant remember why, it had something to do with talking about Peggy, oh you had asked how long I've known her, which is for 20 years! Or even longer at this point, we met when we were 13. The story is recently I started a new notebook and to decorate it I made a self-portrait of myself on the inside cover. I was most engrossed in doing it & it took me an entire night, Marie helped me color the hair which I decided to make all the colors (we were working with colored pencils with water). Marie kept looking at it & saying this picture and you look the same, and I kept saying well no they dont exactly. I've never been a good artist & whenever I make a self-portrait it is kind of fixated on some image of myself as a very young person, so I knew it was wrong but I was just having fun. Then I began writing in the journal & I began writing about the drawing which compelled me to try and represent myself in another drawing which would be more accurate. First I used the mirror, then I used a photograph, then I tried to make one without looking, just drawing from a thought of what I looked like that could be communicated to the pen without using my eyes. Well I wound up with quite an amazing group of pictures & a short verse on images. The next day I showed Lewis the original one of me & he said, you dont look like that & I got mad! So I just wanted to tell you that story, I think in relation to your father's photograph. What I do look like these days, more and more, is a picture of my father which was his union photograph, on his union card, where he is grinning, kind of wrinkled against the sun or the flash, and looking, to my mind at the time I first saw it, rather older than he did. In NY It's impossible not to think more about your "appearance" whether it makes any difference or not, as in my case it doesnt because I wouldnt even have time to deal with it if I wanted to (thus I'm still "out of the 60's," which I resent, it's just that my clothes are so old, and I keep wondering if I'm not missing something, like bedecking oneself on occasion?). What happened to me about clothing (this is a great discussion we're having) is that I was put through all the normal bullshit of being a girl, wearing matching hats, shoes & pocketbooks & gloves, etc. & being concerned with fabrics of all kinds (my mother sewed alot & taught me to sew too), and it's a memory my sister, in her work, has never quite recovered from—& then when I became independent of my parents I didnt pay attention to my clothes much except to wear black leotards (after Leotard, French aerial performer) alot, until, when I was living with Ed at some point we came into alot of money and I dallied with buying things at Henri Bendel's etc. to see what that was like, which was fun but alot of work, I remember I always felt like a different person when I had new & carefully sought out clothes, and then I just dropped it & have been wearing old clothes or gifts of clothes ever since, Anne used to give me alot of her old clothes, and since she devoted so much attention to them, many of them have lasted me to this day. Now Peggy is concerned with clothes & gets me things from time to time, in fact today Ted said to me: where did you get that dyke jacket & I said from Peggy, which gave him the chance to say oh of course that makes sense, etc. [→ Ray also always gives me the shirt off her back.] I must admit I wouldnt mind having a tailor though because I still know exactly what kind of clothes I'd like to have, made for me! Perhaps in my old age I'll take up sewing again?

I had a good time at the New School reading just reading a mixture of old and new poems, which I've never done before, and I found myself amazed that I noticed that the old poems still leave the audience in the lurch, they dont respond to them, I felt like I was losing them, somehow spoiled by my previous, always, efforts at reading so tensely only what is totally new. I liked what I did though and especially enjoyed (what

Lewis thought was perverse) reading this poem called untitled which is in POETRY which is a long series of dictionary definitions for a small paragraph of ultimately meaningless words, because all of a sudden I could read it well?! Then I proceeded to be totally depressed about the reading afterwards which was simply my pay I guess. But, though I still get stage-fright and always will, I now thoroughly enjoy reading. (It's only that it causes me, perhaps, to get drunk afterwards!). Bill B. said, which I may have quoted you before, that after listening to all the tapes for the record, he surmised that it took us all 15 years to learn how to read our poetry. I dont agree, but in a way I do I guess. Some part of me still hates the spotlight so I keep thinking I havent learned yet.

Now here I go into more practical matters: it is, yes, the OM-1, not the OM-10 that I was recommending; I'd guess, though I dont know for sure, that the OM-10 has alot more fancy and unrecommendable appurtenances or switches than you'd want. If the OM-1 isnt available now, let me know and I'll check with Ed about what you should do. These days the cheapest film, in a way, is the fancy new 400ASA color print film, because the cost of slide film is so great in the developing that unless you really need slides (& you probably want prints, at least eventually) it's not worth it (it's all because of the cost of silver, & other forms of democratization). To shoot a 36-picture roll of color print film it costs about $15 in all, for both film & developing, which is not so bad if every print is usable (& for what purpose?). Recently I shot a whole roll of penguins at the Coney Island Aquarium, which is just about the best place in NYC to take children—I shot it to find a cover for MIDWINTER DAY in case Eliot Porter is not forthcoming, and I was amazed that I managed to be able to make the sunlight, by sheer force of will, look like snow on the film, since I wanted snow & there wasnt any! Though I'm going to have to go back again & do it over for other reasons, but meanwhile I get to see the whales there & I can write about them while drinking beers outdoors on this terrace from which you can see both the whales and the real ocean. Enclosed is a picture of Marie & Sophia with a beluga whale behind them! And, the face of Grace in the whale! (I've known Grace as long as Peggy).

Problem solving Dream is an old work (from about 1974?) that was supposed, ever, to be published in some issue of the Coldspring Journal which never came out, so I dont know if you ever saw it. Turns out my idea for short prose book isnt going to happen because Lewis & I were planning to "fund" that book from the New York State Council on the arts which says somewhere that they wont fund presses who mainly publish the editors' work! So we decided to list some other books as possibilities & I dont know what will happen—I had to secede! I need a publisher! That book which includes all the pieces you reminded me of, would be a good one I think. Also, Annabel told me she was asking the same NYstate council for money to do a book by me! which she of course will never get around to, but that made Lewis think not to mention me! Because the poetry project too, in my name, is also asking them for money! Too many erstwhile Bernadette's, & none of them the real one!

So this is adult life eh? I love MINE and read it as is my wont (I think I have to stop using that word), slowly every night along with Hawthorne, Scott & Amundsen. It is inspiring & full of great ideas I hope you wont mind me saying, it is indeed philosophical in the best sense, in fact, if you and I play our cards right, we might be considered downright philosophers if the western world gets to continue in anyway properly, especially you. Hearing the philosophers speak makes me see that that pretension is changing its field, I dont know how to say that, it's the subject of another whole thing for which I and you have to be patient I guess, but the kind of "knowledge" in MINE is what? I'll let you know when I know. Now I'll to my bed of swimming which is

)oh dear over) **[Page break]**

what I do each night I think, lying on my stomach in some posture which makes me feel like a frog, and then I can think some more. I'd give anything at this point for limitless time to think, please let me know what you think.

I think of you & Celia & Susan all the time,
*with love,**
Bernadette

*couldnt we collude in the summer somehow?

FRIDAY 6 MARCH **[1981]**

Dear Bernadette,

Time gone by and so many things to respond to I'm afraid I won't be able and will forget half of the most important. But it's somehow a relief to realize it's impossible to get everything discussed in conversation as well! Your DESIRES (I love being able to refer to it as simply that!) is so wonderful and endlessly thoughtful and I want to say spine-tingling that I was sorry to have to read it initially in rush of everything else in preparation to leave here. Too fast, but I couldn't resist, and anyway I got a taste of the whole form of it that way it leaves so very much to savor at leisure later. I want to say something like, it's a momentum of pure thought in a midst, which is a sort of abstract way of stating a high desire I have for my own future work. It so inspired me that I immediately started writing another prose book without any planning or thinking about what it would be and now I've got 15 pages that look like Wittgenstein all in short paragraphs! I'd thought I wanted long ones! Anyway, to give you some immediate response I wrote the enclosed NOTES in midst of reading your midst(!), I'd leap up and write a paragraph after finishing one of your sections, so hopefully it's hot off the focus but it looks so incomplete to me now, you give so much to write from! (god, all these exclamations) Your work gives me a great hungry push toward trying to say all those things I think I "can't say" because what you write has so much of that momentum toward the unsaid. I recall I used to resist that maybe because I wanted the language to do something else (what? now I've forgotten!) or because I just felt stupid "commenting" on what I was afraid "everyone else probably knew." So, you give me confidence, and even more you point so unerringly toward the mystery. And I realize we really don't know what the words can do, so many so-called limits have proven broachable (I think I mean breechable) along the way so far. My thoughts about writing are also in that upheaval mess you describe, which maybe just means that so many things are in motion (as they should be? what about the desire for stillness?). Or that to the poet the word Theory is never singular (what Ted means by his "all my theories"?). Vision of great interlocking chains or bands, a congeries of crystal charms and lapping voices. Your discussion of forgetting about the lines and their possible and disconcerting ends is great, my feelings too. I've grown increasingly impatient with all that tricky bric-a-brac of line-stops and recall after years of fooling around trying to understand all that "measure" business of Williams/Creeley et al. the great relief and joy of finding how Kerouac wrote in his pocket notebooks. I think the really fascinating play of all that goes on within the sentence anyway, no? I feel like when I've got it all working with all possible whirling potential at any moment that play is going on to greater effect without distracting pointing or underlining. Line-breaks sometimes look like somebody pointing to a sign that says SHOES. Also it can be a matter of confusion that stops you: too many options. You could spend forever shunting the train in the yards when what you need is to put it on a track and go. Or it can be like the barber taking too much off the one side and then the other etc. Or (god, this can be endless!) that Fee Dawson story about his lining up his cigarette pak and matches with the edge of the bar and Pollock walking in and smashing them flat with his fist and saying WRONG! Anyway, maybe I'm just becoming a Master of Forgettal!, but somedays I stare at what I just wrote with a kind of awe and fascination, intention having become a mere trigger. Has anybody ever written about the myriad of sorts of spaces that occur within writing, between its particles? And then the other day I got hung up meditating on that entre/entree/entrar word(French/Spanish), how it's simultaneously a door and pure empty space. Shit, you're right, this Everything will be the end of us! And, speaking of line-breaks, the only way out of this paragraph is to just stop it.

The word "political" is confusing to me in so many of its present uses since I always think of its first meaning concerning those who actually govern. and I feel more and more distant from them. Plus I suppose I share the artist's classic anarchic indifference to all that, anarchically disinterested might be a better way of putting it. And now the word seems to have wishy-washed out into whatever happens between persons, maybe among poets that issues from Olson's "polis is eyes" business at least with those who need to speek with such intellectual back-up. I've never had a clear view of how "political" is used by the Language gang, at least among the more interesting ones like Charles who doesn't seem tainted by the stupid neo-Marxism of such as Sillyman. I suppose they're intrigued by some vision of poetry having use in some wider field of "big doings" but that seems naively youthful to me and later just seems to blah out. I mean we all get indignant and fume and piss at politician's assininity and probably bore our friends in person with it and it does affect our writing I want to say like many other goads do but to then say after such transformations that the writing is "political" in some major way seems to devalue it hideously somehow, or it's just naive to think said writing can affect the price of life etc. Actually Alice said it best: "Politics is the misuse of words in order to get power," that's my feeling too and my outrage. And then I love it when she goes on to say: "The only real politics I have is write my poems and destroy anyone who tries to keep me from it." Who among us could argue in the heat of that?

I get a big cartoony view of government affairs as big rough shapes that go bump in the daytime, our instinct says to avoid. It's hard for me to take seriously somebody who looks like a big aged HowdyDoody (Reagan), I keep looking for the strings. Of course what's so seriously horrid about him is that his instincts and his language are so tenuously connected. One thinks of dinosaur brains. But I have trouble keeping any of these public personages in foreground of mind since, for instance, when somebody says Al Haig I immediately think of a musician of the same name who used to play piano with Charlie Parker. I think it's most truly a matter of just who the persons are who inhabit the plane of your imagination your dreams. They are just there and you have to deal with them but you can hardly decide that those precise ones shouldn't be or that other ones should take their place. Guston met Nixon in his dreams and so some sort of "Nixon" entered his paintings and this worried and troubled (and amused) him. Of course there is the sense of relief when there is finally no choice. And Philip's Nixon promptly sailed off for Chinese adventures on an ancient piece of toilet piping.

Policy (Rosenthal, Bernstein, et al.) seems an odd monaural gig for a poet to be concerned in since the writing instinct causes one to deal so continually with so many conflicting elements that sudden changes of mind if not utter indecision must be the dailylife result. I keep seeing Ted here as the reminder of one who seems bound to delight in displaying the moves of a poet when away from his poems, though Ted would say that a poet is never completely away from his poems and I wouldn't argue. And no doubt the display is more delight than the moves always are. But I'm think for example of his all-purpose "yes" as another way of saying "no" or "later." And then for some reason I think of Flaubert at the funeral of his sister (or father, they died so close together) telling the assembled relatives that his mother should only die as well, and when they expressed shock saying "yes, if she wanted to jump out the window I'd be the first to open it for her." Or Gregory at Kerouac's funeral wanting to grab Jack's body out of the coffin and throw it on the floor, but a conflicting instinct prevented him at the last second. What's with all these funerals!? Oh, by the way, that Guston quote you wanted is: "I do not see why the loss of faith in the known image and symbol in our time should be celebrated as a freedom. It is a loss from which we suffer, and this pathos motivates modern painting and poetry at its heart." (printed in catalog for a show he was in at the Whitney in 1958)

Disinterested is perhaps the word to bring in here on our coldhearted discussion, at least in the way the French use it: sans personal bias. And it generously includes the word "disinter," bring into the light, reminding me of your moth (in DESIRES) that is like poetry that brings in "something else," or more precisely something in the poetry brings something unforeseen into itself to generate further, etc. Sometimes I confess to feeling disembodied, staring in disbelief at a tendril of my own passion. Or at whatever portion of the world, persons, thought. Sometimes I think I'm just(!) arriving at the realization of feelings all the great old artists knew so well. I'm reading Flaubert's letters now, which are full of precisely these things. He was epileptic, locked himself up and wrote hard, had immense doubts and countervailing highs, was another guy who lived most of his life with his mother, surrounded by jerks who pestered him about "making it," felt the creation of pure Beauty as in ancient Greece was no longer possible, that he lived in a period of "transition," and when the electric telegraph was invented envisioned governments falling in attempts to keep up with the New, meanwhile he was inventing a "new prose"—it all sounds like yesterday today and tomorrow! He says things like: "For my part, until someone comes along and separates for me the form and the substance of a given sentence, I shall continue to maintain that that distinction is meaningless." I remember Guston exclaiming to me: "There is no form and content!" Reminds me too of your "Stop and think is an impossibility." And, re disembodied/disinterested, your saying in STUDYING HUNGER JOURNALS: "There's something about concentration that makes it impossible to be you." Shit, is anybody else ever going to read and think on these things!? I mean, how seldom has anybody ever said to me (preferably somebody out of the blue) "There's something in one of your writings that I've been thinking about" and then gone on to develop it further on their own so it becomes something interesting to me. That's the only kind of "audience out there" that makes any sense to me. The trouble with these times seems to be that anything one might do is taken up and dropped so quickly that hardly a thoughtful word gets to reach you. It's almost as if this century of art has been a boiler factory that exploded in the midst of a city without a piece of it hitting anybody. Or a whispering gallery where the secrets all fell on the wrong ears. Shit, this is going to get despondent and silly in one big shout.

I realized the other day in trying to "plan" my mind for this South American jaunt that my consciousness has become so present-tense momentary (and I've worked for years to make it this way) that anything as out of the ordinary and geographically displacing as this trip is has no reality for me. Until I'm actually there and in it. Somebody is going to come next week and take me away and plunk me down in a totally strange place, it feels like that. Some days the very next room could be the far side of the moon. Okay, I'll be a visitor in all (and hopefully the best) senses. And I'll really try to take a look of it, right. And one can hope that such dislocation will drop some of the barriers between waking and dream life. Flaubert said that before he went to Egypt (they called "the Orient" in those days) he had imagined the landscapes so fully that when he actually stood there it was the people that totally fascinated him. The other day I wrote: "Soon we will be in Peru, site of the lamps." And what will I find about that?

By the way, page nine of DESIRES got xeroxed so askew that half the words are missing off the side of the paper! Please send another when you get time, it drives me crazy to miss a single word. God, I wish I could sit down and tell you precisely what every single word of that work makes me think of! Your voice of address seems to desire that response and makes it all the more a desire of my own to do that. Why isn't there more time in our lives for exchanges so needful? My enclosed NOTES seem such a piddling excuse for what my mind wants to do. And I want to tell you, Consider everything I write from now on as some kind of response to that book.

On giving readings: I have the impulse to disagree strongly with Bill B. that it took "us" 15 years to learn to do it, since my memories of my very first reading tell me it was great, exhilarating, audience up throughout. That was Ted's series at the Folklore Center, summer of 1966, were you there? I remember seeing you at one of the readings in that series, Ed Sanders'? Ancient history of flickering images, I should remember better. I think those of us who are any good at it were that pretty much from the first outing, except for a few tricks of pacing, talking or not inbetween poems, just which poems sounded best aloud, picked up quite quickly in the act. Though there may have been some change since I've been reading recent shorter poems, as Bill remarked on Long Island this summer that I seem to be sitting up straighter(!) and gesticulating high in air with pointed finger (I'm not sure I like how that sounds!). I tend to chalk that up to surprised enjoyment in reading those particular works. Actually though I must confess that I've always been disappointed in my inability to make the works sound the way they do in my head. There's probably a real and even interesting reason for this though having to do with the unreproducible properties of sub-vocal speech so the best one can do is make a reasonable approximation aloud. This is the kind of subject I always wish neuro-physiologists (if not all those boring linguists!) would write interestingly about, but I fear I'll be long gone before they ever do.

That photograph of Sophia Marie & the whale (& Grace & you behind the Olympus!) is gorgeous! Amazingly clear color. Is that the 400ASA? Marie has a serious Lewis expression, Sophia pure Bernadette joy and attention. And the whale seems included in a block of aquamarine (beryl). I put it up above my desk next to a Saint Jerome by Joos van Cleve the Elder I wrote a poem about. Also next to that lovely portrait of Susan in dim bronze light you took in Lenox a couple years ago, my favorite picture of her and even she doesn't mind it too much(!) Thanks for the info on the Olympus OM-1. Right, the OM-10 is totally automatic I think. There's now something called an OM-1N, god knows what that is, probably more uselessly fancy than yours(?) Anyway this is all for naught as it turns out since no Olympus is available around here, at least quick enough for my purposes of imminent trip. So I got a Nikon FE, which seems comparable to the OM-1 in operation though it's more expensive. Typical with me I procrastinated till I had to grab the best available within reach. The FE automatic mode is what they call "aperture priority" and can shut off totally to give you manual control of all functions so I guess it'll do me. Thing is now I've got only a couple days to master the controls! I've been studying a big Nikon book which tells all sorts of needlessly-complicated-sounding matters like "exposure compensation for back-lit objects," depth of field, etc. which'll hopefully make practical sense once I have the machine in hand (I pick it up on tuesday). I thought slide film was always cheaper than print film, has that radically changed recently due to increased price of silver or something? Shit, I was looking forward to presiding over endless after-dinner slide productions! Guess I waited a bit too long.

I love what you say re philosophy and MINE. Really the best compliment since I've been secretly sliding in that direction for years. I always loved it when you told me about philosophical writings since you always made it sound wonderful in conversation but when I looked at those guys' works themselves they always disappointed me (excepting Wittgenstein) since the words they used seemed dull and I just couldn't read on. Maybe there's an interesting "problem" there we could discuss? I want to go on with this but find I have too much busy stuff to get done before we take off for the tropic attitudes. More soon, I'll steal you a piece of Machu Picchu!

All Love,
Clark

[→ P.S.—The NOODLE arrived, a perfect present! But I fear the party favor fared ill: shattered white plastic fell on the rug. What was it?]

APRIL 17 1981 WHY IT'S PRACTICALLY
EVE OF EASTER!

Dear Clark,

It's also eve of Passover & how do you like this "orchid" paper? When Michael Palmer was here someone whom he described as taking a veritable Ph.D. course in flower arranging brought him some parrot tulips at his reading & he very generously gave them to me & they are the most amazing flower, a kind of filigreed tulip, most complex, which I have before me right now.

I cant wait to hear all about Machu Peek=chu! Many thanks for your card which was hilarious & will I think stay in my mind forever. The picture on the card was all the more amazing because though I've seen photographs of the place before, just as dramatic, I never tried to imagine you and Susan & Celia there before! with all those views of the mountains in clouds (& smoking Winstons the entire while!), Well, what do you have to say about it all?

It seems nearly importunate to write back as to a normal letter, your having been so much elsewhere but I have to say how much I loved your notes on my DESIRES and I treasure your notes as a way of knowing what my DESIRES! are! I read from them (this is carrying things too far) at a reading with Ted Greenwald in a kind of erstwhile theater on 18th St. & 5th Avenue to an audience of 10 or so, and, having chosen to read the last sections closest to giving birth, I realized that no one in the audience had ever had a child but happily it didn't seem to matter except that no one laughed at the funny parts thus forcing me to read in a most intense & tense way.

It's so wonderful to me to have your comments on the book because, in new york, I'm still subject to criticism about my work, and frankly I dont need it. It's like when people say, oh well that person needs guidance, or that writer needs an editor (like James Mellow or Roland Huntford—but not me I hope!). But I also see that what goes on in the city is dependent on everyone's moods and You I mean one can't take any of it seriously at any one moment, it's just that I'm not used to it, and I'm not used to giving a reading where nobody shows up to hear, this, my new work.

Bill B. asked me in a question recently (we are involved in interviewing each other through the mails) is there any such thing as a new sentence? Ass a new sentence. Oh well, so much for that. I think I said no. Except there is.

I just wrote a work—I got disgruntled by giving readings and feeling fixed to my so-called style once again—and I stopped writing for as long as I could bear it—and then all of a sudden I began writing this work addressed to Admiral Scott about the space shuttle and I wound up writing it in lines of 28 characters each so the poem would be a perfect typed rectangle, also in rhyming quatrains, and then in the search for each line to be the right length I wound up writing each one over and over and I left all that in and now it's a very funny work where one (orchid?) tries to find the exact line ending to make the whole thing look and sound like a poem, like perfection in those space crafts, I dont know what I'll do with it but I wonder if anybody'll notice it's funny.

Whenever I cut the hair

of people in my family I shout out in anger: I really wish I didnt have to cut everbody's hair in this family because I'm not very good at it & then when it's cut and people say who did it you'll say it was me! Meanwhile who wants to go to the barber or beauty salon? Thus, our lines. As you say.

The Language gang—not to get so far afield so startlingly from barbershops—seems to think political means how you use words—that is, um, do you use them in a politically freeing way or a restricting one (this weird information I got from the Poetry & Philosophy workshops & it's got nothing to do with "politicians" either, as far as I can see but it does have something to do with Harvard & Yale because you cant understand the terminology unless you went there, or else you bothered to read all those boring philosophers). It's funny when you quote Alice saying: "The only real politics I have is write my poems & destroy anyone who tries to keep me from it" because I found when I read those words of hers that I was shocked by them because to destroy anyone (& then I thought one's children & husband, say) is not what I'd do, in fact I'd be much more likely to destroy myself in the attempt, but the atmosphere of destruction itself seems to be beginning to be shocking in there and it was the one line in that piece of Alice's that astonished me in that way. I'm not arguing about the heat of that, as you say, but that anybody, poet, could say, "destroy anyone." I've been thinking about it ever since

Ted called to attempt to say just about everything he could manage to say to me about everything which took along time.

Now the Nigerian man who accosted Lewis on the street today and tried to give him his $2500 so nobody else (who was not honest) would steal it from him, as opposed to Lewis whom this guy kept saying looked like his "boss"—& maybe the guy was crazy & maybe he was forthright when he said that a porter at the airport had induced him to pay him (the porter) $25 to let him hold the key to a locker wherein the Nigerian man put half his money & his passport & all his belongings—this is what happens when you go uptown to see a few shows (& look like the boss).

Meanwhile, speaking of al haig in the palm or plane or plain of your dreams I'm reminded of a dream I had last night of bob holman where it turned out his penis was a calculator, of a very fancy sort, which he had bought recently, for about $40, which played tunes from memory, like if you set it for your birthday or wedding anniversary, it would then play the appropriate meoldy melody. Meanwhile too I dreamt that United Artists was having a benefit reading by punk groups, then when I awoke I told Lewis & he said, what a good idea! And too I naively dream all the time now I am driving? the space shuttle (I never dreamt about Reagan's shooting).

Disinterested as I am I would love to disinter all those bodies I know about, to remind me that even though I havent read everything in the world—so therefore I dont know nothing—I still can feel free to be prolific now, in a very "dispirited" time! Ah how awful I feel at this point in time, I cant tell you, I feel I cant write, I dont know what to do about what I write (nothing new), I feel that all of life and writing takes so long that I'll never be able to learn about it (I'm both too young & too old), I feel positively orchid, I feel I'm all wrong about everything, I feel I ought not to even say it, and when you say "It's almost as if this century of art has been a boiler factory that exploded in the midst of a city without a piece of it hitting anybody. Or a whispering gallery where the secrets all fell on the wrong ears. Shit, this is going to get despondent . . ." then I feel well at least one other human knows how I feel & that there is no future, as you say about going on a trip, and I think all the time about how I've trained myself, so non-cynically (that's a word Ted was arguing with me about tonight) about all life and now i can exist in the present but at poetry project i constantly exist about two months into the future, or else twelve years, and then, observing children, one is catapulted into the slowest time (e.g., four years from now, Max wont pull things down from the tables in Rosemary's loft), meanwhile I wonder about love's devotion, and in the midst of a spring among the poets, all of whom are most affected by it, as I'd forgotten human beings could be—why it's as if the flowers and newest buds were behaving emotionally the way they look they are!—,—it's impossible not to want some perfection (of the works from what one has learned, of the person from a love of other human beings (if that doesnt sound too silly, but it is perspicaciously said), of the environment, just from old-hat ideas, the normal ones . . .

Oh lord what am I saying? I'm going mad, yet of course I'm not, but I've never felt so driven to find out about something as I do now. Well was Peru the sight of the lamps, or not?

I so wish to know everything & not to be laughed at, then I see how little I'll get to know, I'm to be 36 on May 12th, & I havent yet read . . . . I'm not upset about my age so much as I am wondering about whether I'm in the right place at the rfight time (right time, not fight or fright time!). There is indeed something frenetic, hysterical and quite parrot-tulip about being here right now. I'm still terrified (about our talk about early readings) at the mesmerizing demands other poets place on one, as if one could really stand up and be perfect—say everything that needs to be said, read it beautifully & change the world (I got in trouble with Laura Riding about this—she wrote to her publisher saying that what Lorna Smedman said about my ideas about changing the world were not her ideas; however I was flattered that she mentioned me by name: "I've never heard of this Bernadette Mayer who talks of changing the world & I dont agree with her" (I'm quoting her loosely)).

It's funny, ever since I heard that description of you reading, gesticulating I've been wanting to be able to point my finger too! And when I saw you read at Philip Guston's night, I wanted to be you. Still there's the problem of making the works sound like the writer hears them, but I think you were able to do that, and I've been trying to plan to do that but you cant plan to do that, what with all these parrot tulips on one's desk, etc.

What a life, I constantly say to others; Ted says, oh god what a hard life it is (so you see we don't exactly agree).—And now, is that the difference?

I'm jealous you have a Nikon, because though it is bulky, it's much better than all the others & I'm sure you have millions of amazing pictures of not only macho peekchoo but also selves & other illuminating subjects & objects (the only reason slide film is more expensive now or comparably expensive is, yes, due to the price of the silver, so you can have prints for about two dollars more per 36 than slides, which is alot less than it used to be, not counting the cost of prints from slides. So everyone is catering then ground-hog-like to the idea of instancy.

I really feel I must impress upon you that you ought to come "down" to the "city" more often—after all there's no reason not too! And then we oh we could have some talks, after all Lewis & I went nostalgically to see Breathless the other night & found we had it memorized, and you know Louis Malle has a new movie

I dont get to have many great conversations here, mainly because we either husband out time or people dont want to converse greatly, except for Ted who of course will converse greatly but then he always leaves me out of it. Many people in ny are so involved in their own lack of tulips that you cannot have a decent conversation about poetry, or else there doesnt seem to be the time.

Now the "boys" (as Sooh-phia and Maa-rie call them) are bouncing the basketball audibly and some are playing the disco radio, and I wonder what spring's libidinous attitudes (I just translated three of the "dirtiest" epigrams of the Greek Anthology (not the best ones!) with Rosemary for an edition of THE WORLD) will bring me, surely a more consequent love of Lewis, among all the problems of that (he waxed mad when I came late to the New School to introduce him even though I do believe myself to be a sanity-saint in terms of obligations! then again Lewis is getting to be feeling a great need of being relieved of all the duties of parenthood so that he, as I feel too, can be free to walk out unburdened into the spring city to see small shows, meanwhile I get appalled when I see that Ted keeps Lewis supplied with speed & I dont know when he's taking it & it makes me mad & it makes me mad that time has to go so fast &, with the children, so slow, & there's no way I can complete the parentheses or the sentence, oh well this must be the newsentence then! I dont love new york and often wish I were out of it, I am not complicated enough to be able to do the politics that are within it, to be able to know what to say to this or that person, even Larry who is always playing games, I dont know how to or like having to think and know about all that, I dont know what I'm supposed to do next—everybody seems to know and have some opinion about it but I'm sure that they dont dont know much more than I do! (whether you might express it as a double negative or not) (or whether you might know any of the Greek forms or not), it's a mis-shaped miasma for everybody and now I know a whole lot of things I dont particularly want to know.

I'd like to take a course on all the trees and flowers and shrubberies, I'd like to know all that—it turns out I know a bit more about that than some others do, and there are starlings in ny this years, baby ones, but everybody in ny seems to want to know something that everybody else doesnt and after all the time still does go so slow—I'd rather be in some place where the seasons acknowledge that & where I didnt have to worry about the self I've been trying not to notice so much.

Michael Lally said in some interview recently that he wanted to be a saint (in "Little Ceasar" magazine) & I thought to myself, well that's true, one does want to be that. There is a whole lot of organizing among the poets against being a saint, because it's just as good to be a sinner (drug-addict, not so much adulterer any more) (CYNIC!) so my stance, if you'll forgive me for mentioning it (politically?) is that I teach by example and now no other way (cause I dont teach)

Poor old thoughts just get jammed together like this **[Page break]**

Another piece of orchid paper makes me want to say quite honestly (as maybe you're not supposed to say) that the fuck=up of new york for me is that I dont always want to feel overwhelmed or frenetic about every thing & person, I want to have time to think about it for myself and though I'm learning to do alot of things I dont know how to do, and then I get to see especially psychological messes I would never otherwise know about, still I want to be alone, to be waiting to see what happens without that because I believe that what happens without that, in any given time, is the same thing as what HAPPENS WITH IT (am I going out of my mind? I think I might be ribght I mean right)

Max walks now, Sophia talks a blue streak, Marie is practically a grown-up, Lewis and I are alternately loving what each of us see, mad at the work, oh and forbidding each other from complaining at it, and wondering how it could be that these good-looking and healthy children could come from such parents who feel so ancient, so derived from their own parents (I think this is the trouble with being a poet who has children—you're not supposed to come from anything or anywhere! Is that true?) . . .

Remember when Beethoven said his parents must be the royalty? Recently Bob Holman's girlfriend, who's a woman I had gotten to know and like very much, very completely freaked out in a psychotic way & that all made me remember our dedication (I'm not saying this to scare you) to our work, and how completely headlong & ultimately non-neurotic etc. it is. We work, I assume, despite the fact that I am writing way past my bedtime, because our task is simply & normally this and it doesnt matter about little daily interferences (& I'm not saying those dont enter in), but, if you'll forgive me, we are called to our task and we just do it, I hope. And if we have to trance ourselves beyond death, then of course we will and I'd hope by that time we'd have learned from others how to have some sense of it.

Oh sorry to be so dour, alas I'm wondring If anybody knows nothng, like me, silly exigency & I'm at sea, but at least I have the time to be. As you say. NY spring—well it's just people as far as I can see and I go to bed wondering about each of them

& it's true it's too engrossing but if I can wait to see what happens, I might find out something.

Do you think so?

Love & hopw (hope) (future is dim present)
Lost is not-so-silly the rest,
Old Ideal Love,
Love nevertheless,
On target
In ruins
As you like it,
peek through the time & let me know,
yours,
in great love,
silly untoward & prissy sensation of
normal old-fashioned love
still sensate & full of its
convex concatenations I hope
& all know (evrybody)
(I apologize for feeling backwards,
but not so backwards as the rest),
Unharming Love,
Bernadette

[→ P.S. Seen Alice's new book?

P.P.S. Hope this letter's not boring homiletic or queer, or jejeune (sp?) demimondaine or choucroute, it's just the full moon at resurrection time.]

MAY 22, 1981

Dear Clark,

I am writing to you in an attempt to eloquently exhort you to communicate! It's been a long time! No one's heard from you since you've been to Macchu Picchu! Where are you!

Oh I dont mean to be mean or importunate or overbearing or even worrisome but we do miss hearing from you and hearing all about everything & meanwhile, your having been to other continents, it makes you seem all the further away when we dont then hear from you.

My typewriter is set on double-spacing! because I was humiliatingly typing out double-spaced poems for a caps grant application! Oh woe is me, I realized in doing it that I hardly ever put my poems into some final form because it's aforesaid or whatever the word is, that no one is going to publish them, so I simply put them into my folder (lately entitled Poems NY!) in their rough-shod? rough-hewn? states in strict chronological order, and it's very easy to read from them but they dont look particularly nice. Recently at a reading I held up a poem to show people what it looked like, it was shaped like a sideways triangle and I realized what I was showing was not just the poem but also some added scribbles by Marie all over the page.

I keep thinking of things I want to tell you and as they mount up I realize [→ from their accumulation] how long it's been since we've written. Of course right now I cant think of a single one. No, I'm only fooling,

new paragraph, recently I've been embroiled in the most eschatological (I dont even know if that adjective applies) & outrageous sort of local politics you would ever imagine—a sort of battle among the members of the poetry project's advisory board to choose two new members. It's the first time the board & the bylaws have ever exercised their muscles without the guidance of Ron who created them. And a great stalemate developed between the advocates of the so-called younger people (which means people younger than me, like if I'm 36, a younger person is 33) and the so-called older people which means someone who is between 35 and 43! In the middle of all this I suggested that the next director be chosen from the children's workshop (ages 7–14) so we could be sure of being au courant, or whatever it is. Anyway everyone who was nominated to be a new member of the board seemed appropriate to me & at some other point when everybody started battling I suggested they all resign and just elect 8 new members since we had 8 terrific candidates (oh dear, am I boring you?). But then the unfortunate thing that began happening was that the people on the board began taking sides for and against Ron being one of the new members, and it began to be obvious that the ones who were against Ron were being influenced by ideas of Ted's!

Well, I'm sworn to secrecy about these meetings but suffice it to say that in the midst of many hours of phone calls during this week-long "stalemate" I became very much in the middle of things (I dont have a vote at the meetings) and I not only became privy to much stuff I didnt want to know but also felt for the first time since I've taken this job that I'd been emotionally downed by it. What a mess! Alot of people seemed to feel that the former director should not immediately be incorporated into the board, but Ron, having not been elected, cant understand why his accumulated expertise is not being made use of.

Oh well I wont go on about that anymore, it's funny I feel a great desire to talk to you about it and at the same time and great reluctance to indulge in any misbegotten revelations—does it all sound silly to you?

I've been so involved in that and in creating the first meeting of a Friends committee to try & find more ways of raising money—all this when I thought I'd have little work to do at the end of the so-called season, and also I've been sort of thrown a curve in the budget-cut mishegoss, however as Robt. Creeley would say onward!

And past that, well Sophia saw the dentist yesterday and Max & Marie saw the doctor today & Marie is 44 inches tall and weighs 44 pounds and the doctor then said, aghast at my interest in this boring coincidence, that often "at this age" a child is "an inch a pound"!

Other coincidences that've happened lately are: Lewis took down a book he'd never read that'd been given to him by his original girlfriend Allegra, then on the same day that I met two people I hadnt seen in 11 years, Allegra, whom Lewis hasnt seen in 11 years, sent him a postcard saying she was in NY & wanted to see him! (Hannah said that these things happen all the time and are very ordinary). Actually Lewis has had a string of coincidences happen to him lately, mostly involved with dreams he's having, & which leave him astonished.

We are all embroiled in trying to find a new school for Sophia to get her out of the bureaucratic, rigid headstart environment & that all involved yet another coincidence: we took her to a dental clinic which wound up being housed in the same building as the local Montessori school, which we then got inspired to inquire about and it turned out they're desperate for "girls" & would be willing to hand them scholarships!

In the midst of doing all this, whether it's dentists, doctors, schools or girls or boys, one winds up walking in new york city, about 5 miles a day—partly for fear of public transportation, and partly for the ease of going around with children without having to deal with it. I went with Marie's class to the circus at Madison Square Garden & aside from the fact that one poor boy got his cast caught in the escalator, we also had to deal with losing half our entourage to a train and the rest of us couldnt get on! All the while Marie's teacher was leading the group in and out of the subways and up and down the streets with a fearless posture and a banner arrogantly declaring that we were all (immune from disaster because we were) from "P.S. 19"!

I wrote my one-week journal—I cant remember if I wrote you before or after I did that—and ever since then I've been engrossed in the kind of enhanced noticing of things that doing that kind of work always leaves me with. One is tempted to think, in a way, oh I wish I were recording this and this and this, still recording everything. But the odd thing is that one still is, as you know. I have great plans for the journal, it will be my summer's work to try to make something of it, using books and even my memory(?!)

I must tell you I've been using a typewriter at the Poetry Project, since our old one was stolen which is so amazing as to make you feel, after you get used to it, that you might rule the whole fucking world! It's a [→ IBM] Selectric III or some such thing and when you "turn it on" the "dashboard" lights up to indicate whether you're using 10-point or 12-point "balls."! It is also "self-correcting." I would like to make the daring suggestion that if you can afford it and you feel you would not be intimidated (I began to type intimated) by such a monstrosity, that it does have its advantages, puerile as they might seem. I spent about 20 hours non-stop composing letters on it this past week and I must admit I feel like a pauper now at this my mere machine.

So much for balls. In writing, lately, I've been at a loss. There's no way I could've expected working at the poetry project not to affect my work, valiant as was my attempt to not let it stop me from having the time to write. But the way it affects me finally (finally being end of year) is that I cant figure out what to write (as if I ought to), I am so glutted with poetry and notions about it and also about politics, willy-nilly, that I've begun to think when I sit down to write that I have to actually know something, or that I cant write what I know I'll write, or what I dont know I'll write, but that I have to eliminate about 12/15ths of the possibilities in advance & try & really save the world! I'm assuming this is a temporary state and will lead to some further knowledge, also assuming my health holds out. I find myself hard-pressed not to want to totally speed through each day (I mean speed in my own idiosyncratic way, not like my confreres) & then when I get a chance to be completely exhausted and I have time to think and meditate, I am fascinated and also turned on by that leisure & by my sort of daring to indulge in it.

So you see, if you dont write me, I'll wind up talking and going on and on only about myself! It's odd, one can have about a million fascinating conversations in new york, quite accidentally, but if one doesnt have the time to seek out the conversations one wants to have, you're still left feeling you have no one to talk to. Or never to have the "perfect" person to talk to!—a feeble concept I believe at best, but nonetheless one that persists with me, along with my erstwhile 19th century grammar.

One of the results of my work in the city has been—silly as it might sound—that I do indeed feel old. If I bring this up to anybody (while in the course of complaining) people inevitably say to me, oh it's just because you've been around too long. !. There is such a consciousness of the artificial generations and there is such a hurry among everybody but now that I write that down it makes sense to me—it's just to hurry to get one's work seen & known I guess, without which . . . . . oh I dont know about that. The odd thing is it doesnt seem to result in ambitious projects long poems etc. One of the ways one feels old in the city, in this environment, is that one knows one is old because one is so fucking literary. In the middle of all this shit about politics on the advisory board I simply threw up (I wish I had) my hands and said Oh dear I'm just a fucking intellectual & I dont belong in this job! I should be sitting home writing my books, etc. And then someone very kindlily pointed to me that I did indeed have a job and as a worker I couldnt expect not to be involved in whatever reverberations of the world that would involve, and until that moment I hadnt thought of working at the poetry project as a job, really. But I never dreamed I would be almost forced to learn so much about politics in this my 37th year. And I am learning:

some say the poetry project should not be "open" to all groups, others say it should; some even go so far as to say it should become even more "cliquish" than it is accused of being, no matter who reads or has read there. Well it sounds simple, and as if you could have a sensible response, but . . .

Whaddayou think? Do you think what I'm seeing and learning leaves me better off than the kind of thing you wind up doing teaching at a college? Of course I do, in the end, because I can actually wind up, in the part of my job which has nothing to do with poetry exactly, helping people in some practical ways.

But here I am going on about it some more! See, if I had a letter from you full of stuff, I wouldnt be doing this. Now the magic loud radios are playing because it's warm out, and this has been one of the warmest prettiest springs I've ever seen in new york where the wind blows enough to make the air clear all the time & moths fly in, even here.

Did you read about the 20 geniuses chosen by some foundation to be funded? As geniuses, for five years. It was interesting that in the category of public geniuses, there were so many poets among them, it did wonders for our credibility among people like Lewis's parents. Other than that I'm afraid the choices left me cold, except I do like Robt. Penn Warren's prose sentences sometimes. However I couldnt figure out why neither you nor I was among them.

I would like to write a work that peddled my thoughts (not just them) as if they were merchants on a butcher block. No, but I cant figure out how to get past poetry. No that's not what I mean. I'd like to figure out, no I dont mean figure anything out at all. I'd like to write a work. . . . When I listen to poets read their works now, after listening alot, often I think to myself, oh that's poetry and that is, I forgot about that, but it isnt anything, I already know about how that is that but how could one really amaze everybody! And dont mistake me, I'm not having these imperious thoughts as if I knew something! because at the same time I am thinking, having given myself a rather rigorous course this year, that my own work is stuck in some morass of alternating obfuscation/clarity tour de forces combined with a facility for old-fashioned sentence structure and maybe some observation of everything that I can do and the only talent I feel like I have that nobody else does, except you, is to have the energy to put it all down because I dont wait for inspiration and so on but I think I can still tell when it's coming even though I'm writing all the time through it anyway. At this moment I am dying to know what to do. I feel I could do it if I knew what it was, I almost feel I'm on the verge of knowing what it is, I sure dont want anybody to tell me, but I also feel like if I dont find out soon something awful will happen, like being stuck in one's style forever. [→ I also feel like nobody (one person) ever knows what it is & that my lack of generosity (if you will) to other poets might be purely concerned with narcissism.] I dont feel inspired, I dont feel there's anyone to emulate, I dont know what the times mean. I'm getting involved with the times too much, that's obvious. I can no longer write the kind of thing I was writing before, I keep wanting to learn something new.

So, I warned you and I'll warn you again, if you dont write you'll have to hear more of this sort of thing! There's some homily about it I cant summon up like fair-warned is fair-earned or something like that, well-warned is well known about? What is it? Oh dear that reminds me of the Pope (master of homiletics). The news here is that Eileen Myles is going to marry an Arab who otherwise couldnt stay in the country. I'd guess I better end.

Write soon! Love, Bernadette

MAY 27 1981

Dear Clark,

Perhaps I'll inundate you with written materials, as they say, till you write me a letter! Here's a poem I wrote about Admiral Scott and the space shuttle, taut conservative as I am.

& also here's page nine of my DESIRES to complete your set. I just happened to have to have it xeroxed & of course remembered you.

tonight we are being inundated with disco music due to the heat (which I know doesnt sound sensible but that's how it works) & now I've just succumbed to calling the police, after trying the environmental protection agency, which said to me: "we are not equipped to deal with the activities of people"! (They claimed they would need to be armed! We debated the industrial vs. the personal—is it personal?)

Love,
Bernadette

Police not come yet.

[On Poetry Project letterhead]

JULY 26, 1981

Dear Clark,

Here I get to write you a real official letter.

We would like to invite you to give the opening reading of this coming season, as they say, on October 7th, at 8 pm, with John Cage. The honorarium is $150.

I hope you will want and be able to do it. I'm just getting to write these letters now because I've been waiting—in the midst of normal waiting and also all this politics—to see if I was going to be able to raise the honoraria from their old pastry, I mean paltry $100, and yes we can (Oddly the House & Senate seem to be "on our side").

I just came back from visiting Alice, who, upon returning from a trip to Providence, wound up in a cab accident on the way back from Bob Wilson's and has two shiners! She seems to be in almost buddhisticly good spirits though. I brought her raspberries, Mooseheads and begonias in the hope to cheer & all the while Ted was throwing out copies of Nimrod & the White Dove Review & even The East Village Other with stuff by him, plus astonishing photographs of his families and of old telling paintings of him by George Schneeman.

Meanwhile I'm working, in a way I havent exactly worked before, on my new book, if it is to be one. I've jettisoned the Poetry Project journals altogether from the utopian project and decided to write "an utopia" in the traditional question-and-answer form, if I can. However, now I'm stuck (having planned to read all these books and steal from them) not knowing whether I still have to read the books at all! Also, I'm fascinated by the books; on the other hand I'm dying to get started writing. I've been trying very very hard to just read and spend an inordinate amount of time cleaning up & rearranging the house, ostensibly to make life into a life of total ease, as if? I had been my own maid, in the future. . . . Saw "Numero Deux" last night and there is a wonderful line about memory coming out between a woman's legs. It's a movie—have you seen it?—that one would want to have the text of, with so many spectacular speeches, all set against such theoretically dull visual backgrounds(?) that one wonders how Godard can make the language so fucking fascinating, and there is alot of fucking in a way.

But hell, I'm not supposed to be going into all this in this voiced formal letter on stationery, it's secret pleasures?

I only cant resist adding that I've been reading HEAVENLY BREAKFAST by Sam Delany, ISLAND by Aldous Huxley which is a really mixed up book and enough other utopian texts to lead me to believe that (except for Delany's book and Godard's movie to some extent) the entire field of utopian scholarship is the most sexist enclave I've ever come upon in any discipline. But despite that Max who's still nursing has learned to talk a bit and if he demands an apple when he means a tomato, well it isnt lost on us who are attentive to forms (he often behaves now like "a bruiser."). & Marie has learned to swim and all three of the children, more or less with Sophia as the ringleader as they say, have become so obsessed with the foods of summer (they dont even know about baseball) that when a bag of fruit comes into the house there are six little hands grabbing at everything full of such a simultaneous sweetness and greed as to make one wonder about philosophical formulations about the nature of human beings.

Please let me know as soon as you can about the reading, I'll be here, home, for the rest of the summer, so you can write or call or whatever you would like.

Sweet dreams I was tempted to say, my dreams have been monumental lately—while in Guilford I was plagued by Poetry Project dreams; now back in NY I am plagued by lengthy dreams about communes and Guilford too, I am actually grateful to these dreams for teaching me something about magic which has to do with this book & the writing of it—& if you'll forgive me for going on longer I realized that one talent I always had in writing was to do something interesting as a result of thinking I could create magic or a magical language. Dont get me wrong, I dont know if the magic ever resulted but when I was aware of what I was trying to do in that way—like create something much like Fournier's THE WANDERERS (though that might be a bad example), I would wind up doing something that I could do, that's all I have to say about that now.

Much love,

much love,

Bernadette

TUESDAY 4 AUGUST [1981]

Dear Bernadette,

I've been writing letters to you and tearing them up, also writing many others in my head. It's terrible, I guess I don't like what they say. I look at them the next day and they seem to be written by somebody else. Sometimes my work seems that way too, quite often lately actually. I'm going through a peculiar period. I don't like a lot of what I'm writing and that is very distressing. My old work, especially the work of ten years ago or so (which I'm afraid most people know me by), I dislike so much I can't even look at it. I think I was really trying to do something quite different from what appears. But it's getting very difficult for even me to remember what that was. There's such a confusion in me right now about all this and other things too that I find it very difficult to write a letter, especially to those few I feel close to. I feel as if I should start traveling (anywhere) and keep going (probably impossible right now), or else sit very quiet for the time it takes to find out what has become of me.

I can't accept the reading. It's hard to describe why exactly, this involves so many feelings, many conflicting. Mainly it has to do I think with my present upset about my work. And an overall feeling, very strong since returning from Peru, that the poetry scene has become very stupid and trivial, the whole "art" scene actually, an isolated island full of foolish people whizzing around trying each to gain his/her little advantage to very little purpose or effect. The connections I once thought I saw, between individuals, between works of art and people's lives, are lost. It's all a depressing swim. Great loss of definition between and within. I get the feeling we should all be very quiet for a while or else go away(at least I should). I never really thought of poetry as a "career," but now I see it as totally not that. It would be ridiculous to think so. It's just something I do that I can't stop doing, and I sometimes think now (more and more) that I would stop doing it if I could but I can't, it's too late.

Also I realized very clearly lately just how much I hate New York City. It seems the end of things. Especially the Lower East Side, about the most depressing place I know. It's something I don't need to fight against right now. I never want to have to sleep on the floor in dreariness again. Actually I can never forgive New York for refusing to remain the vision I first had of it when my folks brought me there as a child (Kerouac's descriptions of it in the Forties in Cody are the closest evocations of what I mean). I keep getting the feeling, ridiculous as it may sound, that if I should ever go there again I should be put up at the Plaza, taken to the best restaurants, driven around in a limousine, a whole layer of glory laid over all that distress. I ask myself, don't I deserve this? Is this unwarranted?

Maybe this all sounds crazy(?) and I really shouldn't be writing you this kind of letter (I feel the urge to tear this up every other second but I'll ignore that and press on). Maybe anything would be better than silence from me at this point? But I do feel a great need for silence. I know, I'm fighting a big depression and have been ever since we got back from Peru, something I'll have to find the way to fight through somehow. I especially don't want any choices at the moment, they drive me to immobile distraction. Like Jane Bowles I could spend hours just looking at a menu. I hope you'll forgive me. But don't call. I hate the phone (as you know) more than letters. And right now our phone has developed a case of static that makes it so I can't hear anything though the other person can hear me fine.

Anyway, thanks for asking me to read, but I just can't. The main reason is that I have nothing I want to read at the moment.

Love,

Clark

AUGUST 4 NO 7TH 1981

Dear Clark,

I'm so glad you wrote, but I'm sorry you feel so horrible. Of course everything you say makes absolute sense to me except your dismay at your own works which I take as not only an inaccurate perception due to whatever but also, more strongly, a perversion that could do great disservice to everybody. And though I vow to respect your silence for a hundred years if you will, I wont not say that as some part of you knows your writing is enlightening to all (& dont even count me). Maybe it's even disturbing to think that one's writing has already had an effect on the world, before one even knows what one is doing, but that way of not knowing what one is doing and being able to be radical, like Philip Guston, is as I know you now, the best way. I wish you didnt feel awful and I sure wish we could converse regularly so that I would know more about what you are thinking. For myself, I've begun to ruminate that it's self-indulgent to take what goes on in the world as an excuse not to go on with what one has a physical and mental impulse to do—thus of course your mention of not being able to stop writing. And if you'll excuse me for going on about myself, which might seem like an invasion, I'll also say that my idea lately is to cease to focus anything on myself and to take a clue from what I can perceive, I hope accurately, of the world, now that I'm 36 or whatever I am, that notice has been given, both in terms of my own age and of my age, to the end of the obsession with self, which is something

I feel I've dallied with alot. and I'm confused too, especially so by having heard so many poetry readings, as I told you, but, though my instincts are almost physical feelings, it's hard to change. I read old notebooks over last night (not old but from the past two years) and I cant tell you how many times I was mentioning that I wished I were a painter. I cant tell you how many times your letter brought images to me about Philip Guston too. I am not saying that any of us are the same, I am saying what I am thinking as a result of thinking of you. Ultimately none of it matters the present moment excepted. Only thing is I feel so close to you that it's hard for me to write **[Page break]**

write sensibly & to try on a small page to respect your silence when I just want to hit you! I want to jolt you out of your thoughts! but that's exactly what you asked me not to do! oh shit well of course you're absolutely right as I said before except about that one thing about which you're dead wrong. At least I can say that I know about your writing & all about it and its everything. & that's what I can say. Oh god Clark, I dont mean to add to your problems but this whole thing makes me feel awful. Let me say this & be done with it: I think you should be more generous—share your work, I dont give a whit for careers or anything, and I'm not talking about giving readings, so then I'll say just know what your work is, you couldnt possibly not know that, I cant believe that.

Please I hope you feel better, I often think it would be wonderful to have someone to talk to about what I think about writing at this moment, I dont. But we are the cupbearers, which I know is a misuse of the word but it's the word I've picked nonetheless, and we must still be doing this, your or my mishegoss notwithstanding, I know that much—dont you? And I dont mean just we, but I know I mean we. I hope you'll forgive me for my ranting, and if I've missed the point, well tell me! nobody else will! & please continue to tell me everything else too, otherwise I'll say the wrong thing. Cant we be blunt with each other, if any people can? It's a step forward to be so, unlike the mothers in the park who are saying the same things to their children that their mothers say to them. Well you are my consanguinity too—I dont know exactly why—so I can make demands on you (should we have a self-criticism?) something otherwise I'll fucking mourn

Oh dear I'm sorry I know we do deserve the limousines according to our everything, yes it's true, to hear is not so far from the red fox or the illimitable rock.

Love,
Bernadette

[On Poetry Project letterhead]

SEPTEMBER 15, 1981

Dear Clark,

Alan Davies mentioned to me that you might indeed come to read so I'd like to invite you for Wednesday December 16th (8 pm). If you'd like to read solo, the honorarium is $200. If you'd like to read with another, the fee would be $150, and please feel free to tell me if you have any thoughts about with whom you'd like to read. Also, we'd like to ask you, if you will, to do a workshop on the following night, Thursday September I mean December 17th, also at 8 pm. The workshop fee is $150.

When I say workshop of course it can be whatever you would like to make it—more of a lecture, or whatever. Let me know if there are any specific ways you'd want us to describe either the reading or the workshop in the newsletter, on the poster & in press releases. Otherwise, for the workshop, we normally simply say "Special Workshop with . . ."

When I talked with Alan I told him I'd mention the 16th to you, and that he would invite you around that time. If that date's no good, let me know.

I sure hope it wasnt the reading with Cage that soured you on coming to read at all because, I assume you know, if you want to read alone I think that's great. I'd just gotten obsessed with a vision of the two of you! As it turned out I had to cancel the whole first week anyway! due to an unfinished floor!

Also I'm supposed to mention that WBAI has been taping and broadcasting our readings on alternating Saturday nights. Each reading is not necessarily broadcast immediately after it's recorded, but eventually it is. If you have any objections to being taped for the radio, then, let me know.

Write soon. It's finally raining here, after a very sour Indian-summer-type (but too early for that) hot-dry spell.

Love,
Bernadette

MONDAY 21 SEPTEMBER [**1981**]

Dear Bernadette,

I'd better get this off to you this morning as my typewriter's going in to be fixed this afternoon (platen replaced, cleaning) and I'll probably be without it for a week or so. I talked with Alan Davies the other day again and suggested January 23rd would be a better date for the Ear Inn, no doubt he's told you by now? The week before Christmas is always a crowded family time here, plus I think a "mid-winter" break in January would feel right. So, either wednesday before or after that saturday would be okay with me, you choose and let me know. I'd prefer reading solo if that's possible. And I can't, at the moment anyway, imagine preparing anything for the workshop, so better skip that this time around. Fine with me if BAI wants to tape the reading.

It's been a truly terrible summer, but I think I'm begging to (hmm, nice slip) . . . beginning to get hold of things again. Finally it feels like I'm indulging myself in this depression, nurturing it like a plant indoors. So fuck it. Autumn, time to start things again, clear the air, starting with the typewriter. Fixing time. So I tell myself anyway, hoping it works. But I do feel better. Your last letter helped, but I was by that time too far from the habit of letter writing to reply. I did need a good kick in the head! It's peculiar. Coming back here from Peru has been really hard. Everything began looking really ridiculous and insubstantial, trivial finally. I've never felt so removed from things, the country's things, the art scene, even myself in a strange partial slant. Michael Palmer just got back from a month in France and is undergoing a similar malaise. Hard to feel this place is real again, on top of the well-known feeling of unreality as any kind of artist in this country anyway. Double askew.

But I've been writing the while, but writing blind sort of. Any kind of thoughts, not to mention "theories," about writing seeming hopelessly useless and silly. "Not knowing what I'm doing" for real this time. A prose work I'm calling THE TIME has been accumulating in short paragraphs, takes and blurts about and throughout all this. While I was doing it I thought it was really nuts, certifiably neurotic maybe, but now it's beginning to look amazingly sane. Don't know what will become of it as I can't imagine any kind of "end" for it. Maybe it's just one of those interim jots, something to keep me going no matter what? Will see. I've been reading a lot of novels, mostly pulp junk, seemed to need to do that for a while, usually there's at least one funny detail or whatever that sticks out in even the worst of them (ever notice?), and realized that I have always taken any fiction as <u>real</u> (any writing actually), so maybe that's my problem with writing novel, that I can't take writing as imaginarily optional(?) Reading a Joan Didion novel I realized that she had taken some facts from her own childhood and made a fictional character out of these and "other," something I can't even imagine doing. I must operate in some irrevocably other framework/wavelength, impossible to define. Well, blah.

Further. I'll be reading in Buffalo (with Don Byrd of all people) on Nov. 13 which is a friday and maybe nobody else wanted that date? Hopefully it'll be a workout toward getting back into the swing of reading anyway. Did you notice that Annabel surprised the world by actually coming through with my book? I'll send you one soon. What else? We bought a new car (Subaru) and two weeks later smashed the whole front end in hitting a deer one night on way to movie in Williamstown. Terrifying and stupid. $1000 worth of body damage, insurance covered luckily. /// Anyway, let me know about the reading date. And I'll try to fill you in further on everything when I get my machine back gleaming like new.

LOVE,

Clark

[On Poetry Project letterhead]

OCTOBER 26, 1981

Dear Clark,

It seems like I've been so busy and also preoccupied all the time I dont have time to turn my head around, not saying that to be complaining though, I've been having a great time. & I've made some progress on my utopia, which sounds silly to say though the main thing is it seems when you start writing a utopia your life begins to reflect your concerns, but I guess it always did. I'm not meaning to sound mysterious but cant get into it all now, I'm writing to you from the Poetry Project to confirm that you'll be reading January 20th 8 pm (the fee for a solo reading is $200, I guess I told you all that before). If you change your mind about a workshop, let me know by November 25th, and we could still schedule one. OK?

I seem to be imitating you and have completely ceased writing letters, except for the Poetry Project for which I have to write so many letters all the time I cant conceive of writing a real one. My life seems to become more and more involved in this little dense geographical space and less involved, as the mailbox shows, with the so-called outside world, though in other ways, oh here I am waxing mysterious again, I seem more involved with the outside than ever. Boy I am far from eloquence today! AMERICAN ONES is a great book, I want to write it too. Where is your other book? The Annabel book? I havent seen it. I'll send you some portions of my book when I feel like I'm really finished with them. I dont know how to proceed with it at all, it's been like this for weeks, so perhaps the book is done, it's resting. In fact my writing is all quiescent unlike this room I work in: hammering, sawing and banging all around me, the poetry files in boxes surrounding our desks, our wallpaper a shiny silver stuff that every few feet says "Johns-Manville fiberglass insulation" interspersed with wooden boards hung with what I think are some kind of bands on which to put plaster, six bare bulbs hanging from long wires from the high ceiling & no heat, no light, a weird cave. I'll write soon again or

maybe I'll see you soon.

LOVE,
Bernadette

WEDNESDAY 28 OCTOBER [1981]

Dear Bernadette,

Getting back to my letter-writing pace (I hope!), and just got your letter (confirming reading date) so thought I'd sit down and say something it's been so long. Drove down the hill to mailhouse without my glasses (!), first time I've forgotten those. What's to become of me? Result no doubt of big hassle getting new glasses a month or so ago, a whole other needless story too construe to review (turned out I didn't need a new prescription after all). But, feeling better overall, autumn doing its big quickening number on me as ever and much more appreciated this year, what with worse summer doldrums than ever. Decided it's time to push, drive for that totality (of work at least) I always said I was after. Maybe time to get back to the LongWork, I dunno. Musing over possibilities of changing structure of that to conform(ha!) to such newer thinks as MINE etc.

Meanwhile big hill of poems here on desk is rattling at me to get it collected 'tween covers of some sort. But I can't find anybody to do that! Wrong timing, Clark. Thought of maybe Geoff Young's FIGURES and have put out feelers, but except he's either moneyless or self-limited to Bay Area types (?) Wish I had put the touch on Mattingly before he retired, I envy Ted that big book so. But it sure would feel better (right) to have these poems in BOOK, I'm so hooked on old-time notions of substantiality?

Feels like little to report, or lots but I forgot (time between). What's going on? Newspapers feel like a mess, collages of little bits stapled together by idiots. TV worse (vacuum cleaner). At least I finally(!) got my typewriter fixed as you can see (new platen, cleaning/oiling by a guy out on Dalton Avenue who's pretty good/fast) so hoping to hold onto it for many years future. I know you disapproved of it but I'm used to it, and when's the last time you saw a typer made of solid steel?

Celia's now in highschool marching band with a big orange plume (feather) on her cap. Likes it ok so far (the school), though some senior boy is already teasing her in halls and she wonders what's the right approach(!) I told her if he pisses her off enough that she gets furious it's alright with me if she punches him out. What am I coming to? What is she? She probably needs your advice more than mine(?) I think you two would have a great time now putting heads together over whatever. Too bad, all this distance, lives, jobs, divergence.

I'm going to read in Buffalo on November (friday the) 13th, with Don Byrd of all people (at least he's got a new car with stereo tapedeck). But, what the fuck, I haven't read since the Guston Memorial, plus hope to get to see Creeley again after all these millions of years it feels like. Hope it doesn't snow!

Got some great slides on Vineyard, best being portraits of my mother Celia etc. in post-sundown light with 400 film. It's exciting but I'm trying not to go all nuts with it so I end up buying 10 rolls a week or anything. Maybe try some black&white. No doubt we're in for a great slide evening (yours & mine) sometime in future.

I sent you copy of Annabel book, sort of fucked up (irregular inking, tiny type, spine title printed upside down) but I'm glad she did it finally anyway, and I do sort of like the cover blend (her notion totally). Turns out I could send it 1st class for only a few pennies more than book rate (just under a certain weight I guess?). I'll never understand the post office.

Do send some of (or all of) your utopia when you're ready. I'm dying to have a look. An idea that would never have occurred to me I must say. How did it happen to you? Not that we don't sorely need some utopia about now, but that seems too simple a reason. Contrariwise (always wanted to use that word!) I feel the pressure toward a deep obssession with self, which I'm sort of fighting but maybe I shouldn't and just work through it, see where and what I get? It's resultant of this monkish isolation no doubt.

Can't think what else to say at the present, just wanted to catch up a bit while the mood struck me. I just read a biography of the Marquis de Sade and found myself wishing I had read it in highschool, don't ask me why! Some kind of adolescent aid?

Well, so much for now. I think of you much and have imaginary conversations. Maybe we should have a phonecall soon? I'll do my best with that infernal organ!

We're all well, excepting total sneeze from house dust (I think). Hoping you're all well. Anne wrote and said she can't stand the street scene(!)

Write again soon. And I promise to do better quicker.

Love,
Clark

Colin MacCabe's book on Godard (IMAGES, SOUNDS, POLITICS) is sort of interesting (as all Godard books somehow are) though full of abstruse bullshit (& a horrid "feminist" chapter by somebody). Worth a run-through if only for the pictures (though most of them tiny) and up-date on "political" and video works post-70. But why can't I see the films?!!!? I envy your chance at Numero Deux! Write and tell me about it?

NOVEMBER 22 1981

Dear Clark,

Seems like about two millions years ago that we sat unexpected at your table & I guess I said this sort of then but I have to say again that I was astonished at how lush! your house seemed to me, I mean lush like all the plants were so much bigger and there seemed to be so many birds and so many great things as always it seemed like your whole house with all the things and people in it was one big thriving plant! & of course you remember my brains, as you said yourself, were "fried" at that moment so I assume my view of things was relatively accurate—ha ha what a formal way of putting the result of "fried brains." So I just wanted to say that despite your summer doldrums you all looked very good to me & what a pleasure it was to see you. Actually I'm sure we looked horrible having had little sleep and less peace and I, for one, feeling traumatized by having to endure the ride home with the kids rolling around in the back of the black-windowed truck, but it turned out pretty smooth and when we got back to the city it was late enough that the famous Ralph Lee Halloween parade was "getting out" and all through our ride in the downtown streets we kept seeing the most astonishing Draculas and Frankensteins and people who'd got themselves out in great detailed costumes, often with two-colored faces or some two people tied together some fantastic way and many ghosts & witches (they all looked kind of expensive) and babies in tiger costumes & really a Halloween parade is the perfect occasion for new york because that is what people like to do anyway, look weird, well I guess I dont mean that altogether yet I do. Anyway Marie told us scary stories all the way down in the truck . . .

. . . isnt

that a good transition? A few phone calls have now taken place, all of which were necessary, I mean not just fooling around having fun talking on the phone that infernal machine on which you can enjoy yourself, I had to talk to Shelley about meeting with the head of the Marlborough Gallery tomorrow about a benefit for the Poetry Project when Larry Rivers' show opens, then Rosemary called to pursue an interesting conversation we'd begun this afternoon and I didnt have the instinct not to talk though I knew this was the beginning of the end of my "night" then when the phone rang next I assumed it was Ron returning my call about the benefit but it was Harris apologizing for cancelling Lewis's birthday dinner after I'd already gotten a baby sitter because he had to go to a proofreading job at night on Wall St. doing legal work which was a nightmare he'll never do it again, then Ron did call after getting fed up with the james bond movie he'd been watching when I'd first called him and now I'm gonna do something I think I've rarely, if ever, done before, which is to finish writing to you at some time in the future!!! because for me it's sleepytime and I am old and tomorrow I have to confront, at some really early hour, a man named Pierre Le Va who runs the marlborough and whom I'm quite terrified might be the kind of person who will terrify me unless I go (well rested and) absolutely certain to the meeting that the Poetry Project is not begging for anything but is a well rested group of staid individuals, perhaps not as well fed as this guy, but maybe some of us are, that deserves not only this benefit opening but for the gallery to pay the cost of the printing of the invitations as well! What a funny life, I am learning not only (my main Latin construction: not only . . . but also) about human nature but also about direct mail advertising and society "ladies" as they say (It's not me who says that!) as well.

Before I go I'm going to make a list within this letter of what I'll be wanting to tell you about when I resume it:

How was your reading in Buffalo?

How ours was at MIT, and how Lewis's was in Baltimore, about John Cage's reading & what he said to me afterwards, about utopia, Jane Bowles perhaps, Herland perhaps, about starting over in writing, about time (not pretentiously, just having time) & how dreams are as if I'm not having them,

about the family & everybody in it, about Lewis's haircut, about being "an idiot,"

well, there's many things, last night I dreamt I was at a college to read and from the library which was very disappointing (interesting word) I could see a glass-enclosed gym or health club in which millions of people were doing fascinating health-club type things, why they were even dressing up in firemen's costumes and falling down pipes into a swimming pool, meanwhile "I" couldnt understand why I couldnt be permitted to get upstairs to the second floor of the library and I finally said to somebody, "well even if that only meant I'd have a better view of the gym!"

Then I dreamt a woman, much like the mother of a friend of Marie's, was having a fight with her son who had admitted to her that he smoked ten marijuana cigarettes a day but before the real fight began they were kissing and making out on the street they then screamed at each other (this dream just a function of my continuous observance of how weirdly parents and children treat each other: this same woman asked me to take her child to school the other day because her new baby was nursing so constantly she was too tired, but then when I picked her up I had to wait twenty minutes making everybody late for school & then the child made a fuss & got fawned over by the mother which made me even madder so that I kicked trees), well this is trivial but often these are my concerns; I cant understand why mothers and fathers behave the way they do, both Marie's and Sophia's schools are still in uproars which I have to constantly get involved with, and then other things happen like Rosemary who's seeing a therapist refers to this to Marie as seeing a doctor because she's sick, then I have to explain what a psychiatrist is later to Marie, and I say "oh that's a person that helps you not to be crazy" but I cant understand Rosemary's reluctance to admit to a child that that might be needed in this world which Marie is already so much a part of, & Rosemary says to me oh I just thought it was embarrassing in some way. Meanwhile I'm engrossed in trying to figure out a way for Rosemary to recuperate from an operation she has to have in January, so that she can be provided with constant care and meals for about two weeks—it breaks my heart plus it breaks my political brain to realize that I cant have her here in this house because it's so small, here where she could belong most easily in that situation & some part of me thinks well what the hell if we all lived in China we could do this, we would just do it, it would be normal. So now I'm engrossed in trying to make these plans. **[Page break]**

Well it is another day but I cant say that that says much for me as I've been engrossed all day in situations like how much it costs to order ice cubes for the Larry Rivers Poetry Project benefit—I mean what is my function? I really feel like a person with no identity lately, I could simply be anyone a good half the time, but that's not true, I've got a better "job" than most people in the world where I do get to be a person, I just cant stand dealing with uptown art-gallery owners who, after you have a conversation with them, you have to call two people up to find out what it meant. I've just put together an accumulation of love poems by many people to read in Anne's class in Hoboken tomorrow night.

Our reading at MIT was desultory, 12 people, not much response, many dinner parties though at Corbett's discussing endlessly the Russell Banks-Fanny Howe end of their affair (Corbett's moralistic, Fanny miserable but looking very good, Russell looking like a person who's in mourning, though he's about to get married!)

I wonder what would happen if everybody in the world just suddenly began to tell the absoulute (see i cant even spell it) truth right this second—i would guess there would be a great shifting like glaciers melting and endless migrations and probably even more refugees than already exist, and it would be unhealthy like a plague of truth & the torture of dying of it would be equal to that. Forgive me I am an obsessed person I dont get to dream and read enough in this life.

Lewis's reading in Baltimore, on the other hand, was rewarding as many people came & he was courted and wined & dined also & treated the way one should be, as you know; he was very happy. Since he's got his hair cut believe it or not to be this sort of short haircut which looks a little bit like Caligula in the ads for public television, everybody has been going around telling him how great he looks (I'm the only advocate of long hair for men left in this world), and his mother actually said, "I never thought I'd live to see the day" which she actually hasnt yet as she wont see him till Thanksgiving this Thursday, another dreaded occasion (as you have your summer doldrums I'm afraid if I have to be around other human beings at this time of year, and not just controlling my own destiny and dinners, I get the creeps around Thanksgiving). Anyway Lewis has been getting all these compliments, not only about his hair, but simultaneously about his poetry, and this is making me quite jealous because for completely other reasons I'm feeling very unhappy about my own work and neglected that I havent been asked, petty as it sounds, to read in Baltimore or Buffalo, in fact if I dont schedule myself at the poe. proj. I'll have no other readings this year which is a masochistic situation I sort of enjoy in a way too. I'll sit here, I say to myself, and write my works really really slowly! I'll show them! However I cant do that and either write fast or not at all, but when I was putting together these love poems by the likes of Jimmy Schuyler & the Greek Anthology & Wyatt & Huang O, my own poems seemed to pale in comparison to theirs & I have this sensation lately that my poems are so sloppily flung about the page as to never mean anything to anyone who doesnt know me, if you know what I mean. Nor can I conscion this desire to be less involved in just the process of writing them. Also I really do mean that I feel like no one, this is partly a result of trying to write this utopian book, which no one has any sympathy with, in fact I am constantly being made fun of for trying it, and since I like to talk about what I'm doing, so much the worse. And any prose book I've ever written has seemed to result in what? I cant think how to describe what I mean, all I can think to say is some sort of rearrangement of my personality, which sounds horribly psychological yet it is true. Do I always have to get to be no one? Then to top it all off—my feelings of ridiculousness—I was in the Gotham Book Mart today perusing the dismal poetry books and happened upon the back page description of Mark Strand's latest & it talks all about being no one in this most pretentious way it was almost as if the gods or whoever were trying to prove to me that I was a total idiot in my recent way of thinking.

Well I almost feel that I am haranguing you, and I hope this is not too dull to listen to, I dont mean to jeopardize our correspondence by being either so full of myself or threatening a hovering craziness which is actually no worse than some healthful dreams, yet I am exhausted and in my writing, though I can write much about sex and love, I cannot figure out what else to do, and even those things . . . I become torn between wanting to write something that seems like a poem, even a perfect poem! for the first time in my life! & at the same time wanting to go on and on, and I never know which to do. I keep an interesting journal but it is such that I could never even show it to anybody! I had a fascinating time in the bookstore opening random books, like Flaubert's letters, and finding always that what I was finding had everything to do with what I've been thinking about lately—I am feeling so much a subject!

I have a great desire to describe some scenery!

Please write soon, it'd be a great pleasure to be really writing to each other again.

Love,
Bernadette

MONDAY 7 DECEMBER [1981]

Dear Bernadette,

Yes, it's funny, I also thought you looked so thriving that day here! What does it mean? I guess my old dread-NY feeling that you'd seem plowed under by it all. Maybe it's just absence that allows us big creaky constructs, mainly askew? Also letters allow us to endlessly complain. A need. On the other hand I've been feeling Big Energetics here, Fall has turned the key for me as usual (praise be!). Taking on all kinds of too many projects and feeling it's all vast to the good. Even if I don't accomplish most of them. Activity that makes me not remember details of dreams so well, almost as if I don't so much need that constant overlapping meditation on the thing, the dare. Anyway, was wonderful to see you, just wishing we had had a big raving discussion of exactly where we are today (your wondering about telling the absolute truth?).

Funny too, there were exactly twelve people at my reading in Buffalo too! (too many toos) If I could make big numerology numbers like Duncan, say, I could grow a big significant deal out of that. Maybe it was because Friday the Thirteenth? Or the rumour we heard afterward that Allen DeLoach told his workshop to "boycott" the reading. I don't have the slightest what that might mean, never met the man. Anyway, it's an odd room to read in (did you?) with all those mirrors, as if I was supposed to practice dancing or something thewhile. I kind of enjoyed it, though more as a kind of workout after long absence from "the stage" (hadn't read since last December's Guston Memorial), trying out new numbers, for instance read my new (god, written last January) RESEARCH poem, if it is a poem, felt a bit overlong but somehow interesting. What audience there was attentative (huh? such a word? attentive I meant), especially one guy who had come out of Rochester especially to hear me carrying a copy of QUARTZ HEARTS (which he said he'd been reading on the way) and wanted to talk all about Smithson. And especially Jack Clarke, did you meet him?, old friend of Olson's and Blake scholar but actually an old hipster unregenerate bebopper so we got to yak about all that till dawn in house of a guy described as "a Jungian analyst" whatever that might mean in practice, young freshface guy with obvious money, expensive stereo equipment and mounds of cocaine. Anyway, this Jungian wanted to ask me all about if I cut things all up in my poems or if I just saw the world that way, and I told him no cutting (at least in the sense there were "halves" of everything missing) and that yes I spose I do "see the world that way," how else to feel finally? But the main interest I take away was from Jack Clarke saying I should definitely take up playing the drums again, in fact "have no right not" to play. Maybe the nudge I needed after all these years of avoiding same due to thinking I hadn't time for both writing and music, would have to neglect one or the other since I couldn't feel myself being full-time serious about both at once, etc. So, here I am beating my knees black&blue with sticks and scraping the rust off my drums! Who knows? Figure to give it a shot, a winter of practice and see if the physical side comes back at all (after 12 years, god!). It's certainly a "side" of myself I've sorely neglected.

And, would you believe it?, Creeley was in Alaska! Feels somehow fated that we keep just missing one another here and there over 6 or 7 years now. Buffalo felt gloomy like a city at the end of the world with little definition, aimless streets under chemical cloud. But also it's the start of the midwest and I could imagine just keep on driving west, a bit of the old On The Road feeling. Perfect weather for the traveling and the very next weekend they got a foot of snow there!

Here I've just finished reading Mariani's vast WCW biography, a great chance to meditate in deep on the fascinating Williams life (somebody should give Alice a copy for Christmas). Though he was willful as hell, and vain enough I spose, he also had a great sense of being another "worker in poetry," like, Let's all get together and work on the idiom, etc. and of course was eventually disappointed. I was amazed to find out just how much he allowed Zukofsky to severely prune his book manuscripts. I imagine he must have felt sometimes "dumb" like I do at the vastness of the field of attempt. And in fact he kept trying to organize writers to get together and read their works and mull it all over in person but of course everybody kept falling out by the way and he always ends up by himself again making his big dumb statements about variable feet etc. I get big pangs of sympathy. And I remember how you were once talking about being a "worker," and how Godard keeps trying to work with other people on projects but it always seems to come to the same disappointment. I don't know exactly what I mean here, in practice, I guess, but it's got to do with feeling each of us like isolate boat heaps. We talk over it all so little and then put out our little poems and people criticize or just ignore mostly? Agh, it's horribly confusing, and I keep imagining useless conversations with non-artists who ask why I'm not "doing" anything meaningful to world and I say but I am I'm writing poetry, which comes to feel more like some hard kernel of no matter if anybody does read it. If I keep on like this I'll work myself into another deep mind mess!

But I must tell you I do feel very like you describe yourself, "writing fast or not at all" though I too have over&over promised myself "Now this time I'll write real slow and have the space to see everything before proceeding" but it always comes back down to getting it down quick before whatever else intervenes. And, yes, all those poems I started writing after the OWN FACE impulse were an attempt to write something that "seems like a POEM," yes! In fact, if I get this big collection of the poems together in print I'm thinking seriously of calling it POEMS (1978 to whatever), a titling I never thought I'd consider even, just because it finally meant something to have poems(!) be the result of whatever I've been doing. I'm still trying to figure all this out, and in practice, because of course I still have the other impulse to become closely involved in long woven strands of fine details that require almost ULTIMATE attention on part of readers, if not, as you say, that they actually know me. Sometimes when I'm reading to an audience I even have time to think, shit, all these so many things are going by so fast how will anyone be able to grasp them a flicking second nevermind meditate on each of them at length as I have. How can anyone "hear" all these things that continually (it's part of their very life-process?) hide themselves variously behind eachother and sometimes dart out and cast strange lights here and there and on themselves?? I always end up guessing that it ultimately comes down to just what you can do at any time, which is I guess just another way of saying who you are helplessly and can you change yourself as radically as you might sometimes have to imagine? I too imagine great gleaming constructs (god!) like tiered cities on the horizon. Romance of the impossible? But I just keep stepping toward that unknown whatever, it must all come out of that?, no matter the consequences or what all I might "like" to do or have done.

Somehow apropos, I got a lovely note out of the blue from John Cage the other day. He said he had heard from somebody (a conversation with you?) that I was feeling depressed about my work (or my "work and society") and he just wanted me to know that he loved my work and wanted more of it (& please come visit etc.). It brought tears to my eyes. And we haven't seen each other in years. He is a great man.

Lyn Hejinian has been urging me to contact Geoff Young (THE FIGURES) about a possible book, so I just wrote to sound him out about maybe printing a big collection of poems. Then immediately Bill Berkson wrote me that Young's "out of money" but "don't let that stop you"(!?) This bizzness is coocoo! But it's surely time to get these things out of the growing heap and off my desk and out of the way of new writing. The impulse is now and I'm afraid that if somebody doesn't make a book of the poems soon they'll just relapse into unmanageable stacks for too many more years. You know the feeling. They want covers! Also this would make me look through them all more carefully in putting together book-sequencing so I can see just what I've done. Not "if they're good" or anything, I know what's what there, but Where now? Who now?

And, would you believe it (yes), Corbett just wrote me about that sheaf of poems I sent Ted&Alice asking if I could send it to him to be copied and (mainly) so he could have a copy of "my new book." I had to tell him it ISN'T a book and I don't even have a copy of that "manuscript" here, just the work sheets of the poems. His antennae are atwitch as ever! Actually I am planning on sending him whatever collection I (hopefully) make up since he offered free Xeroxing. I told him to write me a letter, ok? Is he really that hurried/harried? (all those unanswerable cards) I suppose. His new book/poem makes him sound prematurely aged with all these unreconcileables that won't go away (his father et al.), but they really can't be called "obssessions" at least the way I see obssession as a generative thing. I was thinking the other day how much I love the way the surrealist poets (at their best anyway: early Eluard, Breton's NADJA) could make their obssession with love/sex/woman into a hard gleaming OBJECT of obssession that therefore would stand and transmit. I have a (maybe unfinished) poem somewhere, called PROCESSIONS OF THE OBSSESSION, which takes off from that NADJA feeling. And I just bought a Gallimard edition of CAPITALE DE LA DOULEUR (my favorite!) in maybe vain(?) itchy and myopic attempt to peer into the French.

Why do I insist on putting four s's in obsession?

Flaubert's letters are great, especially the ones to Louise Colet full of sex details but also, though it seems she wasn't a very good poet, all those writing secrets. Here's one that really rang a bell in me, he's in midst of copying out the first part of BOVARY and says "I should like to be able to read these one hundred and fifty-eight pages at a single glance and grasp them with all their details in a single thought." Right? That one really jumped at me. I've felt like that about my long prose, and sometimes almost thought I was about to be able to do it, but as it grew longer . . .

Writing erects such a silence that it seems we should be able to do so many things in it. But mostly it proves a most evasive silence, medium for only what actually is (has been) done. It lingers and covers like a hum that mostly just obscures many of the possibilities that have just lit there. This bothers me. And makes me think that maybe Beckett is right, we write just to be able to stop, to erect such an impenetrable silence that nothing further will itch at us. Or would this be a kind of "living death"? Or is living-death in this sense something else, a going-on I can't foresee? But this immediately gets, if not scary, imponderable.

We went to see REDS the other night. Started out interesting, details of recreated oldtime etc., and the interviews with real "survivors" (Henry Miller, Scott Nearing et al.) are great, big heads looming out of the darkness (especially the women actually), but then it gets confused and finally boring as the "romance" intrudes, lovers running around searching for eachother in a big world that grows helplessly smaller as it gets oh so well known. There's some funny problem about overlays of sentiment on history. Of course the movie-details of such sentiment are by now so familiar, you find yourself drifting away imagining what could be instead and I got really tired in the part after intermission (it's 3½ hours). But Keaton is great I think, I like the way she can get a really scared look in her eyes. And there are a couple great fights like pictures full of soft light with nevertheless sharp edges. But, though I started out with a real curiosity about John Reed (only know about him in flashes through reading about Mabel Dodge etc.) I finally realized I wasn't getting to know him at all but instead purely Warren Beatty (I don't much care to know about).

So many movies now I can get wired up about tiny details but then realize I'm taking them to where I might develop them and have left the existing movie behind! Trying to nurture oneself on tiny glimpses? Such movies give me a bound up feeling, like the makers were scared of busting out and showing some amazing secret developments, truly extended thinks, true moves in imagined world. I guess we surely know the reasons for this and they're boring.

I hope I didn't give you the impression that I was uninterested in your Utopia, quite the opposite! I'm fascinated to see it! I can't wait to see what kind of imagination it is. It's odd I think that people wouldn't have sympathy for such a project right now in this crapped-up time. But then, who are these "people"? Cynical NewYorkers who have to think it silly? Isn't a (an?) Utopia one of the grand tasks in literature? Would it take great hubris to attempt? Or just getting pissed off enough? Maybe people think it would be a big embarrassing revelation about yourself? All the more reason to try, no? Odd how the Greek root means "not a place."

One of those bright blue days here today after 8 inches of blowing snow yesterday (but not the two feet or so that evidently buried R.I. & Boston). Winter all arrived in one day! Ready or not. And today Celia's home with a cold, after two nights out at "slumber parties" (do they still call them that?) at a friend's house. Where they seem to have spent most of their time watching video-tapes of such as FRIDAY THE THIRTEENTH PART TWO (what's a parent to do?). Maybe she mainly just didn't want to go to school, "expected" a snowday, like I used to(?) She wants earphones for Christmas, and tapes. She likes THE PRETENDERS now. Where will her version of rock&roll lead? It's like trying to imagine a Utopia?

Of course another side of this whole project is to just start writing and make a sheer EVERYTHING work and never stop and just let the chips, something I've yet to dare to do, would you have to stop everything (else) in order to include everything? A work of the pure endless(?) consciousness striving? Wonder if after decades of writing one would just have accumulated the "chops" to write on and not worry about "form" et al.? Then I get into my hassles about not being able to write (in hand or type) FAST enough. This sounds, too, like your "shorthand" ideas for such a project, we keep coming back to it don't we?! Then, of course (ha!) one runs into (inevitably?) the resistance effect, wherein (I was just out taking pictures in the snow) as in photos just because a thing stands up "out there" there's no assurance that it will stand up in a photo (or in words). A feeling off this like we are always making up the whole world all over again & again, maybe those Buddhists are right?!

This is where my speculations start to mummify and fall off the table. I too would like to describe some scenery (there's that urge to travel again!). A new landscape, a new world, a new mind, and Hello Doctor Williams. A beautiful day the cat won't go out in.

Lewis' new haircut sounds as hard to imagine as a Utopia (send me a picture?). A change like that can be mindfully necessary and it'll always grow out if it don't "work." I always seem to be inbetween on the issue of men's hair with mine. But Flaubert said, "No middle course! Life!"

Hey, you didn't tell me about some of the things on your list and left me intrigued! What did Cage say about Utopia? Did you read the Jane Bowles biog? What is "Herland"? Write soon and let's keep this going!

Much love to all (& give Rosemary a hug for me),

Clark

JANUARY 12 1982

Dear Clark,

I havent had time to write to answer your letter much as I've wanted to but I have, also for a long time, wanted to tell you how much I loved your poems in the manuscript you originally gave Ted + Alice. They're amazing!

Make heart beat faster + more in tune, stop + start, made me weep for joy at possible emotion, + took me higher + out of this often too busy or too some thing life, like the sense these words on paper are as they ought to be. So if I dont have a chance to write a real letter before I see you, I did want to say at least that. Funny coincidences in your letter—we had just seen Reds too + thought the same as you of it. I've been embroiled in the New Year's Benefit, which went well. It'll be great fun to see you next week.

Love,

Bernadette

FEBRUARY 6, 1982

Dear Clark,

Ah finally I am done with this hideous Larry Rivers Benefit which has been taking up so much of my time, we made some money but not enough for it to be worth my trouble and after one more season of this social service work I'm ready to retire, I often wonder if I'll live a long enough life not to resent even this much! Anyway—other problems—Rosemary is fine and recuperating fast enough to be bored and bitchy at having to sit still so long at this point, she has the most amazing environment for herself in her loft just normally, but now in her recuperation it's even more eccentric and she reclines in a room filled with overgrown plants like trees and pots of hyacinths and what are the first spring flowers, you know [→ crocuses] the ones that poke through snow from time to time! She demands an inch of wine and the rest of the glass filled with water! She's well.

So as you said in your last letter which was well nigh two months ago (but now the work of the money-raising is pretty much done by me & I'll be faster after this, I promise), I'm a worker, I've always thought of myself as a worker (you were talking, in case it's too long to remember about William Williams and his workerliness), but now I'm afraid I'm turned into a sort of social worker! I dont know what to do about this but to take it as fate, I doubt that anybody winds up doing anything in the world (if there's any choice at all) that they I mean he or she doesnt secretly partly want to do or be doing, like in love, dont you think? I always think in love that you wind up having things happen, even if they seem bad at some moment, that you wanted to have happen, having recognized at the outset of falling in love with another human being what that person's nature is and all that is and would be inherent in it. When I propound this idea to others, they give me trouble, but I believe it. It makes me (perhaps too much so) adaptable. Now it's time for a big belly laugh and to listen to a really sad and heartrending Tom Waits song. Oh lord what is this life, and so on. I seem to be called upon to spend alot of time helping other people these days, so much so that it's even more than I can do much less to consider time to write, or read. I dont know what to make of it all. I want to help and I have a sense of an ethical life that involves helping yet I want to be having all the time in the world for myself, my dreaming, my sleeping, my thinking, and finally the writing that does result from that—I'm afraid I've a slow hand. So I begin to think of this time, as I told you, as a temporary situation where I have to be wholeheartedly doing what I'm doing and hoping it's worthwhile, meanwhile trying to keep writing, seeing how it affects my writing, and learning as rapidly as possible all I can about human nature. But oh fuck it, I'd rather be you, often. I know this life (& the life of the world in general) forces me to go too fast, and as a result I get literally unhealthy and then cant work well, but how at this point can I ever again excerpt myself from the life of the world?! I secretly know the answer to that question, first off I'd like to return to the country somehow, then take all my children out of school (ha!), then, well this isnt practical, but to be able to move around to a certain extent so that they as well as me would be studying nothing but society and our own thoughts—short of living in some workable community (like utopias!) where others are truly present, it would be nice wouldnt it? to be able to work, truly. **[Page break]**

Your readings were wonderful, what a pleasure to hear in the midst of my hearing so much of contemporary poetry I could get an inspiration from your works, of course, which is simply that the words must be, like in that Beethoven Last Quartet where he phrases musically "It must be." Nothing unnecessary or even gratuitous (a word I normally like) in your work. & oh the feelings, not to be spoken, about justice and truth, which I can only tell to you—what's that all about? Sweet truth like a penny, the most revolutionary. (forget about all).

(Remember everything).

Obssession ought to be spelled for the rest of its life like that or like obbssessionn.

Makes the word sound at the end like John! or Eon.

Old-fashioned Anglo-Saxon johns and eons, we've had enough of them, havent we, better to be a person from outer space, but please I beg of us we wont seem crazy in the world, we'll be perfectly sane on the surface because of our love.

Meanwhile, in the normal world, MIDWINTER DAY is due out in five weeks, so given the condition of publishers I'd guess sometime in April, with no cover by Eliot Porter but a plain cover with just print on it, well what the hell. I must admit I dont care & have now developed a slightly paranoid feeling that my publishers dont care either and are thinking of this as one of their books "that wont make money" which of course it wont, but shit I havent had a book now in four years. & you know what MIDWINTER DAY seems like to me now? it seems like a practically buddhistic meditation on pleasure and evenness like the moon that (also practically) has ceased to exist in the world since it was written (certainly for me). Well this is narcissistic going on I guess, but like a lover who finally comes around after you've lost interest in him or her, I feel embarrassed about this book about my own feelings about it. Who cares? I say to myself, it's just this thing I wrote four or five years ago, perhaps I have a distorted sense of time (Ashbery in a recent interview says all poetry is about passage of time, what a bore) but I feel like I'd much rather have a book of most recent poems being published instantaneously—dont you?

Surely writing could conceivably never stop, I would hope so, I would hope it could be so—to be such a lunatic would be sublime, thus the silence we speak about. Somebody someday has to do that work of never stopping, of going as fast as it can be gone to the point, dare I say it, of eliminating existence at all so that, and that would be an interesting moment, which gets gotten to sometimes in poems, or in Proust, you've finally gotten to the end of reminiscence and all experience and certainly all knowledge (if you have it)—well actually poems do this all the time I guess, like Rimbaud—and get left with the great and wonderful high blank of no purpose at last but a mind wherein you can know exactly (ha!) how you and everyone else too exists in the world at this time (not the times but breathing). Oh am I being pretentious, I hope not, because I do mean it. My sister's lost loft is such a fantasy of her world, she maintains it at great cost and has done so for many years and it's full of objects and sculptures and wonderful things which create a new world in her home for her; very few people do this—her place is like a version of Disneyland, for her, perhaps too individual, certainly not commercial, her works are not salable at "this moment in time," it's fascinating. I dont want to be anybody at all, I'd prefer to be nobody, but a nobody who could actually unveil all the amazing secret developments of the whole fucking world. I have to get to work, or back to work reading again all the new physics books and the books about how life has begun to be discovered to have begun on this planet—dont we need to know all of this? dont we need to know everything? have I given it all up and become temporarily a social worker and less of a hermetic philosopher than I'd like to be? None of these terms fit me, perhaps because I'm a woman. I feel old in the sense that I dont know anything that "entertains" me, nor do I want to go to jail, if you'll forgive the leap in my logic. Beyond all the possible helping of other people and the keeping of the Poetry Project going, which I'm "ethically" committed to doing for one more season, I find much of what goes on in this community not worth my time, compared to my desire to do my own work and devote that time to it. I'm not talking about cultural events—all the millions of great dance concerts I dont have time or money to go to—I'm sure they're inspiring. I'm talking about the world I wind up being consigned to, for lack of time for the rest, which is a weird combination of the poetry community and the great big larger world that exists in the newspapers. [→ The one is trivial, + in the other I'm helpless.] Oh I am waxing homeopathically corny, I know. Sorry.

Sophia tonight is at a "slumber party!" with three other children, all little boys! I cant believe it's come to this so soon. I find the whole thing pretty humorous but I'm serious when I say I think parents rush kids into things a little bit too fast—all these slumberers are four years old! Not only that but they're all expecting to catch chicken pox in the next few days, from another nursery school person. & tomorrow's Max's 2nd birthday! he being born at 3:30 this morning, just a few hours from now in anniversary, in Henniker, in a whole different life, wherein my student pronounced him a definite person from outer space—a cone-head, and indeed his head emerged from me when he was in the act of being born and for many minutes his body wouldnt, so that the midwife, not knowing if this person was a boy or girl—the ultimate question of birth?—was saying to him, oh hello welcome to the world, and I was shouting, oh dear baby why dont you come out. Now Max is a real kid, growing up faster than he even needs to because of his sister's constant "teaching" and this birthday certainly marks the end of my dealing with infancy (except in adults?). I'm glad in many ways and love having the children be older, be companions, but I dreamt last night of nursing a baby again. And then I dreamt that Anne Waldman was "freaking out at a benefit" and I asked her what was the matter and she said, well you gave me the finger, and in the dream I lied to her and said, oh no I didnt do that, but actually I had. & there were so many other sort of star-struck people all mixed in with the babies and the taking care of babies. I dreamt I went to a place for a vacation, and the place was flooded, and I thought why did I bother to come here, to deal with these floods, but I found high ground. Such rhetoric in one's dreams!

I'd like to write on and on, in this letter, and everywhere I'd like to write till like Freud said only fatigue or hunger would stop you and Kerouac had a solution for that. I'd wish for no exigencies in life, especially as I get older, I'd like to be a stone I think, a stone like a big head on top of a tree which collaboration made me at least look like a human being and I could only just sway immobile in the wind. But I'm here with moving body that goes up first and second avenues all the time, and even beyond there, to some completely undramatic purpose. I hope, often, I'm not a total fool.

Love, Bernadette

THURSDAY 18 MARCH [1982]

Dear Bernadette,

You're probably wondering where I am(?) And I'm wondering if maybe I haven't run out of things to say, except in the writing (and I want to say: of course). Maybe that's what it'll (this writing "we" "do") come down to: furled into a particular warp, the only one we'll finally be able to use to "speak"? What a notion! And yet and yet . . . One of the things the writing tells me, this.

Actually the other day I realized I don't like the word "writer." Something wrong with it, like wet cardboard around a black metal chair leg. Anglo Saxon, that, "to scratch," which should be okay, but somehow . . . The Greek and Latin ones are better, no? Logos. Scriptor!

(which reminds, warmly, of first mechanical pencil we probably all had(?): SCRIPTO). Are we scribes? I certainly get the feeling I'm "taking things down" from somewhere(?) As if I would be a clerk (British pronounce "clark" anyhow)? And thinking of Kerouac's "sketching," when I wanta get relieved of my head and its endless routes.

Thinking of Kerouac anyway since Larry's been after me/us (did he write you & ask for piece?) for ROAD memories/memoirs. By the way, I used a great sentence from your last letter in mine (sentence about the Great Everything Writing, which just perfectly set down all I wanted to get in there about that), hope you don't mind(?) I had to laugh since Larry claimed your sentence/thought was "pure Hinayana Buddhist" concept. Just shows you what (or how little) an alternate set of terms can do for you. Rumour now is (you've heard?) that Larry is about to take on the Vajrayana(sp?) course-load, maybe even go for one of them "weekends"(!) Too much. Or could that be one of the "terms" for splicing up their marriage?

He's still got me on the string (vagueness) re whether I'll be asked out for the JK wingding in July. Must say it sounds more & more the waste of time, what with all this amassing of Steve Allens & ex-wives & skid-row buddies. Doubt I'd get in more than 2 or 3 sentences on a "panel" or whatever. Did you get the Naropa Summer Schedule thing? Cracked me up: on K's "methods of writing, poetics, composition et al." panel they got Ferlinghetti, Robert Frank & David Amram(!) Wow, good thinking there, Allen. Actually I think they'd best give a reading of his complete works and go home.

And I hardly want to get into the Tom Clark invite matter. Sufficient to say that the potential for suckerdom in that locale seems strictly unlimited.

Oh dear, how boring all this gossip. It won't even stick in the ground like a post. Travel may indeed be the ticket. Now that the bucks for same grow shorter by the hour. Take the kids out of school (permanently!) and just keep moving seems a most attractive idea (at least, unattached to any other considerations). Would we could etc. How much is fear, how much willpower, how much practical thinking about all of life together in one big carseat lump? I dunno. But I do know that my memories of Peru have already entered the lighting and proportions of childhood memories.

And how quick they did that! Equality of intensity and etching-in, no matter one's age? Anyway good to see the mechanism's still firing.

And speaking travel, I've been jaunting about a bit (much, for winter?) myself. A week in Frisco to visit with Palmers (saw only a few others, by plan, Lyn, BB & Meltzers). Then a quick peek into mere corner of Manhattan last saturday for the Cage event. Tomorrow Susan & I are escaping(!) for weekend on Vineyard, something we've promised ourselves all through the Fall etc. Maybe we'll get snowed in down there & have to stay for weeks!

Lots of talk re the Big Sex Work (challenge) in the air. Michael P. & BB both interested in trying such. Bill says he's decided he can say "she" but not "you" in matters of sexual address. Hmmm. I don't know if that's a distance he feels he needs or any kind of intrinsic necessity. Seems to me such a thing is close to well-known dangers of "She walks in beauty . . ." etc. Michael said all the sex letters in Penthouse are written by one person (a man). He knows somebody who knows this guy. Heavy stylistic models we all grew up with (Miller, Lawrence, pulp-porn etc.) are no help: I used to try using porno texts, cut 'em up, rearrange etc., but all you seem to end up with is a Burroughs-type shake-down. Sade's mechanistics are sorta interesting if you read a lot of him. Funny how some of the sado-takes are more interesting as writing somehow. Ballard's Crash, for example. Funny too how Bill B was a bit perturbed by my Fucking At Night poem. He actually asked me if I was referring to sadistic action(!) He must've taken it I meant leather when I said "belts" instead of garter as I intended. Ha! An area full of quicksands.

The Cage scene was amazing. Packed house, the biggest I guess I've ever read in front of, lines around the block throughout. They were quite quiet and attentive though. John gave me a very kind introduction, after asking if I "minded" if he did so(!) I went on between a Cage percussion piece and Paul Jacobs playing Schoenberg, not bad company? I got the strange but exhilarating feeling while reading (sections 1 & 3 of Am Ones) that the work was finally on its own, hardly needed any touch at all from me anymore, I could almost watch my lips moving and felt at one point like I was sitting in a corner of my head responding ("hmmmm," "What!?", "yeah") to my own words. The only at all uncomfortable thing about the whole scene was that this is evidently the kind of event where all your past "acquaintances" tend to come out of the woodwork. Like, a guy who claimed we'd been at Brown together that I still can't recall at all. Another guy I'd forgotten all about (20 years at least) who's now conducting the pit-orchestra for Chorus Line. Also somebody I'd met on the boat in the Galapagos showed up. Glad I don't get to do this kind of thing very often! Overall though it was great, the music et al., and I had fun. The only poets: me & Jackson, who now looks so tiny and frail with his beard shaved off and his hair cut, I almost didn't recognize him!

Well, not really much more to report from this slushy neck of the territory right now. Oh, Celia had her first period the morning of the day I flew to California, doing her best to act totally cool about it. A lot of her school friends had already had theirs and I think she was beginning to worry she'd never get hers. Now the problem is that Hancock is wanting to move all the kids from here up to Mount Greylock High, and of course Celia doesn't want to leave her friends, feeling she doesn't want to go through that initiation twice (she just entered New Lebanon High this year). I don't blame her. It's not at all certain this change will take place (would be next year anyway), but if it does we may find ourselves in the strange position of having to pay the difference in tuition to keep her in Lebanon (which ain't such a hot school anyway).

This is sort of an interim note I guess. Hope I have more to go on longer about next time. Feeling kind of hurried right now, not sure why. Really want to get a lot of work done in next few months here before the summer traveling madness hits again. Oh, please tell Eileen I enjoyed her book, in case I don't get to write thanking her properly. Also, do you know Steve Malmude's present address? I promised (after my reading) I'd send him some books and then promptly lost his address(!) Typical poet behavior. Feeling oddly scattered, maybe 'cause I'm trying to read 4 or 5 books at once and working on 3 Or 4 different works? Maybe the Vineyard will help (though rain, snow & other varied sky horrors are predicted). Anyway . . .

Much Love,

Clark

APRIL 29, 1982

Dear Clark,

I just finished reading your poem! "Flight from Hartford to Los Angeles" to the AERIAL's audience, which was of course mostly the AERIAL's contributors, and what a great pleasure it was! First of all, I and you (thru me!) and Reed Bye were among the few people who had the perspicacity to read just one work, plus Joe Brainard who though he read four, read briefly. Man, after about two million poetry readings at this point in the season any poet who reads more than one poem in a group reading must be insane. However, on from that, your work is wonderful and what a pleasure to read it. I rehearsed about three times, not daring to write you about it, for fear you'd decide against it, and now having had the chance to read the work aloud with all its fast-talking (I read it fast) and words like globigerina & Elasmosaurus, well I couldnt have had a better time & would wish for a chance to read all your works aloud, would that there were more chances to do so, I found myself beating my feet on the floor in time to the work & wishing I lacked timorousness enough to throw out my arm at some "beat" moment. Actually it's Elasmosaur just before Stegosaur (sic, ha ha). I pronounced everything right & with feeling, I had more fun being you than me tonight (my own poem luckily takes about one minute to read), and thank you for the chance to do this! Yvonne, & also Mimi Gross & Michael Scholnick and others praised your work afterwards. It was a funny sort of wooden reading as a whole, where when you stood up to read you felt like you were in school but there were some loosening moments, especially Kenward's singing of "Eggs" & Joe's nervous looseness & an unexpected piece by Rudy about looking up and down and looking at Yvonne, & a tape of Edwin dutifully un-homaged by Rudy who placed the speaker on the reader's table & said, "well this is Edwin I guess." Anyway a real agglomeration of the NY poets which showed both how living and how dead they are. & how sometimes glowing & sometimes wooden. Then Lewis & Peggy & I had the perspicacity to abhor any further socializing & simply go out to dinner together & we went & had a wonderful meal of antipasto, pollo mimosa, veal & cannelloni with lots of wine & the first chance we've had to talk together that unrelievedly, without children around, for about seven years!

Our life, mine and Lewis's, has been rather boring lately—suffice it to say it is mostly involved with a rent strike and acoustical and political problems at the church, which, if I related them, that relation would make you think I was another! Most recently no hot water again for days, then no mail (landlord harassment) for two days, even worse because we're expecting a sort of live-or-die grant announcement, and just briefly our landlord (who is not a person) is harassing all the people in our building to try & get them to move out so he can turn it into a cooperative & since we as a result refuse to pay our rent, we spend much time at rent-strike meetings & in court. It's especially unconscionable because for most of the winter there was so little heat as to (the intent) drive out the older tenants whose rent-controlled apartments & senior-citizen status make them the most desireable for the greedy landlord to want to get rid of. But us rent-strikers (only about 1/10th of the tenants) have accomplished something, at least in scaring the landlord into making the building a little bit safer to live in, though I doubt that he'd hesitate to sabotage the lives of everyone in it if it were "in his interest," and we are the ones who dare to have "nothing to lose." Anyway I did say didnt I I wouldnt bore you with all this & now a child is crying. . . . who is now calmed down. I wont I promise tell about the acoustical problems! I wont!

Acoustically Max though is quite amazing & can speak wonderful sentences like the one he said to me this morning, at age two: "I have these paper cups because Lewis daddy gave them to me to play with," which is all the more complex than it even sounds because it's a lie! Which type of sentence has graduated from the sentence like, "Need more one books Max." It's astonishing to me to converse with this person, age two, with whom I can have a nearly normal & regular conversation, his being so small—we can talk about almost everything (at least that is important to me). & subterfuge is not the least part of it, because one of Max's original sentences was, either, : Sophia did it, or, Marie did it! Not to be outdone, Sophia has most recently given forth with one of her greatest Steinian lectures, which she gave originally for the benefit of Anne & Reed at dinner: how she was going to invite, when she was ten & could cook the dinner & Marie would be 12 and could light the stove, all the people of the world to dinner including the clouds, stars, rain, snow, rainbows & trees & lightning & thunder (but none of them would do anything at the dinner because we wouldnt want it to be frozen or rained on or . . . , they would just sit still). & Marie recently outdid herself as an incipient adolescent by stealing a $20 bill from my drawer to trade at school for some "stickers" that her friend Hui had told her could only be gotten by him from New Jersey, if she would give him some money, she only to be caught in this transaction by her teacher who laughed and saved us the twenty dollars, which to Marie could as easily have been $1. So adult life begins, maybe. So amazing that Celia has had her period! Just after I got your letter mentioning that, Marie was asking me all about my period, & I told her Celia had just gotten hers for the first time, then later that day Max said to me, oh mommy you have a penis! after which I gave him a little talk about life too. He seemed to have the impression that all grownups were men and all "sisters" were girls and that was all there was to it! However, why not?

I've been working, as much as I can, hard at my utopia book, and I've nearly got the first draft, which is really the third draft, done, and just last night I solved the problems of the end of it which has been obsessing me for a long time. & when I do have it done what I'm going to do is make copies for a number of people and send them out & ask for contributions and emendations & footnotes & whatever anyone would want to contribute, so you'll see something of that soon. I'm so amazed at having come close to finishing some version of it—& it's all a question of structure in a way, a way of making myself think harder & trying to make a decent or new structure for some work—anyway, I hope you'll find it worthwhile. It's a book I'll have to write again and again, but why not finish it for once now & try again later. Or maybe the next time I try it wont be a form as naive as "utopia" but something else, anyway I've done it or nearly so. & what a stupid struggle to do the book against the odds of having to work at the church & also wanting or feeling I have to go to certain other things in NY, all the while lately simultaneously reading Wm. Williams' biography, strange as it is, and feeling empathy with all that doctorhood since I seem to have been led into so much taking care of.

dear clerk-clark: I don't know about scribes, but we are cupbearers an image I'm sure I never liked which has come and come to me & now I see that it is just waiting, that is what we do is waiting, holding onto something (not for anyone). & in the midst of the waiting, passing the time, staying in shape, exercising, sketching, even journalizing. It's not that there isnt much else to do but when you're on this particular train already, well if you can get elsewhere through your gravity-prone veins swell, like machu pichu or even boulder or frisco old-home but I like to say in a little manageable corner & lower east side is much like lenox, but I'd wish to be here (there) on my own terms (fresh air, no hours), I've no choice about the air, at least I can make my own hours, & do some valuable political work, I hope. I must admit I feel old, oh shit I must admit I must've said that before, but I like feeling old (grownup) but dont like it too (old in other ways). & "of sex" I believe bill b was only disturbed by your "belts" as in their being not "enigmatic" enough! dont you think? Belts of any kind are after all not stones. I remember once when I was pregnant being told by a man who professed to love me, well what's in your belly must be a stone, when I felt most distinctly that it was a monkey! **[Page break]**

Anyway, what were we talking about, change of page, sex poems, in early middle age! & how to manage one's life and love for one's lover and sex too in the midst of this desire, shit it's not even a desire it's unconscionable, to write at all hours which doesnt exactly make you exempt from the human universe, I would wish though to be exempt from this job which makes me too speedy and to drink too much so that I dont even know what it feels like to have two weeks of peace with my own thoughts, which maybe I'm not supposed to now that I'm a grownup & I often think maybe I've been a grownup too long, it's time to do something else! (also consult confusing Williams biography on this). The women poets, but for Alice, if you want to say this, have not grown up, but rather grown down. I cant say this.

&

now its spring in Ny available for your notice, but I dont notice because to some extent I've grown to hate myself here, and if I were to truly grow up I wouldnt do that. I do need what they call a vacation & Lewis and I are hoping to find one this summer. I find it hard to accept that the feeble but beautiful signs of spring in the city can go along with the feelings in my body about the season when I'm simultaneously engulfed in the fumes of landlord harassments & poets acting as though you've insulted them for spending the nights of their readings doing your own writing. Fuck it, I actually only care about my own writing and my children & Lewis—why should I care about anything else? This job I'm so dutiful toward, I wouldnt do it if I were able to find some other better way to earn money, or just had some money. It's dismal to be caught up in this identity, which I've made as nought of as anybody could, but still it's that, it's there. I hate the expected importance & I hate the politics (though I like the politics of being able to use the job to change things, oh fuck I didnt want to be writing about this, I'm just doing so because I'm tired).

Twelve thousand trees are in bloom in the st. mark's yard (one of our best playgrounds) against the wishes or with them of my white shirt or the whitest shirt I can find to wear under my vest to go and read uptown, the vest to hide my unfashionably Raphaelesque belly from the white queers who are our cohorts in poetry, oh I dont mean to say that & I'd guess I cant send this letter though I will send it, hope you dont mind it, my heart is under the weather and I would like to write a new kind of work, as always, also so many people's parents are sick and even dying I dream very often now I see myself so that I'm not a feeling person in my dreams which drives me crazy, I even attacked myself in my dream the other night as a bear ("bernadette") & before that as a vulture (leonardo)

Ah but I'll let you go,
in great & difficult sanity,
WITH LOVE, *Please write me soon, I beg!*
Bernadette

SATURDAY 8 MAY **[1982]**

Dear Bernadette,

Glad you liked reading my "poem"! I'd forgotten all about how Yvonne wrote and asked who I would pick to read it in my absence and I wrote back and said you or if you didn't want to then Yvonne herself should read it. But I must say I don't think of that writing as a poem, it's really just a notebook entry, and I never would have thought to publish it or even type it up except for Yvonne's asking for things aerial. Good it all worked out for the best anyway. And by the way, please do feel free to read anything of mine you want out loud anytime, you hereby have my carefree permission(!) I'd love to hear you do it, if that wouldn't make you nervous. In the case of that airplane entry, I'm sure it gained lots by your "fast" reading of it, since it's really a lot of separate takes surrounded by (too much?) air. It'd be great to hear you read some prose of mine (like MINE) sometime.

Which reminds me, you once promised to make a tape of Elizabeth Browning's sonnets for me (I won't hold you to that!).

And speaking of MINE, I got a great surprise phonecall from Geoff Young last week saying he was reading mss of MINE (evidently he copied the copy Barry had copied from the copy I sent Michael) and was all enthusiastic to publish it "by the summer." And at that point I was about to send a poem-collection mss, which he said to send anyway since he might want to do that too(!) Certainly is a great Up, with my groaning about publishing possibilities being about dead these years etc., though I hardly know the man, hope it'll all work out as he stated without the usual publisher hassles one tends to discover along the way, when it's too late etc. I'm probably just trying to keep myself from getting too excited. MINE is the work I'd most like in print right now, but had just about adjusted to the "fact" that it probably wouldn't be for a long time to come. Odd detail too is that he's moving to Great Barrington this summer, for a year or something fairly temporary, I don't understand why. I guess he has money(?)

That's the biggest news for now from here. Otherwise we're trying to get our summer plans straight. Which isn't exactly being aided by Larry's procrastinating about the Kerouac thing. He called the other night to say there's now a "90 percent chance" I'll get asked. Meanwhile my enthusiasm has been diminishing for the whole scene, which sounds more&more like some kind of carny-seance I'd be lost in amidst all the attendant Abbies & Timothies. A couple of panels and a reading (w/ Ted & Creeley, L. says). Ho hum. Who knows? But we plan to go out to Cal anyway, probably 2nd week in July for a couple weeks, then I might just fly home by way of Boulder, Celia & Susan going straight home at the same point. But I'll have to give Larry an ultimatum soon since it's getting already kind of late to book flights.

And speaking of Creeley, can you believe his overweening (to put it mildly) remarks re Corbett's books in the newsletter?! He must be missing some vital brain cells. Or is that all a kind of Boston nostalgia? Anyway reminds me how Bob's been afflicted by blurborhea in recent years. Everybody a "boss poet," etc. Somehow I find that term insulting. Or just too callous. And finally meaningless.

Bill C. has been very nice

lately about doing limitless free Xeroxing for me. But I spose he figures he's getting a good deal since he gets to keep a copy of everything he wants. Which does make me feel a bit funny, since there certainly are several people I would send copies of my work to before him. Oh well. Bitch bitch bitch.

That Mimeo Argument seems sure to start a great brouhaha, no? Might be fun. I find myself more on Eileen's side so far. I've never had any great love for mimeo as mimeo. Too instant fallapart and grunged under-shoe in backrooms all over. Paper held together by tiny metal pins run through it seems bound to be torn apart. But I just can't shake a love for the well-letter-pressed page, hardcovered if possible. That's the only "real" book to my mind, and if that makes me a booboisie so be it. And it ain't for reason of money (all I ever made from Space was a $250 advance) (strangely about the same amount I got union-scale for the Serpent Power sessions). It's just the fact that well-printed/bound books do tend to last more than a few years. And I must say as I get older I think more about wanting my works to exist for readers beyond my lifetime: I was surprised to discover this just a few years ago, typical middle aged feelings I spose(?) And lacking such a book I'd rather hand around copies of mss, yeah. Most typewriter faces are easier-reading than most mimeo-jobs I've seen anyway, plus you get to choose who you send 'em to, more personal that way. And didn't the Russian poets tend to hand around original (even handwritten?) manuscripts, if not actually memorize and speak back each other's poems? I could get more of a romance going for that procedure than I could for mimeoing. Does this argument tend to hit into some more basic feelings about ourselves as active poets? Some kind of litmus test? I mean I do dig your spirit of disconnect from any capitalist procedures, but show me most mimeo poetry and I'll find myself saying, oh well I spose it's better than nothing . . . Like being forced to eat Velveeta for the rest of one's life? I mean, a glossy puff-job of somebody's nothing verse is one thing, but a mimeobook of some good poet shredded under the kitchen table and forgot ain't so great either. Quikness & cheepness have always been the mimeo virtues, but now it seems soon such cheepness will disappear as well. Ah, well, something else to argue about when we're not actually doing anything important!

And what is this importance of what we're doing? I keep getting the strong but indefinite feeling that it's beyond what we say about what we do. Certainly not publishing, careers, desires for fame or the right response. Not even glory. I don't mean to be mysterious, just think it out a bit further. Respond to a feeling that nags me, a feeling that I'm missing something in the very act of the work itself. I dunno, some pattern, some angle I keep missing that would give me a line to follow. A lot of the time I feel like I'm pursuing something blind, something I haven't been provided with the right integers to count. But it's there somewhere in the work, a work which I've managed to supersaturate with . . . what? so that the route has gotten obscured by maybe my own momentary fascinations? What do I tell myself? This is strange and deep and maybe even gets left off the memory side of dreams. But I keep thinking the data is there, somewhere, I've even written it, maybe over and over again. Maddening! A thing, a thought?, that makes notions of poetry seem trivial and sideline. The times you say "I can't say that," so you say something, the momentum must be kept, a movement in time to stay aware. Of what? Poetry being an act of transformation, and so fast the changes, must also be an act of obscuring. What do we let go by? The writer "has assassinated the natural day," Melville in Pierre. Sometimes I think I will have nothing at last but the words to go by, having lost my way among them. How much we have allowed into the field of words, and thus how many changes in the natural order we have made. An erected field to get lost in. Authorship seems a very odd title for such a doer.

Of course I've far from put this right. What do you think? And I don't think there is any "natural order," meant simply the state of things before I performed the operation of words upon them. I certainly haven't come up out of this hovering construe with much. Maybe I'm mostly jamming my own frequencies? Jumping around in the doubting mode. But there is a certain kind of knowledge possible from this field we alter and wander in. And the jumpy feeling withal that to speak of it is perhaps to silence it(?) Certain things come up . . . Like, the strong feeling that time has a lot to do with light, somewhere their secrets intertwine. The painter-writer relation seems to illumine this. Painters, to the writer's mind, condensing the time of momentary acts into the light of image. Image to the writer is of a very different order, often image hinders the momentum of his procedures. Maybe this is why something in me rejects the novel, say, since its heavy construction of images blocks the flow of the pursuit line(s) I am setting up? Is this crazy? Unclear enough to stop the conversation? Paddling in murk. I'm continually bedeviled with the question of whether the patterns I follow are my patterns or universe patterns. It would be so easy to get so blocked off in one's own tiny closets, and never know it. Or, worse, think of them as purely patterns of outside matter. Shit, I know the two are inextricably linked (thus the problem right there?), but I want to know just how far one side or the other of the line I am!

Have I salted myself too much with a certain vocabulary, say, making all the red areas blue? Are the lines of inquiry (they are received lines anyway?) wrong? Sometimes I even flinch from picking up a certain book (doesn't matter what) for fear that reading it will fill me with the off-matter that will block signals I was but a moment before all set to pick up. I've written so much by now that it's hard to remember, even what I had wanted by it. As if the act of walking through streets of a vast city were enough to change all of their names, not to mention buildings and people. Fated never to look back and to walk in circles, so that when we come back into the same streets they can't be recognized, they have been changed utterly. It's 2 A.M. and I'm usually circling myself anyway at this hour.

The windows are black. And last night we saw what looked like a vast fire, as of oil refinery or even whole small city blazing on the horizon. Nothing in the news about it today. The "news" obscures itself anyway these days, lines that might be followed nearly impossible to pick out of all the strew. Blabber blabber, but trying to say to you who have some chance of knowing what I'm up to/against.

So pissed off today with John Updike's piece on Melville in the NewYorker. He's such a businessman in the pulpit. Or as Michael P. says of such writers: If he's a writer then I am not, I'm something utterly opposing, and should have a different title. Or as de Kooning said to Greenberg, Only I should be allowed to speak of Cezanne. I know, I should avoid reading such things (even in the bathtub!).

Here's a great and terrifying thing in a letter of Kafka's: "My whole body warns me against each word, each word, before it lets me write it down, first looks round in all directions; the sentences literally disintegrate for me, I see their insides and then quickly have to stop."

Wrote the above late last night in midst of mind somewhat confused, frustratedly, wanting to talk it all over face to face (if only we could!). Today it's all one of those seamless greys. Young squirrels bounding & banging around on the deck up there. Makes me wish I could take on guise of bluejay and perform strafing missions(!) Sunday, midday, and it's finally the season of the tiny greens starting to show. Next week it'll look like full summer. And then, they say, the gypsy moths will start tearing it all down again. "You can hear them chewing in the night" etc. And I'm getting over my usual Spring cold, we've all had, lots of honking and coughing in the household. Just had to unclog the garbage-disposal with a gardening tool. **[Page break]**

So. And so what else? I haven't heard from Bill B in a month or so. Before that he seemed all doomed and clotted in hassles of dmoestic(ha!) domestic give & take. So many things seem to prevent him, and how many of those has he chosen? He keeps talking about Europe (Italy mainly) but I don't think they will go. How strange to feel stuck in Bolinas at this point!

By the way, my Kerouac "remembrance" piece was printed (the most instant publishing I've ever experienced!) in Naropa Student Newsletter. I still think your sentence is the star of the piece. Only problem is they spelled your name wrong ("Meyer"). Have you seen? If not I have an extra I'll send. Larry's talking about making up a book of all these JK musings, did he ask you for one too? I told him to ask you. Would be interesting to see everybody's responses, though they might turn out maddeningly similar(?), On The Road having been such a central point for so many of us. Bill B sent me his and it's such an amazing full graph of names dates & places. He could do such a detailed memory work if only he would (?)

Celia and I have great detailed movie discussions these days. She tends towards the horror & sci-fi, as so many kids now seem to. We watch Doctor Who (funny British sci-fi show) together every day at 5:30. You should see her, it'd be almost like meeting her again after all this time (of growth). We're really hoping you can find a way of visiting us here this summer. Please try! Looks like we'll be away for most of July (plus early August on Vineyard), but any other time. Maybe in June? Let's see if we can get something figured out.

Can't resist showing you this dream I had a few months ago. Just as I have it in my notebook:

I'm with a bunch of people (3 or 4) (events forgotten) and go out, I have to go to the bathroom, & sitting on the toilet I discover I've changed into Bernadette, my body anyway, and I remember thinking: Now I can find out how it feels to have breasts, and I start to look down but I've got an open book in my hands and have to finish what I'm reading first.

(ha ha, but true) (strangely mundane and funny) and that's all there was to it, I never did find out anything, can't even remember what book I was reading! Dailiness quick to close over the secrets again, even in dream . . .

Guess I'll close with that event, get this off soon enough that we have some chance of recalling what we're talking about(!) The greens filling the grey almost as you watch, and the birds exchanging chairs.

Love to all,

Clark

[BM: *thinks that's the only way to protect the true preciousness of a vision but, having begun something else too, involving people, how can illuminated writer be anything but generous + whole-hearted (thus, outer space) also, childhood "all is incorporated in me"—Whitman!*]

OCTOBER 2, 1982

Dear Clark,

Well now that I've got myself acclimated or whatever the word is to being in new york, after three weeks of having this city glare at me & also blare at me & be its most blatant self full of all the quarrelsome people so badly that you think it must be the atmosphere or something, now i'm finally used to it like some physical exercise that feeling is, now i'm ready to go right back to Monterey! Lewis and I were just consoling each other that we'd rather spend the winter in the cabin there where we'd have to live in the upstairs bedrooms to keep warm than here in this rather old-fashioned state of nausea. Well I'm sure this is not something you want to hear all about and I've tried to put off writing you a letter till I had something more, how do they say?

upbeat? to say & in the meantime I've reorganized our entire house & literally touched if not cleaned every object in it, washed the windows and the veritable walls, all in an attempt to make it somehow approximating the beauty i've gotten used to yet though i hate analogies intensely i cant help thinking that all the trees are replaced now for me by the faces of people (including their bodies too of course) and if you ever care to know what super-realism is, try spending a long while in the country and then returning to the city of new york, still looking as carefully and well as you were doing in the woods. It hasnt helped that for most of this time the weather here's been one huge gray cloud hanging over at the very least (as Calvin Coolidge wouldda said) the Lower East Side, holding all the exhaust fumes in, nor would i even notice all these things so exactly if i hadnt succeeded in emptying all parts of body including brain of course yes that too while at Lake Buel of what i considered to be the unnecessary stuff so i could ha ha experiment in trying to think clearly once again. Well where does this leave me I mean in terms of the letter! I seem to be at the door of telling you about this fight between Ted & Lewis which, if it hadnt happened (oh the syntax, i cant finish that one, i was going to say there were two days where i felt back to normal) then Ted & Lewis proceeded to have a giant fight the repercussions of which have to do with all the bullshit of living here, including people's relative envy I guess of our own rather tentative but apparently better than their financial situation. Ted took all the hardcover SONNETS & signed some and sold them & kept all the money, returned the rest to us unsigned and then felt guilty about it, so laid into Lewis in giant speed-rap that it was all Lewis's fault because Lewis is not a good friend, then he said well i'm sure we wont be speaking for months on account of this. So now all of a sudden this! becomes the event of the day which I have to spend time thinking about, not dissimilar to the way it was when I left New York in the early summer when all kinds of feuds were going on, and it doesnt help for me to refuse to get involved in them, no one seems to pay any attention to the fact that i'm refusing, i think the only possible refusal would be to leave town! Now i'm stuck with thinking thoughts like shit i try to be a kind and thoughtful person, etc. No doubt it would be better to be a hideous creep who was ambitious, competitive & cruel. All the time. The very same day that all this was taking place in my house, I was at the Poetry Project meeting with the Committee for International Poetry, which is

Simon Pettet and Bob Rosenthal & they started talking to me about a reading they want to set up & using words and phrases about money I couldnt even understand, like let's roll some of this around the tree like goats, I forget what they said, but the gist of it was, we know you have money & we're in debt to you so why dont you give us your money for no reason and we'll return it to you to pay off our debt. Now here I was in a roomful of men and I said I dont understand what you're talking about. They all grinned then & said oh Bernadette she's always like that, then I get sort of nudged in the ribs by various men saying, oh this is a good deal, or this is ok. Now I dont feel that the poetry project has anything to do with big business and if other people want to make or pretend they're making big business deals, well then they should try another corner of the world I feel. Meanwhile, at this moment, I'm feeling exactly the way i felt when, the other day, i was at a meeting of what they called the mothers of the kindergarten children & when I complained about some way that I felt was unfair that the teachers were laying on the parents, all the other "mothers" in the room started shouting at me, "Oh you dont understand, those are the rules & we have to obey them!" Can I really be living in a world where parents let themselves be treated like children by teachers & where poets pretend to be businessmen, even ones we know, and where best friends are so drug-addicted that they take pills to feel righteous when they feel guilty? Well yes I guess I can & am. It doesnt help much to think clearly, much less to be able to write clearly. Old friend Ted says to me, you and Lewis are suckers (for giving him his own books!). Well shit I am going to be a sucker for the rest of my life I would hope and if not that, then i'll turn into a total crank, I dont see too many other alternatives today. It's very hard to contemplate keeping the Poetry Project "going" the way I feel, though in some funny way i'm relieved that it's in my hands. It's much harder to figure out what writing I wanna do because apart from & also involved with all this it seems to me that i've done some good writing in the past much of which i could probably devote the rest of my life to getting published, the way that goes, and if you'll forgive me for having & worse expressing such a hardcore thought, there really isnt much future sitting around waiting for us to give our works to it for later use, as in what they call posterity or even immortality. Now this may be my plain old bad mood & this may also be what i've begun to think of as a disease of new york, yet i've lived in new york for 30 of my 37 years &

have not always had this disease, far from it, i've been a fucking optimist! I can imagine spending alot of time reading and observing now, simply waiting to see what happens, but i am not of the whatever you call it makeup spiritually to do that. So here I a relative intellectual sit around saying I want some action, intellectual action, I would even settle for sexual action or political action but I wont settle for living among the desperate drug addicts & the cirrhotic if that's a word. Nor am I wanting isolation either, isnt that funny. I dont think my self is particularly important but I do wonder what my self is doing here & can do here. To write poetry & raise children & work at putting on public poetry readings ought to be a pretty glorious series of tasks, no? Yet I feel like I am wasting most of my hours & never doing as much as I could be. There is so much work involved in keeping our house just going & all the dealings with food, cleaning bathrooms & kitchens, etc., none of which is work i particularly mind doing but when i have to do it at a moment where i feel like my entire brain is denied its being & my body too, no way to use that except in cleaning, i begin to wonder what the hell i am doing. It is often astonishing to me to remember that i'm a smart person who can think complicated thoughts and also express them in some new way. What are those thoughts? The old "train of thought"? & when I "work on" the poetry project, is it of any use that I in particular be there, with my blatant truth-telling, is it even communicable or does it show? I doubt it. I dont wanna be one of these life is shit people, like Ted is now, that was also always my argument with Ed & i do believe that alot of the ways people around me are acting have to do with that belief. Do you think it's a question of getting older that you then eventually believe that (I'm not discounting the astonishing questions of the times). I am apparently about to change fields & I think almost any field among these would be preferable to poetry: philosophy, sociology, political science ha ha oh i cant go on. Maybe I'm just thinking that if I actually do die when my parents did, well then this right now is my old age! But I dont think so & I can dispense with that thought in one second. But I dont see having any particularly traditional or even less so ideas about writing right now. I can of course imagine writing for the rest of my life simply to keep doing it and amuse myself and have something to do that I'm good at, and possibly to help to change the world which is a thought i dont have when i'm writing a letter so much as I remember that feeling from writing & maybe the final thought is to be able to really translate the present into some words, or not the present but thinking which then, for me now, cannot help but have to do with the outrage to my dignity and the dignity of everybody else at living in this world, which if you can find someplace to live in it relatively unmolested the way you do seems less of an outrage, and since i've seen and experienced that too I know what the pleasures can be of a real possible life, even today, but dig it, if you and I can choose or have that, and I dont even know if i can still choose it, then we're among the few who can, I mean a large few too, and the reason, if I can use that word, that the world we live in is as it is, is because hardly anybody has that choice. So whaddo we do, we write our talented works because we're the ones who feel & know everything & can, but we are lost! There's only this world, set itself on fire. We've gotta hurry up, at best. Sitting around in our cultured manners doesnt seem to matter any more, I feel. Though I do feel that we are keeping alive what poetry is, I dont doubt that. I went to a block party in the neighborhood today, where there was a poetry reading. I was going to read but i lost my nerve, partly because the poetry was so bad & because the people listening were so making fun of every poet, I couldnt do it because i hate to be the fool, which is exactly what i am, and you are, and we all are! We are idiots and lunatics and all the rest of that & i would guess that we'd better catch up and begin acting like those things instead of pretending that we're somehow so smart as to be the closet academic ones, since we do know so much. Is everything not lively because we're all getting older? Have we given up on things? I dont wanna be a highly regarded minor American poet in my old age, nor do i wanna be a major american poet either, in that exact sex ha ha i meant to say sense. But i do wanna have some belief in what i'm doing beyond the fucking afterlife because i do disbelieve in the immortal dont you? It's difficult enough to be a person much less a poet; i am no longer neurotic but I'm still scared of what i see. I know we're not supposed exactly to talk about these things but i cant not (I saw a man and woman in love in the park today kissing & happily being together & I actually thought to myself, how can this be!). I also dont want to pass, like with thoughts like these, into that peculiarly american state of being an old(er) person who has been forgotten because he is not established as one of the great ones in the decades dealt with. In fact I cannot deal at all with being one person, I have never been able to. After all it makes no sense, the prison of the body, the limited time to sleep and think, the idea of a history much less a family. It does seem absurd to devote oneself to living as long as possible! Just to get by that! "I never did anything, therefore I am one hundred years old"! Great! Catherine never smiled, to retain her youth. To lighten my tirade which I apologize for subjecting you to I will tell you this dream which makes me so happy that dreams can be so greatly literal when you need them to be, also I saw a most wonderfully literal movie by Wim Wenders where everything in it was an expression of the total exactness visually & every other way that you could envision ever having, plus the movie could've been criticized easily, as i'm sure it has been, as being totally simple-minded and provincial, which it is. This kind of thing seems to me now to be a philosophical question which is the most complex kind of that kind of thing, do you know what i mean? Anyway the dream was that enormous blisters erupted on my arms and legs and they were moving, so i looked at them & tore the skin away to see what was underneath, and in each one, and what a long and tedious dream, was a scorpion (I have never seen one). So I laid around wondering in my half-sleep what this all meant because in the dream i was travelling across country & when I got to Georgia I got to the ocean & could see it & it was performing, even on the public beach of the dream, in great threatening waves so beautiful as to stun you, magnanimous too, and then i totally laughed at myself awake cause it took me (first i insisted on travelling the southern route so we'd be sure to see the desert of New Mexico and Arizona) five full minutes to remember that Lewis & Ted & Alice & Simon Pettet & Sophia who's been giving us a very difficult time lately & Lewis's mother too are all Scorpios, plus Hannah and many other people that we know. These blisters did not give me any pain, I was curious about them and astonished that the scorpions hadnt stung me as they're wont to do—the fucking scourge or one of them of the Bible! The reference to Georgia and the beautiful ocean believe it or not has to do with the church and what a refuge that place is to me now, it is pristinely recreated and is, as i keep being reminded by the historians, recreated as what it was—a country chapel! Also, dont forget "i've got you under my skin," thin-skinned, etc. I'm sure I've told you more than I should, for your sake, and sorry not to have saved you from outright obsessions but in the midst of my "revealment" maybe you might have some good advice for me because I am totally at sea. I can proceed sensibly and sanely but i cannot help receiving what's given to me in all the ways i get things here and at this moment. In the terms of being one person, it makes me want to weep. Also I drink alot, though as little as possible, but in order to be able to weep. To move back to the country would possibly mean "escaping" knowing about all this, on the other hand it would be right if there were some real future. Civilization has apparently come to some knowledge of one's relative place in the universe (without relatives!). Forgive me if i sound unconscionably corny, I dont even know how i sound nor do i wanna pretend to be alarming because i've never felt more understanding of my self and other people and things, but maybe you could point me in a way where in the midst of all i've been telling you of, i could do something worthwhile, or just something. I mean tell me to take a membership in a health club! & I will! Or say, you are off the mark, and in this particular way: ______________. I need to find out. Well of course this is asking too much, but then dont we always, I dont find new york unendurable, that's not it, but i cant figure out what to do here. Does that make sense? Shall I try & retrain myself to write no-sense? Wish you were here, just astrally, for a few hours of conversation.

Love,
Bernadette

15 OCTOBER 1982

Dear Bernadette,

Oh hell, here we go again, crossed dismalities! I have some "dumps" going here too. But the writing does not worry, though I endlessly worry it. I'm beginning to know when I should not listen to anyone but myself, though I know it's harder to keep to that strictum where you are. We'll both keep on, I know that. No matter what mess the world.

Advice? I can't stand it! A flighty thing. It seems to come demagnetized, won't attach to anyone. Do you really want mine? Ok, here's some. Which may sound inconsequential considering all the weight of problem you enumerate (and I could equal up my side of that scale here as well), but anyway it's a solid grasp I can present here. The Antarctica by Elliot Porter is now in remainder. If you haven't got it, go out and buy it. Give yourself a present of the elaboration of one of your strong fascinations. Continue it. Look into it before you enter anything else in your day. It's a little trick I use to keep my head up or at least less in the way of the monstrous unbraspabaple. (!!!!!!!!) Ungraspable! And maybe the best reason to own all these books.

I believe in small things. Word by word. The heart is small. The blood even less. Which is on my mind today (I keep having the impulse to type "mind" as "mine"!) since I'm reading all about H.D.'s eerie Moravian background, how they seemed to believe in Christ's wound as a bloody cunt of balm and sweetness. Amazing the foods we are given before we know what best to eat, if we ever do? Eat Antarctica in winter!

I feel I'm being flippant. The sentences shorten to chatter. Probably I'm avoiding deep problem. Questions tend to shorten (unless you're Barry Watten). And some days all my sentences tend to query by the end. This is much mess. Your letter fits right in with my mess. (keep writing) Poem as the straightening out of dinner. Blood on the hands. Do you think we are devils (poets)? Cigarettes and fire water. And feuds and forgetfulness and even writings that are lingering wounds? Do you think poets change the world? For the best, for the worse? What is the evidence? Homer's effect probably was most to drive boys furious out to fling swords. He certainly made war gleam for all time, drew an anatomy of its physique. But this is probably all wrong for your mood? Scott making the ice ring.

Choice? I dunno, more & more I doubt. Think it's probably less choice than chance & inclination. You already are what you "want to" be. As little as you have any choice in matter of fascination or pursuit. Once I say "knowledge" then rushes in all that value forgettal has for art. We are barely balanced on strange bars. Oblique lights to our eyes. Writing to be seen later and unscattered for further and endless care. Does Creeley trouble at what he will wear? What is your view of perfume? And one could elaborate quite a tome on the precise angles at which angels arrive.

How well do you know Fanny Howe? Quite well I somehow presume. She's been writing to me proposing I read all kinds of Gnostic texts etc., which I would probably do if I could find such exact and hermetic volumes. A great mystical Catholicism she seems all bound up in, you no doubt have more clue to than I(?) I feel an attraction there but I've never known to open the correct doors. What books would you recommend? I can't be stuck with that crabby Jerome for the rest of my days.

Maybe I need to get involved with an elaborate new vocabulary. We should find great new texts to discuss. What was that Wim Wenders film you saw? Not that I'll ever get to see it here. I saw only American Friend once and it had that exactness you mentioned, until the last part when Dennis Hopper tore through and drained a psychedelic crankcase all over everything. I read the book his Hammett is based on, a sort of so-so novel though the project was interesting enough.

I wish I could think of something to say perfectly useful to you at this battered-sounding moment! It's hard. I don't have much first-hand of your life and locale now for years! NewYorkCity has receded for me to proportions of dream if not nightmare outright. Uninhabitable locale and growing thicker. Your letters always say it's truly terrible but not really that. I can't think what to think. Ambivalent city of shoots and dives. I always remember that grey dawn we had breakfast just blocks away from where that mob guy (Joey Gallo?) was getting shot in front of stray eaters like us. I can stills see the exact tone of pre-morn light against the mercury vapors. Dreamlike now. As memory and dream are mixed in this something-or-other universe (Kerouac says somewhere).

I wonder why I prefer Fall when everything drains away then. And that peculiarity of the leaves proving radiant just previous to dying away. Rain and wind now tearing away and I have great complicated plotty dreams I can't recall much of later. Though images pop in a lot during stray reading during the day after. Something last night about me & de Kooning (I've never dreamt about him before) meeting in a TV film and rolling around in "electric filth" in the Great Courtyard of Hats. About all I can grasp now with any exactness (though it started a poem) (poems need gaps to occur in?), though it's somehow made me fear I'll now hear he died today. Just some more irrational proof.

Are poems the dreams of empty rooms? Just how much of poetry is unprovoked thought? I certainly am jealous of and do protect my solitude, and now you're losing yours! Thus it will not always be. Thinking time will come. I used to think the world got all changed around every night. Except then Kerouac found that it all slipped back exactly as it was before in a flash before morning.

Oh, Bernadette your self is particularly important! Take that from me anyway and believe it. That's all I particularly want to have you hear from me today. And if nothing else of this makes sense. The middle of life does seem some sort of draggy inertial hinge and if we have to force it then that's what we'll do. Screw the future. I doubt if I do know all that much but if I don't keep writing I'm sure I won't finally know anything. Movies prove to us that if we recognize our selves there it's right now and not in future or past. Which is probably why the present is so difficult, it has no place to retreat. And everything is there!

Had a great quick visit the other day from Chris Dewdney & his girlfriend from Toronto, and they were so young and enthusiastic about everything it made me feel like an old drub! You and I are too influenceable. But good for me to see people who don't care a whit for humanity's failures or whatever morose.

Well, is this the best I can do? Sort of a pep letter to myself with you listening in . . .

Now half of the leaves are gone, but the far ridges begin to appear.

Stick to it!!!

LOVE,

Clark

OCTOBER 21, 1982

Dear Clark,

Ah well I guess I dont really want your advice, better put all those words in quotes, but i sure do appreciate your letter, be it advice or no advice. About two days after I wrote to you I wandered into the Strand Bookstore and found the Antarctica book remaindered and though I had only 20 dollars in my pocket, for other things, I bought one and have been perusing it every day since & never cease to be amazed. Simultaneously I was also lucky to be given by Rosemary a book she thought I must read, it's a "novel" by a paleontologist about the meeting of Neandertal &

Cro-Magnon man! called DANCE OF THE TIGER by Bjorn Kurten. Perhaps I even mentioned it before. But these are two things, call it escapism if you will, that have engrossed me in ways i know i could be engrossed all the time given the choice, leisure, etc. Gee, I forget all I wrote you I know it was effulgent in its dismay at life & all i can (ever) remember is how i felt when i was writing you, i'm gonna use a semi-colon here; I wonder at the thinking of all my thoughts when I see how much totally intrusive mundanity, now there's an ugly word if ever there was one, interferes with, as you said, just the juggling around of our various types of oranges, we are supposed to be people with lives so we embark on a rent strike out of outrage but also out of energy that others dont have, then we know constantly that we are the least equipped to get things done in this world, except for the angels of our rage and love I guess, or angles? I know what you mean but your letter disturbed the very way that the precise angle of my being is being forced to be, because I remember being engrossed in the most leading ways in all thought and now i am constantly doing things and often my thoughts cannot even be had because if i dont remember (& isnt memory the curse of life in all ways) to do this or that, and since i have a "bad" memory i wont unless i remind myself all the time, then something is going to be all wrong—you know, dinner, the eases of life, or the poetry reading, my so-called responsibilities. The funny thing is that i suddenly find these things all very easy, a contradiction i wont bother to explain. At perfume i am usually nauseous as i often am in the mornings of new york city with the fear that lateness, sexuality, looseness of any kind is like a little diadem to be worn on the head of only the king & queen. i'll contradict myself again to say that it's most inspiring to be one of the workers in a city like new york where sexuality and looseness if not lateness are all over the place. yet everyone still has a fear of the lord, and I am (not) joking. I would love to be exempt from this consciousness and i think i could even arrange it, but apparently i've chosen it, as you say in much more inspiring words than these, though why i'll never know. is it my fucking karma? is it because i went to see a hideous freudian analyst when i was desperate/? is it perhaps because my entire life history is really quite rather rigid victorian expressionist sensationalist? i do not mean to involve you in a discussion of my self but i could put it this way: that i cannot for poetry figure out why i am here. I do know Fanny Howe very well & she told me she was engaging you in correspondence & i wondered how much gnosticism was involved, i havent the vaguest in to those texts which i sure never learned in school, nor do i know exactly what's involved except to know practically by rote that mystical catholicism was what was destroyed in "later" years by the likes of St. Paul in a giant attempt (successful) to make that religion just a morality code, just like Dennis Hopper or somebody! But you know religion has never interested me much. In fact, obverse to Fanny, I feel remorselessly angry at the work of religion on me. Lately, looking at my own children, I'm amazed that they're finally getting to the age where i can remember being their age and having the works of a rigid religious environment done on my senses of pleasure in life, all of them! even fucking eating! Yesterday was the day my father died 25 years ago, and as far as I know he died a person left lonely by an attempt at family life because his wife excoriated him religiously for not making enough money. If i were a primitive person, I would rightfully and not ignorantly think that as a result I've had my period now for 25 years. It is not lost on me that my father's name was Ted, though Ted's name is not really Ted. Nor is it less amazing to me that yesterday, in need of an envelope to have printed for a mailing, I pulled one at random from an addressographed group at the Poetry Project, and the one I pulled out was addressed to Frances Waldman. I say it is amazing because i am no longer interested in all these things and feel that i can be a person now without any necessary devotion to anybody's dying but perhaps my own. & I'd like very much to have a little interim period of just plain freedom of thought before i actually do begin to actively die, do you know what i mean? however of course there's no such thing. & i dont mean to impose such lateral logic on you as gets imposed on me. recently a teacher of sophia's said to me, when i was objecting to her being given cake, lollipops, soda and

chocolate bars all at once in one moment, I said just the cake would be enough to please the children, and the teacher in her teacher-role thought she could intimidate me by asking, "do you still smoke?" I was a little bit nervous at her logic since she's my daughter's teacher and asked if that was her perception of logic, dropping then the rhetorical device of saying that if i were a heroin addict i would not necessarily want the future to be mine, however the teacher's point was not lost on me, perhaps that in this world one in desperation seeks pleasure only in the most immediate ways—no care for the teeth etc., because after all what difference does it make? Wim

Wenders is very inspiring because he is such an intellectual and creates in his films a whole category of things that only perhaps you and I and maybe hundreds of other people could see, a million visual jokes about the movies and ways of seeing things and about the influence of Americans on european civilization, plus there is a sustained suspension of disbelief in the relative beauties of modern life, an obsession with modern structures and the building of them (of course a joke on Godard, endless jokes). His movies are totally concerned with men, all the women in them are either interfering, negligible or making some statement. There is an astonishing scene where a young man berates his father who is falling asleep at his old-fashioned typesetting machines; the young man spends the night making a newspaper with headlines of the wrongs his father did to him. This same man who is a travelling repairer of cinemas gets involved with a woman who ultimately says to him, I now live alone with my daughter and I want it to stay that way, so they sleep together in their clothes. Though there's much incipient male love in the movies, there's never any sexuality in a real way. everybody is not having sex. It actually reminds me of Ed in alot of ways. But this is West Germany! & everybody is always humming an american rock n roll tune, mostly bob dylan, and they say at some point the americans have colonialized their sub-conscious! I do wish we had a movie of that morning you remember of eating breakfast at Dayton's Dairy Cafeteria because the astonishing thing in one of these Wenders movies to me was some shots of that neighborhood and i looked at them and i couldnt for the life of me figure out whether they were meant to be beautiful or not. Astonishing that you're dreaming about de Kooning because I've just been having so many conversations about him with Paul Cummings, a friend and Friend of the poetry project, who is putting together a big de Kooning show for the Whitney. Paul visits de Kooning all the time lately and tells me of his total absence of memory, his grouchiness and his only interest in what women and not men think of his new paintings, which are extremely gay, though to the dismay of everybody else he's taken to making millions of drawings non-stop on paper like this i'm typing on. The one thing I know is what you say, and it's something Kerouac says in some other way, that if i dont keep writing i'm sure i wont know anything or even be able to be but it's amazing, clark, as you know, to have come to the conclusion, ha ha what words we use, that we do live in this present and then to have to deal with that. i dont doubt that there is no real retreat nor do i understand what children are because you cannot just be waiting for them to get older, especially now. i really think i think in our times it's easier to just think like a fucking monk than do anything else. it's very funny to me that i was so tempted to become a missionary, just think of that work and word; at age 13 that seemed like the most sensible work to me to do. little did i know that meant teaching people to abhor the normal. i cannot fathom the relation of my self to the world as a poet. I doubt that i'm as wrong now as i might've been at age 13, nor do i miss seeing that many of our friends are getting to be as wrong now, after being "right," as I was then. I regret alot of things in my life too, especially being so shy as to not be able to enjoy the absoluteness of my health, then—do you know what i mean? When I was exactly 22 I remember saying to people, this is when i can do many things and would like alot of things to do. Learning about human nature at the poetry project and being the parent of little children at age 37 is not quite right, i feel & of course this is like your thought amazing the foods we are given before we know what best to eat. aw shit it's so depressing and we've done so little i cant stand it. what have we done? we write and write as if that were making food and then all it leads to is certain embroiling squabbles. Is there a consistent sense in the country because of the things about what they call nature that this isnt so? The only thing i know about this for sure is the feeling on waking up and walking out in the morning that my own self is not important, and is distractable by what is a real way of being in relation to what you see in the world. Max said the great thing, on the dock at Lake Buel, "dont look at me, look at your own self," which could easily be applied to any person or tree. I do not have a nostalgic or weird notion of "the country" but i do have a feeling that there's value in the observances there. & what of those here? Prisons are always indigenous, whatever that means, and i am no longer interested in mine, which is an awful problem. It's horrible to lose friends without beating them up or something, what do you do to them? I'm so sick of hearing people referring to the economic problems of our time yet i know i always wanted very much to understand politics and now i do, because of the city and this job. i've also always wanted to be surrounded by people in some sort of natural community, now that's my family, i've had to create it myself! this further community of poets i've no real comment about. i yearn all the time mostly for love which i seem to still know nothing about because i havent the vaguest idea of what kind of love i'm speaking of. Here in these typed justified on the right hand margin lines i might say this, right? Lewis and me, that is a whole distinct thing, where there will be love for ever, agreed upon, isnt that marriage? or whatever it's called? but i mean a much weirder love of moths i'm seeking, the ones that fell on my head through the light while i was writing in Monterey. Our changing the world must be dependent on something, I wonder what it is, i know it's not advertising, i'm not absolutely sure it's keeping on writing, maybe it's devotion to each other and to proving that love can be, and documenting it, and keeping journals, writing letters, who knows? you & i, for instance feel no cynicism toward each other, we do not involve each other ever in the literary doings. Apparently that is unusual though i never dreamed it would be so. Maybe it's preserving all the you's and i's that can be still intact, lovingly, today. Yet i have such a fear of fighting i may not know what i'm saying. maybe it's just preserving the you as some you and the i as some i that is objectively sensible, so that you can also see clearly & convey that information to everyone, also about thought. Surely somebody should "fund" a conversation between us, dont you think? though i am lost in my own stupidity which is just a sensitivity to the stupidity of this world i'm in & i'm not certain that i dont want to learn more about it though another part of me wants to protectively take my family and flee. I cant tell you how grateful i am for your letter and i know in the rigidity of our thoughts, we owe at the very least each other these letters, though i apologize for being overly serious I guess. Here the leaves have not even turned colors yet but are becoming a little bit tired and falling down anyway!

LOVE,

Bernadette

Index

www.ingramcontent.com/pod-product-compliance
Lightning Source LLC
Chambersburg PA
CBHW051103030726
47504CB00006B/1768
* 9 7 8 0 8 2 6 3 6 6 2 7 6 *